A People of Hope

ALSO BY JOHN L. ALLEN JR.

Conclave

All the Pope's Men

The Rise of Benedict XVI

Opus Dei

The Future Church

John L. Allen Jr.

A People of Hope

ARCHBISHOP TIMOTHY DOLAN IN CONVERSATION
WITH JOHN L. ALLEN JR.

IMAGE BOOKS
New York

Published in the United States by Image Books, an imprint of
the Crown Publishing Group, a division of Random House, Inc., New York.
www.crownpublishing.com

IMAGE and the Image colophon are registered trademarks
of Random House, Inc.

Library of Congress cataloging-in-publication data is available upon request.

ISBN 978-0-307-71849-5
eISBN 978-0-307-71851-8

Printed in the United States of America

Book design by Elina Nudelman
Cover photography by Getty Images

10 9 8 7 6 5 4 3 2 1

First Edition

For Shannon and Ellis, as always . . .

Contents

INTRODUCTION

Historic runs of success always become the stuff of legend. In baseball, Joe DiMaggio's fifty-six-game hitting streak in 1941 still sets the standard for consistent excellence. Basketball fans will always celebrate the eighty-eight-game winning streak the UCLA Bruins put together from 1971 to 1974, as well as the companion ninety-game unblemished mark posted by the Lady Huskies of the University of Connecticut from 2008 to 2010. In the world of entertainment, people still marvel at the thirty-seven-week run of Michael Jackson's *Thriller* album atop the Billboard charts in 1983 to 1984, or the fifteen consecutive weeks as box office champ logged by the blockbuster movie *Titanic* in 1997.

While there's no exact parallel in the Catholic Church to a winning streak or a long run at the box office, perhaps the closest anyone's come in recent memory was the eye-popping run of promotions, honors, papal votes of confidence, and signs of growing celebrity racked up by Archbishop Timothy Michael Dolan of New York from February 2009 to June 2011. Consider the record put together over that span by Dolan, sixty-one years old as of this writing, which, by ecclesiastical standards, is still quite young:

- On February 23, 2009, Pope Benedict XVI named Dolan the tenth archbishop of New York, after serving just under seven years as the archbishop of Milwaukee. In Catholic terms, New York is on a short list of pace-setting dioceses around the world, such as Milan in Italy, Paris in France, and Westminster in the United Kingdom, whose incumbent is seen as a global point of reference. New York is traditionally considered the most important bully pulpit in the American Catholic Church, and since New York is also the media capital of the world, its archbishop is inevitably a premier "front man" for Catholicism.

• On May 31, 2010, Pope Benedict XVI tapped Dolan as an "Apostolic Visitor" to Ireland, helping lead the Vatican's response to that country's massive sexual-abuse crisis. Benedict is deeply worried about Ireland, once a cornerstone of Catholic culture in Europe, and his concern was reflected in his choice of visitors. They included Cardinal Cormac Murphy-O'Connor, the former archbishop of Westminster, England; Cardinal Sean O'Malley of Boston; Archbishop Thomas Collins of Toronto, Canada; and Archbishop Terrence Prendergast of Ottawa, Canada. All are considered among the most influential prelates in the English-speaking world, and Dolan is now on that list.

• On November 16, 2010, Dolan was elected president of the United States Conference of Catholic Bishops, making him the de facto leader and spokesperson for more than 250 Catholic bishops who run dioceses and other jurisdictions across the country. (He'll hold the position until November 2013.) Dolan prevailed in the balloting despite a strong custom in the conference that the sitting vice president, at the time Bishop Gerald Kicanas of Tucson, Arizona, automatically ascends to the top job. In effect, the upset result means Dolan's fellow bishops weren't just following a script—they wanted him, specifically, to be their voice.

• On January 5, 2011, Pope Benedict XVI named Dolan a member of a new Vatican council designed to promote "New Evangelization," which is the apple of the pope's eye. (To be honest, no one yet has a clear idea of what this office might do; what's relevant is that Benedict XVI takes it seriously.) Dolan joined heavy-hitters such as Cardinal Angelo Scola of Milan; Cardinal Gianfranco Ravasi of the Pontifical Council for Culture; Cardinal George Pell of Sydney, Australia; Cardinal Christoph Schönborn of Vienna, Austria; Cardinal Marc Ouellet of the Congregation for Bishops; and Cardinal William Levada of the Congregation for the Doctrine of the Faith. That's a Vatican "A Team" if ever there was one, and the fact that Dolan is part of it, even in advance of getting a cardinal's red hat, speaks volumes about where he stands. (Dolan himself says his first reaction upon scanning the list of names was "My Lord, how did I make this cut?")

- On March 20, 2011, the famed CBS News program *60 Minutes* devoted an entire segment to Dolan, proclaiming him the Catholic Church's answer to its woes of the past decade, including the sexual-abuse crisis and a steady attrition of the faithful. The introductory voice-over for the segment dubbed Dolan the "American pope." In comments after the piece aired, host Morley Safer, who clearly did not share Dolan's views on a range of controversial questions such as abortion and gay marriage, nonetheless said of the archbishop: "He is a genuinely jovial, life-embracing, people-loving man. There's no question of that."

- Two months later, on June 2, 2011, Dolan traveled to Rome for the first meeting of the Pontifical Council for the New Evangelization. He was accompanied by Matt Lauer, Al Roker, and the crew of NBC's *Today* show, the highest-rated morning news program in America, with an average daily audience in excess of six million people. Dolan arranged an on-camera introduction to Pope Benedict XVI as well as behind-the-scenes Vatican access for the *Today* crew, and then effectively cohosted a live broadcast from Rome. During the segment, Lauer described Dolan as the "highest-profile person now of the Catholic Church in the United States," someone with "enormous charisma, a great personality."

Collectively, this was a remarkable rise to prominence in a short arc of time, especially in an institution typically inclined to think in centuries. By the time the dust had settled, there could be no doubt about Dolan's status. Prior to February 2009, one could have made a compelling argument that Timothy Dolan was a key to the American Catholic future. By the spring of 2011, it had become crystal clear that Dolan is very much the Church's present—Rome's go-to guy in America, the prelate other American bishops look to for leadership, and the new media darling of the Church in the United States. Nor is Dolan quite finished yet. Sometime in 2012 or 2013, right around the time his term as president of the U.S. bishops' conference is ending, Dolan will likely be inducted into the College of Cardinals, making him "Cardinal Dolan" and thus eligible to vote for the next pope.

One can celebrate Dolan's ascent or lament it—and, to be sure, there are examples of both views, inside and outside the Catholic Church—but at a purely descriptive level, the bottom line seems clear. Anyone who wants a sense of where the Catholic Church in the United States is headed, at least over the next couple of decades or so, must get to know the man who is now its preeminent face and voice. Further, Dolan's extroverted personality and media savvy suggest that he won't just be a behind-the-scenes power broker, but also an important voice of conscience in public debates for some time to come. A bit like Pat Robertson on the right or Jim Wallis on the left, Dolan is fast becoming one of those religious leaders in American life with impact well beyond the boundaries of his own confessional group.

Easier Said Than Done

Getting a satisfying read on Dolan, however, is easier said than done. In part, that's because he's a larger-than-life character who, upon first contact, tends to overwhelm one's senses. He's over six feet tall and a wide load of a man, reflecting his love for food, drink, and a good cigar, and his relative lack of enthusiasm for formal exercise. He's got a booming voice, a raucous laugh, and a kilowatt-laced smile that could probably power several blocks of downtown Manhattan. He's quick with a joke, the kind of hale-fellow-well-met who never saw a back he didn't want to slap or a baby he didn't want to kiss. Had Timothy Dolan not become a Catholic bishop, he could easily have been a U.S. senator or a corporate CEO, such is his charm and relentless energy.

At a time when the public image of Catholic bishops in the United States is arguably at an all-time low as a result of a persistent sexual-abuse crisis, bruising political fights over health care reform and gay marriage, and a variety of other issues, not to mention the general difficulty of asserting religious authority in a culture profoundly skeptical of such claims, Dolan stands out as a towering exception to the dour stereotype—a truly nice guy who also happens to wear a miter. In general, people tend to be so dazzled the first few times they encounter Dolan that it takes a while for their critical faculties to come back online, so they can begin to ask: "But what is this guy really all about?"

Dolan is so relentlessly upbeat, in fact, that one risk is to reduce him to nothing but a series of one-liners and photo ops. That was the thrust of a 2009 profile in *New York* magazine that labeled Dolan the "Archbishop of Charm"—suggesting, perhaps, that beneath Dolan's one-liners, there's not much "there" there. It doesn't help that Dolan loves to take shots at himself, deliberately playing off such impressions. I once watched him drop in on a meeting of lay movements where he didn't make many statements but asked a lot of probing questions. When I commented on it later, he said: "I figure I can get away with acting dumb for about the first year . . . until they realize that I ain't acting!"

In truth, Dolan is far more than simply a charmer. There are at least three deep currents to his personality, which sometimes sit in uneasy tension with one another. First, Dolan tends to be an ideological conservative on matters both secular and sacred, giving him a strong sense of identity and a clear vision for where the Church ought to go. (In his *60 Minutes* interview, Dolan said that if "conservative" means "somebody enthusiastically committed to and grateful for the timeless heritage of the Church ... I'm a conservative, no doubt.") Second, he's a country pastor, whose implied model for Catholic life is his father's backyard BBQ pit in Ballwin, Missouri, where all are welcome and everyone gets along. Third, Dolan is a keen Church historian, having studied under the legendary Monsignor John Tracy Ellis at the Catholic University of America. That training affords him a striking ability to ask probing questions, to stand back, and to size up debates objectively, being fair to all views.

Part of the drama of Tim Dolan — part of what makes him such a fascinating, and at times unpredictable, force in Catholic life — is trying to guess which combination of those instincts will prevail in any given situation.

Dolan Vignettes

Because of Dolan's outsized personality and complex character, no one anecdote can do him justice. The following are three vignettes that, taken together, capture something of the Timothy Dolan experience. Among other things, they illustrate how Dolan is able to win friends and influence people, both at the top of the Church and at the grassroots, and even among non-Catholics with a chip on their shoulders about the Church. Taken together, these stories also help explain Dolan's rapid rise into the ecclesiastical stratosphere.

"Even I'd join the Church!"

In late December 2009, I spent an exhausting week following Dolan around in New York. The schedule included a stop at the renowned

Temple Emanu-El in order to light the first candle of Hanukkah. (Among other notables, New York mayor Michael Bloomberg is a member of the congregation.) One could make the argument that New York's Fifth Avenue is among the most evocative pieces of Jewish-Catholic real estate on the planet, home both to Temple Emanu-El and to St. Patrick's Cathedral.

On this occasion, the congregation pulled out all the stops to celebrate Dolan's visit, including something you definitely don't see every day: At the end of the service, the choir performed a toe-tapping, doo-wop version of the classic holiday number "I Have a Little Dreidel," which could easily be the anchor track on a *Hanukkah Goes Motown* album. After the service, Dolan was mobbed by people wanting to thank him for coming, to get their pictures taken with him, and to shove pieces of Hanukkah cake into his hands.

I was hovering off to the side, trying to watch the scene unfold. At one stage, a member of the temple's governing board pulled me aside for a chat. He asked what I did for a living, and I said I'm a journalist who covers the Catholic Church. That prompted this proud septuagenarian Jew to launch into a semi-tirade about Pope Pius XII, the mess over Pope Benedict's decision to lift the excommunication of a Holocaust-denying bishop, and what he sees as broad rollback on relations with Judaism from the Church. Having worked himself into a lather, he then asked what I was doing in New York, and I explained that I was working on a book about Dolan.

The guy's body language changed in a flash. Conspiratorially, he drew close, smiled, and offered this sotto voce comment: "He's such a magnificent human being . . . If every bishop were like Dolan, even I'd consider joining the Church!"

"Ah, my friend Dolan!"

One gorgeous Italian Saturday in early May 2011, I found myself in Spoleto, a small town in the Umbria region about an hour and a half north of Rome. I had been asked to say a few words at the opening of a photo exhibit dedicated to Pope John Paul II, timed to coincide with the late pope's beatification on May 1, 2011. The featured speaker was Cardinal Leonardo Sandri, head of the Vatican's Congregation for Eastern Churches, and formerly the "substitute" in the Vatican's Secretariat of State under John Paul II, meaning the official responsible for day-to-day administration of the Church. It was Sandri, sixty-seven, an Argentine by birth who hails from an Italian family, who announced John Paul's death to the world from St. Peter's Square on April 2, 2005, memorably saying: "We all feel like orphans tonight."

Just days before the Spoleto event, I had written a piece proclaiming Sandri a leading candidate to be the next pope. Such perceptions are sort of the third rail of Vatican politics — no one, ever, wants to be seen as campaigning for the job. As fate would have it, I ended up seated next to Sandri at lunch, which could have made things a bit awkward. In the course of conversation, however, I mentioned that I was working on a book with Dolan, and the previously restrained Sandri lit up: "Ah, my friend Dolan!" It turns out that Sandri served in the papal embassy in Washington, D.C., during the same period that Dolan worked there in the late eighties and early nineties, and like so many others, Sandri was won over by the up-and-coming young American cleric.

From that moment on, the ice at our table was melted — an instance, perhaps, of Dolan working his charm even at a distance. Among other things, the loosened-up Sandri told a hilarious story of visiting Los Angeles in summer 2009 for a meeting with the Maronite church, which has its origins in Lebanon. When Sandri presented his Vatican passport at LAX, an official of the U.S. Customs and Border Protection service apparently asked him: "Oh, are you part of the Vatican delegation for the Michael Jackson funeral?" Sandri laughingly said he had to explain there was no such animal.

As the lunch broke up, Sandri made a point of asking me to be sure to pass along my regards to his "good friend" in New York.

"He makes me feel good to be Catholic"

After arriving in New York, Dolan made a point of moving around the archdiocese to visit each of its vicariates, referring to a geographical subdivision of the archdiocese. The usual formula is for Dolan to arrive early in order to have dinner with the priests of the area, offering some informal remarks, which sometimes amount to talking off the cuff about whatever happened during his day. After dinner, Dolan leads a vespers service for area Catholics in a local parish. Afterwards, he goes to a cafeteria or gym, where he stands for hours to personally greet hundreds of people who line up to shake his hand, whisper something in his ear, and have their pictures taken with him.

One night in late 2009, I watched Dolan make one of these visits in affluent Westchester County, where an overflow crowd kept him shaking hands and having quick chats almost until midnight. At one point, a woman spent a few minutes talking to Dolan, got tears in her eyes, and then made her way over to a corner of the room to compose herself. I happened to be standing nearby, so she introduced herself and asked if I was from the parish. I explained that I was a journalist working on a book about Dolan, and she said: "I'm a lifelong Catholic, but the last few years it's been so hard . . . with the sex-abuse scandals, with bishops who don't seem to listen, with all of it."

She told me she was basically on the liberal wing of many intra-Catholic debates and couldn't help feeling that the authorities in her own church are trying to squeeze her out because of her views on women, on authority, and on any number of other issues. Her encounter with Dolan, however, had given her a new perspective.

"I came tonight not knowing what to expect," she said, "but this guy ... I don't know, somehow he just makes me feel good about being Catholic."

The Rest of the Story

That last story hints at a core motive for this book. Uniquely among the current crop of nationally and internationally prominent bishops, Dolan offers a way to tell the "rest of the story" about the Catholic Church—meaning the portion of the Catholic story typically left in the shadows by most media coverage, an omission that often leaves outsiders with a terribly flawed grasp of what is actually happening in the Church.

To explain what I mean by "the rest of the story," I need to inject myself into the narrative just a bit.

My beat as a journalist is the global Catholic Church, with a special eye on the Vatican and the papacy. In practice, that means a considerable percentage of my time is devoted to stories of crisis, scandal, and controversy, the kinds of things that tend to dominate secular coverage of religion. Aside from the sexual-abuse crisis, I've covered political tensions within Catholicism in the United States over President Barack Obama, health care reform, and abortion; interfaith spats between the Catholic Church and both Muslims and Jews, not to mention other Christians; a global cause célèbre about a decision of Pope Benedict in 2009 to lift the excommunications of four traditionalist Catholic bishops, including one who is a Holocaust-denier; and a whole cluster of eternal Catholic debating points, such as priestly celibacy, contraception, the ordination of women to the priesthood, gay rights and gay marriage, ecclesiastical power and the limits of dissent, and so on.

These are all important stories, and conspiracy theories about how the media is out to get the Catholic Church can't dissolve the legitimate questions they raise. That said, these stories nevertheless

leave an obvious question hanging: If this is all there is to the Catholic Church—scandal, controversy, public-relations meltdowns, and bruising political fights—why would anyone bother being Catholic? Surely there's enough pain and polarization in the outside world, so why would anyone go looking for it in church? If one had to assess Catholic fortunes in America merely on the basis of most media coverage, the surprise would not be that there are an estimated twenty-two million ex-Catholics out there, who taken together would form the second largest religious body in the country. The real surprise would be that anyone has stuck it out at all.

And yet, they come. Hundreds of millions of Catholics across the globe, including an estimated sixteen to twenty million in America, still show up for Mass every Sunday. The numbers of young people opting for the Catholic priesthood and religious life are slowly inching up, even in the United States. Tens of millions of Americans, and hundreds of millions more around the world, still turn to the Church for inspiration, for its sacramental life, for its experience of community and service. In every diocese in America, if you look hard enough, you can find parishes that are flourishing—where the music is good and the preaching at least passable, where the parish itself is a beehive of charitable activity and youth ministry and adult faith formation and on and on. That's not to suggest that everything in the Catholic Church is peaches and cream, but there must be something that draws all those folks, despite the truckload of challenges and headaches facing the Church. Given public images of Catholicism, it's often tough for outsiders to imagine what that "something" might be.

What is it? In a word, it's faith. By that, I don't mean an exaggerated religious frenzy that feeds an uncritical view of the Church. Catholics are nothing if not sober realists about the humanity of their institutions and leaders. One of my favorite writers of detective stories, John Sandford, once had his hero, Lucas Davenport, offer this utterly spot-on observation about Catholic psychology: "Catholics don't scream about Jesus. They scream about the bishop."

When I say "faith," what I mean instead is that at some level, most Catholics really do believe that there's something supernatural about the Church, that it's where God calls them to be despite the well-documented failures to live up to its lofty ideals. As a result, most Catholics, most of the time, don't make decisions about the Church based primarily on ideological considerations—i.e., that they happen to agree with the political priorities of the current leadership class—or on the consumerist logic that the Catholic Church meets their perceived needs better than its competitors in the dynamic American religious marketplace. Instead, with eyes wide open, they still believe the Catholic Church is their spiritual home. Given that frame, they see the Church not as a debating society or a multinational enterprise, but a family—with all the flaws and dysfunction, but also all the joy and life, of families everywhere.

That's where Archbishop Timothy Dolan of New York enters the picture.

It's not that Dolan is somehow responsible for the personal decisions of roughly 16 million American Catholics, about one-quarter of the country's total Catholic population of 67 million, to get out of bed on Sunday and go to Mass. Even in New York, where Dolan has a high media profile, probably few Catholics could pick their archbishop out of a line-up. What I mean instead is that Dolan, at his best, incarnates the kind of upbeat, hopeful, affirming Catholicism that's the untold story about the Church today . . . the counterpoint to the Sturm und Drang of crisis and scandal, and at least a partial explanation as to why so many people still turn up at the Church's door. While currents of life are often buried under an avalanche of bad news, Dolan is that rare senior figure who manages to put a warm human face on the Church's public image. As Monsignor Michael Turek, a Saint Louis pastor and former classmate of Dolan, says: "When you meet Dolan, you don't meet a bishop. You meet a real human being who happens to be a bishop. You're not talking to an office or a hat, but a man."

Probably my chief professional frustration is that the Catho-

lic Church I have come to know from the inside—the warmth and laughter one finds in most Catholic circles, the rich intellectual tradition, the vast body of lore, the incredible range of characters, the deep desire to do good, the abiding faith against all odds that thrives even in a secular world, the ability to go anywhere and feel instantly at home, even the love of good food, good drink, and good company—rarely finds an echo in my reporting. I wanted to tell the Tim Dolan story in part because it wouldn't leave me with a sense of dissonance between the inner experience of being Catholic, and the public perception of what the Church is all about.

Affirmative Orthodoxy on Steroids

Some time back, I coined the phrase "Affirmative Orthodoxy" to describe the distinctive character of Pope Benedict XVI's teaching. Both parts of that formula are important. Benedict is certainly "orthodox" in the sense of tenaciously defending the core elements of classic Catholic thought, speech, and practice. Yet he's also "affirmative" in the sense of being determined to present the building blocks of orthodoxy in a positive key. The emphasis is on what Catholicism embraces and affirms, what it says "yes" to, rather than what it opposes and condemns. That spirit of Affirmative Orthodoxy runs like a scarlet thread through Benedict's teaching, yet it's often been obscured in media coverage and public perceptions. In part, that's because of the pope's own quiet, scholarly persona, making him hardly the same media magnet as his predecessor John Paul II; and, truth to be told, it's also partly because Benedict's Vatican team has sometimes demonstrated a special genius for shooting itself in the foot.

Archbishop Timothy Dolan is Affirmative Orthodoxy on steroids. He is, to adapt the marketing slogan for the sugar and caffeine–rich Jolt Cola, "all the orthodoxy and twice the affirmative!"

Without any doubt, Dolan is "orthodox," so much so that most observers would place him firmly on the conservative, if not actually neo-conservative, wing of intra-Catholic debates. When the University of Notre Dame invited Obama to deliver its commencement address in 2009 and awarded him an honorary doctorate, Dolan was among those American bishops who complained that the university had compromised its Catholic identity. When the Catholic Health Association came out in March 2010 in favor of Obama's health care reform package, Dolan told me he agreed with the conservative chorus denouncing the association for appearing "soft" on abortion. He's the kind of bishop who will not tolerate dissent from Catholic teaching on the church's payroll, and he openly admits that he has a second-grader's sense of awe and unquestioning loyalty when it comes to the pope. Dolan proudly proclaims that he's a "John Paul II" bishop, as opposed to the more liberal category of "Vatican II" bishop, meaning someone shaped by a reform-oriented and progressive outlook.

Given the persistent divisions in Catholicism, it's no surprise that some quarters in the Church have been cheered by Dolan's neo-conservative outlook and others frightened by it. Yet whatever one makes of it, it's not really his defining trait, in part because it's widely shared among a growing swath of American bishops. What makes Dolan unique is instead his generosity of spirit, a determination to keep lines of communication open, and a deep conviction that most of life's problems can be solved by sitting down with people over a couple of beers and talking things out. If faced with a choice between reconciliation and recrimination, Dolan will almost invariably prefer the former. For example, while he strenuously objected to Notre Dame's handling of the Obama affair and the Catholic Health Association's position on the Obama reform package, he has resisted calls from some quarters to impose sanctions. Instead, he says he wants to sit down and talk to the leaders at both places, arguing that conversation rather than confrontation is generally the right way to deal with disagreements.

Dolan's guiding philosophy is that when people look at the Catholic Church, they should see a happy place. It's his drive to foster relationships and to preserve an "open door" policy, which insulates him from becoming an ideologue and protects his theology from becoming sectarian.

In terms of the Catholic landscape in the early twenty-first century, Dolan is a leading force in the "evangelical" movement coursing through the Church. Inspired by Pope John Paul II, Catholic evangelicals are tired of internal debate over traditional markers of Catholic identity such as priestly celibacy or episcopal authority. They take a strong sense of Catholic identity for granted, and are eager to use it as a lever with which to transform the world. Though there's nothing necessarily ideological about the evangelical impulse, it tends to be more congenial to the Catholic right than to the left.

Yet, it's striking that so far into his tenure in New York, whatever criticism Dolan has attracted seems fairly evenly divided between the right and the left. Liberals have objected to some of Dolan's public policy pronouncements, such as a blog post in May 2011 in which Dolan referred to proposals for gay marriage as an instance of "Orwellian social engineering." Yet conservatives have also complained about Dolan's reluctance to bring the hammer down. To date, Dolan has not publicly threatened disciplinary measures against New York governor Andrew Cuomo, a pro-choice and pro-gay marriage Catholic Democrat. Dolan himself said he heard more blowback from conservatives after his election as president of the U.S. Conference of Catholic Bishops, mostly along the lines of how he doesn't walk the talk: "There were some on the right who said Dolan's no more a conservative than anybody else," he said. "He talks a good game, but when it comes to the hard choices, he's not going to pull the trigger."

Want an analogy for Tim Dolan?

Think about any movie or play you've ever seen centered on a large, complicated family. If things hold to form, the parents are basically decent, loving people, but who also have a pretty clear sense of right and wrong and who tried to impose it on their kids growing up. There will be those children, now adults, who bought their parents' worldview hook, line, and sinker, and who become almost fanatically defensive when anyone challenges it; there will be a few kids who chafed against it, and sometimes can't even talk about (or to) their parents without those old resentments welling up; and there's usually the one kid still on speaking terms with everybody, and who tries desperately to keep the peace. It's the kid who loves the good in his mom and dad, but who also "gets it" as to why some of his siblings are still smoldering, and whose most cherished dream is putting the pieces back together again. Sometimes everyone loves him for it, and sometimes everybody sees him as a hopeless naïf who's in denial about the reality of the situation. In the end, however, he's the glue who holds the family together.

Dolan is that one kid in the American Catholic Church.

That's not just a matter of a velvet glove fitting neatly over an iron fist. Dolan's soft touch is so celebrated that his critics usually feel compelled to begin their indictment there, suggesting that all the schmaltz amounts to a clever way of masking what the man really represents. They say that Dolan is part of a rollback on the reform vision of the Second Vatican Council, someone bent on propping up an authoritarian and ultra-clerical version of the Catholic Church. To those inclined to skepticism, Dolan's effervescence can seem like a Star Trek–esque "cloaking device" for a bare-knuckles strategy, from a hierarchy threatened by loss of power and control. In other words, they warn, beware the real Dolan beneath the kindly, good-humored façade.

Yet the more time one spends with Dolan, the more one begins to suspect that perhaps the façade is the real bishop—in other words, that his love for people and zest for friendship is what's truly fundamental about the man, not a PR device calculated to conceal some other agenda. That's not to say that Dolan can't, or won't, draw lines in the sand when he believes that core matters of Catholic identity are at stake. He's well aware that we live in a deeply secular world in the West, in which powerful pressures, both subtle and overt, seek to blur the counter-cultural message of Catholicism on many fronts. One key to Dolan's character, however, is that changing hearts, not knocking heads, is always his first instinct.

The genesis of this book is not that Timothy Dolan is the most compelling Catholic story in America. There are 67 million Catholics in this country and just over 400 bishops, which means that without breaking a sweat, one could find plenty of American Catholics who are smarter, holier, even kinder and more loving. The point is rather that those qualities, which are very much part of the contemporary Catholic story, rarely break into public discussions about the Church. Given that they are also very much part of Dolan's own personality, the spotlight he attracts gives them a fighting chance to see the light of day.

About This Book

It's too soon for a conventional biography of Dolan, as most of his lasting contributions as a Church leader still lie in the future. The question I set out to answer is more forward-looking: What will the rise of Timothy Dolan mean for the Catholic Church? Where does he want to lead, and how will a Church that increasingly bears his imprint look, taste, smell, and feel?

Initially, my thought was to approach this project like an extended magazine profile, interviewing people who've known Dolan over the years, including both friends and foes (the latter are more difficult to find, but they're out there), reading his works, conducting some interviews with Dolan, and then offering my own analysis and forecasts. The more I thought about it, however, the more it seemed that not only has that been done before, but it's not the most informative approach. Inevitably, such a book would be more about me, how I see the state of the Church and Dolan's role in it, than it would be about the man himself. To understand where Dolan wants to take the Church, what's really necessary is to get inside his head and then let him speak for himself.

The solution I settled upon was to model this book after one of the more famous contributions to Catholic literature in the last quarter-century, a book called *The Ratzinger Report* (first published in Italian as *Rapporto sulla fede* in 1984). It was a conversation between a prominent Italian Catholic journalist, Vittorio Messori, and then-cardinal Joseph Ratzinger, the man who is today Pope Benedict XVI. In many ways, it was the book that made Ratzinger a star. Prior to 1984, his role as the chief of the Vatican's doctrinal office made him a known quantity among Catholic insiders, but *The Ratzinger Report* introduced him to the wider world. Messori ran Ratzinger through the gauntlet of all the controversies swirling in the Catholic Church at the time, from women priests to liberation theology in Latin America, and Ratzinger delivered the trenchant, crystal clear defense of orthodoxy that has long been his trademark. The book fell upon the world like a thunderbolt, because it offered the clearest possible evidence that the winds in Rome had shifted—a period of reform and introspection had closed and a newly assertive and muscular defense of the faith had begun. The genius of *The Ratzinger Report* was that it allowed Ratzinger, in his own words, to draw a set of lines in the sand that in many ways framed Catholic debate for the next quarter-century.

By no means am I predicting that this book will resemble *The Ratzinger Report* in the sense of propelling its subject to the papacy, and Lord knows that Dolan cringes at even the hint of such a thought . . . though in the deeply improbable event that it should happen, I'd be thrilled to collect the royalties. Instead, I adopted the Messori model of setting the scene, framing the questions, and then allowing Dolan largely to speak for himself. This is really a book "with" Dolan, rather than a book "about" him, which is probably the best way to catch a glimpse of what his ascent augurs for the Church.

Dolan agreed to the format, and over the course of late 2009 and on different occasions in 2010 and 2011 he agreed to sit down for several hours of interviews spread over the course of two days. All together, we spent about thirty hours in formal on-the-record conversation, with several dozen more hours of me tagging along behind Dolan at various events, riding with him in the archbishop's minivan on the way to and from various appointments, and sitting around in his study in the residence at St. Patrick's Cathedral late into the night. I've taken those sprawling, unsystematic conversations and organized them into three basic categories: a brief look at Dolan's biography and its influence on who he is today; a review of all the hot-button debates about Catholicism, and how Dolan thinks about them; and a consideration of the spiritual essentials of Catholic life, including Dolan's reflections on how Catholicism can best offer a message of hope to the modern world.

There are a few revelations scattered throughout, such as Dolan's close friendship with a priest who died of AIDS in the mid-1980s and the impact of that experience on his thinking about the importance of compassion in relating to people who fall short of the ideals of Catholic morality. Dolan also talks candidly about his relationship with two men he's replaced over the course of his career, who for different reasons are polarizing figures: Archbishop Rembert Weakland of Milwaukee and Cardinal Edward Egan of New York. At various points, Dolan reveals a few behind-the-scenes details of interactions over the years among the American bishops, or between American bishops and the Vatican, and he also talks about his encounters with U.S. president Barack Obama (whom he admires for both his civility and his political shrewdness). For the most part, however, our conversations were not about a search for "scoops," but rather an exploration of Dolan's mind.

Here's one other key difference between this book and *The Ratzinger Report*: While the essence of Messori's book may have been to draw lines in the sand, the primary thrust this time around is to try to explain what Catholicism is for rather than what it's against. In other words, the agenda here is to take a trip in Affirmative Orthodoxy with the Catholic leader in America who best seems to embody its spirit. At the end, one can agree or disagree with Dolan's outlook, but one may at least be better equipped to understand why thoughtful modern women and men might still believe there's something worth considering in the Catholic message.

A footnote is in order.

America's most famous Catholic priest, the acclaimed novelist and sociologist Father Andrew Greeley, once said that the original sin of clerical culture in the Church is envy. Anytime a member of the clerical club starts to make a name for himself, murmurs begin to make the rounds: "That guy's an exhibitionist. He's vain, he's a climber, he's just interested in grabbing headlines and making himself look good." While that may be a bit of a caricature, there's enough merit to Greeley's observation that I feel compelled to put the following disclaimer on the record: This book was not Tim Dolan's idea. I approached him, not the other way around. Truth be told, to the extent that Dolan ever agonizes about anything, he agonized about this. He later told me that he went to his friend and mentor, Cardinal Justin Rigali of Philadelphia, for advice. When Rigali asked what was holding him back, Dolan said he worried that people might think he's ambitious. Rigali's reply, according to Dolan, was that such a fear could itself be construed as ambitious, in the sense that Dolan would be turning down an opportunity to evangelize, to get the Church's message out, in order to protect his reputation. That apparently sealed the deal.

As Dolan himself notes in our interviews, he's basically beyond the point at which careerist ambitions would make much sense. He's already the archbishop of New York, so the only real higher rung left on the career ladder is the papacy—the longest of long shots, and in any event, the trash heaps of church history are littered with the carcasses of journalists who have tried to predict the next pope. A much safer forecast is that whatever the future may have in store for Dolan—whether he stays in New York until he dies, whether he's eventually called to Rome to work in a senior Vatican post, or something else entirely—he will be a force in the Catholic Church both nationally and internationally, and it's well worth trying to discern what that might mean.

SECTION ONE

~

WHO DOLAN IS

ONE

The Dolan Story

During the era of Christendom in medieval Europe, maps of the world showed Jerusalem at the dead center. The premise was that God's plan for salvation had to be reflected even in the geography of the planet, so that the place where the faith was born would naturally fall in the middle. In the same spirit, if a map of the United States were to be drawn up to reflect Tim Dolan's own personal salvation history, the dead center would probably fall in the unlikely spot of Ballwin, Missouri, a Saint Louis suburb where the Dolan family relocated when the future archbishop was four years old, and where he would come of age in Holy Infant Parish—to this day, his version of the Platonic form of Catholic parish life.

Dolan was born on February 6, 1950, the oldest of five children of Robert and Shirley Dolan. Both parents were Irish Catholic, and both were part of the broad post–World War II American move to the suburbs. Robert Dolan was a factory foreman and Shirley Dolan a stay-at-home mom, and in 1954, four years after their oldest son was born, they bought a new home in Ballwin for the whopping sum of $11,000. Dolan describes it as a happy home, one in which his parents were deeply in love and in which family was their absolute priority, but he also acknowledges that things weren't always idyllic. For one thing, money was chronically tight. Dolan says his brothers and sisters laugh about it now, mimicking the way their dad would joust with bill collectors over the phone at night: "Didn't you get that check yet? Oh, the damn post office!" Dolan says he now realizes that the pressure to make ends meet for a large family had to be a perpetual source of anxiety and may be part of the reason that his father died at fifty-one.

To illustrate the sacrifices his parents made on his behalf, Dolan tells the story of his ordination to the priesthood in 1976, when his parents insisted on buying his chalice. They had it hand made and included jewels from his mother's engagement ring in a Celtic cross at the base. The finished product cost roughly $300, which was real money in the mid-seventies, and the check they wrote to pay the bill bounced. Dolan insists that every time he says Mass, the chalice reminds him of the "crushed wheat and grapes" along his path to the priesthood.

Though Dolan acknowledges that he can sound like a Hallmark card when talking about his childhood, he nonetheless insists: "The faith is the greatest supernatural gift you can have, but the greatest natural gift anyone can have is a happy, loving family. I was lucky enough to have both."

In many ways, Dolan's lifelong aptitude for building bridges reflects his formative experiences in his family. Here's how he describes it:

> My dad was a very upbeat guy, with a tremendous sense of humor, who would always see the best in people. The kind of people that others didn't get along with, he liked. It was almost like he wanted to give them a chance. We can often remember him saying to my mom, "Honey, they're not all that bad." You know, she'd say, "Do we have to have them here again? Why did you invite them to the barbeque?" Dad would say, "They're not all that bad. They're good guys." Dad's philosophy of life was that if you can get somebody on a lawn chair, outside on a Sunday, while he was doing pork steaks in the barbeque pit, listening to Harry Caray and the Saint Louis Cardinals in the background

with a bottle of Busch, you could win over anybody. There's nobody that
if you eyeball, have a beer with, and really start talking to . . . rare would
be the person with whom you would not find a common bond.

Aside from his family, the most important early influence on Dolan
was unquestionably Holy Infant Parish in Ballwin, which remains his
model for a vibrant Catholic community. There he drank deeply from
the well of the American Catholic ethos of the 1950s—flourishing,
self-confident, still innocent of the deep internal divisions that would
erupt in the wake of the Second Vatican Council (1962–65). He cred-
its the Sisters of Mercy from Drogheda, Ireland, who arrived in the
parish in 1957, along with a succession of strong but loving pastors,
with framing his basic outlook on the faith. His eyes still light up when
he describes his memories of traditional Catholic flourishes such as
May Crownings of the Virgin Mary and Forty Hours devotions. Dolan
insists that he never found this all-embracing Catholic milieu, what
some describe as "ghetto Catholicism," stifling or suffocating. Instead,
he says, it "gave meaning and purpose and joy to life." For him, "there
was a sense of cohesion, even though we were never Shiite Catholics."

It seemed the most natural thing in the world for Dolan, in 1964, to
enter the minor seminary in Saint Louis, Saint Louis Preparatory Seminary, known as "Prep," at the tender age of fourteen. He sometimes
waxes so nostalgic about the glory days of his youth that he's accused of
being a throwback, perhaps representing the best of fifties-era Catholicism but a man out of time today. While he understands the basis of
that impression, he says fundamentally it's not so:

I've often said that when I was a parish priest, subconsciously what
I wanted to do was to create an environment like the one I remem-
ber in Holy Infant in Ballwin. That was such a sustaining, uplifting,
happy period for me . . . I thought that if these kids in fifth grade that
I'm teaching can look back twenty-five years from now with the same

warmth, gratitude, and happy memories that I have of Holy Infant, I'll
be doing them a big favor, because this means a lot to me. Am I nostalgic
for nuns in veils, altars turned around, and that kind of stuff? No, not
at all. But am I nostalgic for what you might say is the best in a cultural
Catholicism where there's warmth, acceptance, and a sense of belonging,
just an innate focus and meaning of life? You bet I am, and I wouldn't
apologize for that. If that's what's meant by a "throwback," bring it on.
But if you mean fiddlebacks and maniples, forget it.

For those who may not be conversant with old-time Catholicism, fiddlebacks and maniples are vestments worn by priests while saying the old Latin Mass, sometimes popularly called the Tridentine rite, which was revived by Pope Benedict XVI in 2007 as an "extraordinary form" of the Mass. For the record, Dolan says he has nothing against the Latin Mass but has no special passion for promoting it either. He's interested not so much in the external forms of the Catholic ethos in which he was raised but rather in what it felt like from the inside—an all-encompassing sense of the meaning of life, expressed and lived in a community where people genuinely knew and loved one another.

One other aspect of Dolan's early experience of the Catholic Church worth recording is his fond memories of the pastors at Holy Infant Parish, especially Father Jeremiah Callahan, who led the parish from 1958, when Dolan was eight years old, to 1967, by which time Dolan had already been in the minor seminary for three years. Dolan says Callahan had a "towering influence" on him, and the traces of that imprint do seem striking. For one thing, Dolan says, Callahan had a swashbuckling, manly swagger. He had been a chaplain to American troops during the Battle of the Bulge and loved to tell stories from the war. For another, Dolan says, Callahan had a great sense of humor, and cut a large swath through the parish—he was a cigar-smoking, back-slapping, vintage 1950s-era Catholic priest. (As Dolan told me about Callahan, he himself was lighting a cigar.)

Yet Dolan also has a clear-eyed recollection of another feature of Callahan's personality: a serious problem with alcohol. He can remember passing the rectory as he walked to the parish school in the mornings and occasionally seeing Callahan's car on the lawn, where he had apparently left it the night before after rolling home sauced. Dolan says he was struck at the time by how such a heroic figure, a pastor who was deeply loved in the neighborhood and an extraordinarily effective priest, could also be such an imperfect human being. To some extent, Dolan now says, the experience inoculated him against the quasi-Gnostic tendency to want a perfect Church or perfect clergy. (Eventually Callahan was removed from the parish by the archbishop of Saint Louis and sent off for treatment.)

Dolan persevered in his seminary studies through the turmoil of .the late 1960s, at a time when many priests were leaving the priesthood and some were beginning to question the faith itself. He certainly knew plenty of priests and seminarians who bailed out, and he says he respected their choice, though he sometimes struggled to understand it. An assistant pastor at Holy Infant named Robert Foley, for example, left the priesthood while Dolan was in seminary, and even though Dolan found that decision "devastating," the two men parted on good terms. (Though they subsequently lost touch, Dolan reported that Foley, now a retired lawyer, recently turned up in New York and they had a "great time together.") As for himself, Dolan says he never really experienced a crisis of faith or deep doubts about his vocation to the priesthood. In one reflection of the topsy-turvy nature of the late 1960s, Dolan says that it was only once he was in the seminary that he actually got a girlfriend—and, he says, "I enjoyed it!"

Dolan's sense of calling to the priesthood ultimately prevailed. Unlike many Catholic conservatives today, Dolan doesn't look back at the 1960s and 1970s as a sort of ecclesiastical Dark Ages or wilderness period. Instead, he tends to emphasize the positive energies he recalls from that era:

I don't have the antipathy to those years that some have. I know they were an era of excesses, and sometimes I'll now say about some loopy idea, "Oh, that's so sixties-ish or seventies-ish." Unfortunately, in the sixties and seventies there were some liturgical abuses and catechetical pollution that we still have to clean up. But I don't have any hostility toward those days. I guess I look back and say, "Hey, they were kind of normative for me too." I can remember the excitement, the promise, the exhilaration, after the council [Second Vatican Council]. That was all part of my happiness about being a Catholic.

Just as Dolan never really had any doubts about the Church, the Church never had doubts about him. From the very first moments of his ecclesiastical career he's been on the fast track to leadership. Monsignor Richard Hanneke, currently an official in the Archdiocese of Saint Louis, is a former seminary classmate of Dolan's and says that when the guys in their class would speculate about who among them might one day become a bishop, there was "no hesitation whatsoever" in pointing to Dolan.

As a seminarian in the 1970s, Dolan was sent to study at the prestigious North American College in Rome (NAC), widely considered the West Point of the American Catholic Church. There he met Monsignor John Tracy Ellis, the most distinguished American Church historian of his generation, and fell under his spell. After his ordination in 1976, Dolan spent three years as an assistant pastor at Immacolata Parish in Richmond Heights, Missouri, before heading to the Catholic University of America to do graduate studies in Church history under Ellis. Dolan tells the story that he applied for a special scholarship offered by the university for a diocesan priest to study Church history. Dolan won the scholarship, and when he arrived in Washington he made a point of thanking Ellis for selecting him from among all the diocesan priests in America. Ellis informed a humbled Dolan that in truth, he had been the only one to apply.

Dolan eventually wrote his doctoral dissertation on Archbishop Edwin O'Hara of Kansas City. Now all but forgotten, O'Hara was a major force in American Catholicism in the first half of the twentieth century, promoting liturgical reform, the minimum wage, Catholic biblical studies, and a host of other projects conventionally regarded as part of the progressive Catholic movement in America before World War II. Dolan said he was especially interested to see where O'Hara might have fit in the defining tension of American Catholic life of the late nineteenth and early twentieth centuries, which was the clash in the American hierarchy between "Americanizers" and "conservatives." Putting on his hat as a Church historian, Dolan describes that tension this way:

> *We're talking about the 1880s and 1890s, with strong corollaries today. The Americanizers back then would have felt that there was a basic concord between the genius of Catholicism and the genius of the United States of America. In general, the Church can get along with culture. Second, they believed that the Holy See is at its best when it leaves us alone. Third, the so-called enlightened projects of society more or less are compatible with the Catholic agenda, such as education, human dignity, social progress—these are all things the Church can and should hook up with. An interesting example was the temperance movement. This was a chic progressive cause, and the Irish said, "We can get into that." Fourth, they felt that ethnic identifications need to be diminished and deemphasized.*
>
> *The conservatives, obviously, differed. They believed that at its core, American culture is inimical to the Catholic agenda. Second, the Holy See is at its best when it's intruding and when it's energetic. The more the Holy See condemns, the better off we are. Third, they saw chic society, enlightened society, as our enemy. The progressives, they believe, hate us deep down. They might use us for certain causes, but in general they don't like us. We're never going to get into their country clubs no*

matter how often Cardinal Gibbons talks to Teddy Roosevelt. Fourth,
ethnic identities need to be accented because it's the only way we'll save
the faith. That was especially strong among the Germans. More or less,
except for the fourth, I think the same characteristics are true today of
both the Americanist and the conservative camps in the U.S. Church.

Dolan concludes that O'Hara probably belonged with the Americanizers, even if the sharp distinction between the two camps is mostly a historical abstraction, and most real bishops fell somewhere in between. As for where Dolan himself fits, he simply says, "I don't know," claiming that he can see merit in each position.

Two features of Dolan's academic background are worth teasing out, because of what they illustrate about the kind of man he is. First, John Tracy Ellis, whom Dolan still regards as a hero and mentor, was seen in his lifetime as a moderate-to-liberal in Catholic affairs. Even though Dolan is conservative in his own leanings, his apprenticeship under Ellis gave him an education in how someone whose views differ from his own can nevertheless possess enormous erudition and insight, hence be worth taking seriously.

Second, Dolan's training as a historian makes him something of an exception among bishops, whose academic background is more typically in dogmatic theology or canon law. Those disciplines tend to impose a systematic way of thinking and a clear—in some cases, perhaps, even rigid—sense of right and wrong, of who the good guys and bad guys are. History, by way of contrast, tends to make one sensitive to the shades of gray, and also to the ways in which even heroes are fallible and even villains have their virtues. A striking share of bishops around the world most often identified as pastoral figures and reconcilers tend to have studied either Church history or biblical studies—perhaps because both disciplines tend to make people flexible in their judgments and inclined to taking the long view, rather than being caught up exclusively in today's battles.

After finishing his graduate studies in Washington, Dolan looked forward to returning to Saint Louis to teach Church history at Kenrick-Glennon Seminary but instead found himself assigned to Curé of Ars Parish, in Shrewsbury, Missouri, as assistant pastor. In the typically brusque corporate style of Church management at the time, Dolan was simply told that the seminary "doesn't need you," even though that's what his years of academic work had pointed to and what, in effect, he had been promised by Archbishop John May. In Dolan's trademark upbeat fashion, he took the disappointment in stride: "I guess I could have been bitter," he says. "I could have been cynical, but I wasn't. I was thrilled."

After his brief assignment at Curé of Ars, he moved to another parish, Little Flower, and never did end up teaching Church history on a full-time basis (although he did end up teaching part-time at Kenrick-Glennon and Saint Louis University). Yet he says that those assignments were "the best thing that could have ever happened to me," and that his eight years as a parish priest were in many ways the happiest of his life.

You gotta believe me when I say that I always wanted to be a parish priest. I hope that's clear. Last May I went home to baptize my new little great-niece, and I stayed with my brother Patrick, who married a girl from Little Flower Parish, which was my last pastoral assignment. It's a beautiful parish, and now they live there. I was taking my two little nieces and my nephew Patrick, who was in a stroller, on a walk through the parish, and I'm kind of nostalgic. Then it dawned on me that I'm doing the same thing in New York that I did here. I'm still celebrating Mass for my people every day, I'm still trying to give a halfway decent sermon, I'm still trying to be good to the sick, I'm still trying to teach kids, I'm still trying to reach out to the unchurched and to be good to the poor. I'm still trying to balance a budget and keep buildings up. Now it's on steroids, it's 2.6 million people, but in terms of job description it's the same. I'm still a parish priest!

In 1987 Dolan was lifted out of parish life and called to work in the Apostolic Nunciature in Washington, D.C., effectively the papal embassy to the United States. (The United States and the Holy See, which is the technical term for the Vatican as a sovereign state under international law, had established full diplomatic relations three years earlier under President Ronald Reagan.) Dolan served there under two nuncios, both Italians who went on to become cardinals: Pio Laghi and Agostino Cacciavillan. It was at the nunciature that Dolan got his first real taste of behind-the-scenes Church politics.

I can remember the first time I took a walk with those guys, and they're talking—not in a gossipy way, but simply because it's workshop talk—about who's going to go where as a bishop. They would say, "Oh, no, Laghi says that guy should be held for this." I'm thinking, "Dear God, I'm in the middle of this. This is actually going on here." This isn't just over a poker game in Saint Louis with some of the fellas, speculating about whether John May's going to get the red hat or not. This was the real ball game. This was like going to the show, as baseball players say of the major leagues.

If Dolan hadn't realized it before, the experience brought home that he was probably moving up the career ladder. He jokingly describes his thought process at the time: "Working at the nunciature and seeing how bishops are made, actually working on it, made me think, 'Hell, if these guys get through, I guess there is a danger of me becoming one!'"

By 1992, Dolan was ready to return to Saint Louis, and in 1994 found himself appointed rector of the North American College in Rome. That appointment came just weeks after Justin Rigali, a long-time American power broker in the Vatican, had been sent back to the States to take over as archbishop of Saint Louis. Though Rigali would quickly become an important friend and mentor for Dolan, he was not the primary force in Dolan's appointment to the North American

College. That role belonged to then-Bishop Edward Egan of Bridge-port, Connecticut, who at the time served as the chair of the college's board of governors, and whom Dolan would later succeed as arch-bishop of New York. Egan persuaded the Congregation for Catholic Education in the Vatican to set aside its normal protocol and confirm Dolan without a lengthy search. Egan was able to pull that off largely because the top man at the congregation at the time was Cardinal Pio Laghi, who remembered Dolan fondly from his service at the nuncia-ture in Washington.

Dolan led the North American College from 1994 to 2001, and it was a critical moment in his career because it transformed him from a known quantity among Catholic insiders to someone with a grow-ing public reputation both in the States and in Rome. Among other things, Dolan agreed to cooperate with a behind-the-scenes look at life in the NAC called *The New Men*, written by Brian Murphy, at the time a Rome-based reporter for the Associated Press. When the book appeared in 1997, it gave some Church officials heartburn for its can-did description of the struggles of some of the seminarians, including tensions over former girlfriends and conflict with bishops back home, but it also painted a warm and deeply human picture of the journey toward priesthood.

Later, Dolan himself became a bestselling author when he published a collection of his own talks to the seminarians, titled *Priests for the Third Millennium*. That book came out in September 2000, just ahead of the massive sexual-abuse crisis that rocked the Catholic Church in the United States in 2002 and 2003. Dolan's positive vision of the priest-hood was seen in some quarters as a riposte to more critical treatments of priestly life and formation in controversial works such as *The Chang-ing Face of the Priesthood* by Father Donald Cozzens.

Yet among the seminarians at the North American College dur-ing Dolan's tenure, the focus in looking back usually isn't so much on Dolan's public persona as on the upbeat climate he seemed to foster inside the college itself. Father Raymond de Souza, a Canadian priest and frequent commentator on Church affairs who lived at the North American College under Dolan, says simply: "He ran a happy house."

Once again, Dolan anticipated going back into a parish in Saint Louis at the end of his tenure at the North American College, and once again fate intervened. In June 2001 he was appointed an auxiliary bishop of Saint Louis, where his toughest assignment was as Rigali's point man on the sexual-abuse crisis. Just a year later Dolan was named to arguably the most sensitive post in the American Church at the time: Archbishop of Milwaukee, replacing the legendary Rembert Weakland, who had reigned for a quarter century. Weakland had been compelled to step down in disgrace following revelations that he had secretly paid more than $450,000 in archdiocesan funds to settle a complaint of sexual harassment made by a man Weakland eventually acknowledged as a former lover, though he denied charges of coercion or abuse.

Those revelations would have been damaging under any set of circumstances, but against the backdrop of the larger national crisis over sexual abuse, they left Milwaukee's Catholic community in tatters. Adding to the complexity of the assignment, Weakland also had a reputation as a leading liberal, and many expected Dolan to lead a sort of "Reagan revolution," shifting the goalposts in the local church considerably to the right. All of that seemed to set the stage for a fairly bruising tenure.

No naïf on Church politics, Dolan knew from the outset that he was in for a bumpy ride. He tells the story of getting a call from the papal nuncio, at the time Archbishop Gabriel Montalvo, who asked him to drop by his Washington, D.C., office. Dolan was under the impression that it was a social call to chew over old times in the nunciature, so when Montalvo began by offering him a drink and a cigarette, he politely declined. When Montalvo then informed Dolan that he had been tapped for Milwaukee, Dolan's first response was "I think I'll have that drink and cigarette now!"

Early signals seemed to augur trouble. Dolan describes his first encounter with the priests in Milwaukee:

> *I was installed on August 28, and I had my first big town meeting*
> *with the priests on September 21. In retrospect, I was probably too*
> *spiritual and lofty. I kind of gave a rector's conference. I said we've*
> *got a crisis, fellas, but I come in with immense respect for you and this*
> *archdiocese. I think we have to see this crisis as a call to integrity, as a*
> *call to holiness, as a call to humility. We have to accent the basics that*
> *make us who we are as priests. After forty-five minutes or so I closed*
> *the book thinking, "Wasn't that great? Everybody's going to stand*
> *up and applaud." Then I asked, "Any questions?" A guy raised his*
> *hand: "Yeah. Are we still going to be able to live wherever we want?*
> *Are you going to keep the salaries the highest in the country, and can*
> *we still retire at sixty-eight?" I thought to myself, "What is this, a*
> *damned Teamsters meeting?"*

In the end, Dolan certainly had his critics in Milwaukee. Victims of
sexual abuse praised his willingness to meet them and to hear their stories, but they sometimes caustically asked what he was willing to offer
beyond a hug. In particular, they faulted his reluctance to release case
files and other confidential Church documents, and his preference for
handling cases through private arbitration rather than formal litigation.
Weakland loyalists and Catholic liberals complained that while their
archdiocese once loomed as "the Milan of America," a reference to the
Italian archdiocese's reputation as a laboratory for creativity and reform,
much of that luster was lost during Dolan's seven-year term. Daniel
Maguire, a liberal Catholic theologian at Milwaukee's Marquette University who was banned by Dolan from speaking on Church property,
opined that Dolan "is in keeping with Church policy that theologians
are to listen and obey"—a stance that, according to Maguire, "turns
theology into a form of magic, expertise without study." Some conservatives, meanwhile, charged that Dolan didn't move nearly far or

fast enough in dismantling the Weakland legacy. Nor was Dolan's af-
fability enough to offset the long-term decline in Mass attendance in
Milwaukee that began in the early 1990s and continued throughout his
seven-year term.

Yet many observers in Milwaukee today say that Dolan proved
to be an enormously popular figure among ordinary Mass-going
Catholics in the pews, with younger seminarians, and in the media,
and that he eventually won over most of the priests and lay leaders
in the archdiocese. (Dolan insists, for example, that the priest who
asked him the question at that first meeting went on to become one
of his best friends.) For a local church that badly needed a shot in the
arm, Dolan's good humor and robust sense of confidence seemed to
play well.

"I think he really steadied the Church at a time when it needed to
be steadied," said Milwaukee mayor Tom Barrett, himself a Catholic,
at the time of Dolan's 2009 appointment as archbishop of New York.
"I'm just thankful we had him here close to seven years."

Moreover, Dolan's conciliatory style took the edge off what could
have been a showdown between the old liberal guard and the zealous
new "John Paul II" set, both of which had come to see Milwaukee as a
symbolic battle zone.

Here's how Dolan describes the approach he took:

> I had to decide early on what the strategy was going to be. You can
> see the choice I had. Was I going to come in as an enforcer? I knew
> that some of the priests and lay leaders, who had come to the top with
> Weakland, were suspicious of me. They thought I was some kind of
> Roman executioner. So what was my strategy? My strategy became, I
> need to win their trust, and I need to be very patient. I hope I can get
> to a comfort level where they trust me, and know that I love them and
> trust them, so that they'll be okay with certain changes that I want to
> make eventually. I hope that worked.

Part of Dolan's strategy in Milwaukee also reflected an old bit of wisdom from Woody Allen, which is that "80 percent of success is showing up." He deliberately avoided getting caught up in affairs outside the archdiocese, in part because he knew he had inherited an archdiocese that needed some tender loving care. Roughly six months after his installation in Milwaukee, Dolan was approached about playing a key role in a Vatican-decreed visitation of American seminaries, as part of the Church's response to the sexual-abuse crisis. It seemed a natural for Dolan given his years at the North American College, and he understood that the Vatican was asking for his help at a moment when the Church badly needed it. Yet in the end he demurred, calculating that the best service he could render would be to help calm the waters in Milwaukee.

Dolan's effort to win trust extended to his personal relationship with the man he replaced, Archbishop Rembert Weakland:

> *Going in, I was thinking that perhaps he was going to be a problem. I thought that this was a guy, from what I have seen and read, who would be somewhat resistant to the reforms of John Paul II. He would approach the pontificate of John Paul II as a blip on the screen that would eventually come to an end, so we could get back to what was intended [by Vatican II]. So, there was trepidation there. . . . [But] there was just no opposition. He was as good as could be. I sought his counsel. I would talk to him. I enjoyed his company tremendously. He has a great intellect, and great wisdom. There was never a word of criticism publicly. I'm sure he was tempted. I mean, he had his groupies who I'm sure were trying to bait him. But he never did it—never, never. I took criticism from some people and some priests, especially outside of Milwaukee, that I didn't tell him to leave. There were brother bishops who thought I should have done that. But he was supportive, he was kind, he was fraternal. At his core, he's a churchman. Rembert Weakland is anything but a flame-throwing God knows what. He's just not.*

As things turned out, the challenges of Milwaukee were simply a warm-up act for the next major twist in Dolan's career.

• • •

By April 2007, when Cardinal Edward Egan of New York turned seventy-five, the Catholic rumor mill in America went into overdrive with speculation about who might take over in the Big Apple. It was generally agreed that the Vatican would be unlikely to make a move until after Pope Benedict XVI's trip to Washington and New York in April 2008, but that didn't stop anyone from positing theories about who might be in line for the job. At least a dozen names were in circulation at one stage or another, but in most handicapping, two candidates loomed especially large: Dolan and Archbishop Wilton Gregory of Atlanta, a charismatic African American prelate who had led the American bishops through the nightmare of the sexual-abuse crisis in 2002. Gregory was widely seen as the candidate of the moderate wing of the American Church, while Dolan appealed more to the conservatives. Both seemed to have the PR savvy and the mettle to handle the country's biggest stage, but each man would represent a slightly different signal about the overall direction of Catholicism in America.

Dolan says that as the drumbeat of speculation became steadily more intense throughout 2007 and 2008, he was aware that New York was a live possibility but did his best not to dwell on it.

Did I ever think about the possibility that I could become archbishop of New York? Yes. It would be a bald-faced lie if I said it never entered my mind. Did I crave it? Was I posturing for it? Did I think it was going to happen? No. But did I think, "These rumors about New York are getting a little hot and heavy, maybe there's something to it?" Yes. I'm not going to deny that, but I can truthfully say that internally I was doing what I could not to think about it. That's for two reasons. First of all, it's not good for your humility. Secondly, it's probably not going

to happen, and if you start thinking about it, you're going to be one
unhappy guy. Spiritually and strategically, I would not allow myself to
dwell on it.

Given Dolan's loyalty to Rigali, it was especially painful for him to watch his mentor end his career in crisis in July 2010, in the wake of a grand jury report in Philadelphia that charged that the thirty-seven priests facing accusations of misconduct had been left in ministry by Rigali in violation of the U.S. bishops' own policies.

In the end the nod went to Dolan. That's an outcome seen by Church insiders as due at least in part to the behind-the-scenes clout of Rigali, the veteran Vatican insider who is still a member of the Congregation for Bishops in Rome, the body responsible for recommending bishops' appointments around the world to the pope. (The Italian cardinal who ran the Congregation for Bishops at the time of the Dolan appointment, Giovanni Battista Re, was an old friend and coworker of Rigali's. The two served together under the legendary Cardinal Giovanni Benelli, the right-hand man of Pope Paul VI.)

In New York, Dolan found himself taking over from a man who in some ways had seemed to leave his archdiocese adrift. While there was never a whiff of personal scandal around Egan, during his nine years in New York he nonetheless acquired a reputation as aloof, arrogant, and heavy-handed. To be fair, even Egan's most acerbic critics generally credit him with tackling a serious financial problem left behind by the late Cardinal John O'Connor; Egan's gift for trimming expenses earned him the nickname "Edward Scissorhands." Yet financial management often seemed to be about the only area where Egan drew high marks. In late 2006 an anonymous letter purportedly written by a group of New York priests made the rounds of the blogosphere, charging Egan with possessing "a severely vindictive nature," being "cruel and cavalier" toward his priests, and presiding over an archdiocese that had never been "so fractured and seemingly hopeless as it is now." By all accounts, Egan was stung by the criticism, and according to some reports he even suggested that it was coming from sexually abusive priests looking to deflect attention from their own guilt. The cumulative effect of such episodes was to create the impression of an archbishop, and an archdiocese, under siege.

Under any circumstances, Dolan's ready wit and self-confident style would probably have played well in New York, but compared with Egan, he came across as Rudy Giuliani, Abraham Lincoln, and Saint Paul all rolled into one. Even the *New York Times*, which is not typically regarded as soft on Catholic bishops, hailed the new man in town as "genial." Probably the single-most common phrase heard in and around New York after the new archbishop made his debut was "What a breath of fresh air!" In fact, the tendency to contrast Egan the Bully with Dolan the Nice Guy is so widespread, in New York and beyond, that Dolan finds it troubling:

> *I'm confounded by the public perception of Ed Egan. He's anything but this unfriendly, stern, reclusive, crabby guy. He's just the opposite. You never want your compliment to be at somebody else's expense. You know the saying that was a favorite of Pope John XXIII: "In essentials, unity; in nonessentials, diversity; in all things, charity." Plus, to give [Egan] credit, he did leave me with a well-oiled machine in terms of administrative things, and an archdiocese that puts a priority on parish life: catechetists, Catholic schools, charities, and communications. He left me an archdiocese in very good shape, and a lot of bishops cannot say that about their predecessor. I'm highly appreciative of all that.*

As in Milwaukee, Dolan has emphasized physical presence during his early period on the job. Unlike Egan, he's made a point of celebrating Mass at seven-thirty each morning in Saint Patrick's Cathedral, and he also takes the ten-fifteen A.M. Mass on Sundays. (Unlike O'Connor, however, Dolan doesn't then hold an impromptu press conference on the cathedral steps.)

He's also made a point of moving around the archdiocese to visit each of its vicariates. I watched Dolan one night in Westchester County when he told the priests about a meeting he had had earlier in the day with Bishop Daniel Jenky of Peoria, Illinois, about the sainthood cause for Archbishop Fulton Sheen, the legendary 1950s-era televangelist. Jenky wanted to bring Sheen's remains back to his hometown in Peoria, which would mean removing them from their current location in a crypt under the high altar of Saint Patrick's Cathedral. Dolan said he wasn't sure what to do, though, he quipped, maybe getting Sheen out of Saint Pat's "would finally let Francis Spellman rest in peace." The priests howled with laughter, knowing of the legendary tensions between Sheen and New York's powerful Cardinal Spellman.

Inevitably, Dolan's honeymoon in New York has ebbed as the practical realities of trying to govern assert themselves. In early 2010, Dolan faced his first tough choice about closing Catholic schools, and by his own account, he didn't handle it as well as he could have. In the end, he decided to close one school and merge two others, a decision that still strikes him as correct. The announcement, however, was another matter. Dolan said he thought it was rolled out only after all the important stakeholders had been consulted, but he learned after the fact that a few veteran benefactors of the archdiocese with ties to those schools learned about it through the media, felt blindsided, and essentially declared that they would no longer support the archdiocese with their pocketbooks. It was a hard reminder, Dolan says, that leadership is not only about making the right decisions but about bringing the right people along with you.

Dolan has also found himself jousting with the *New York Times*, at one point criticizing columnist Maureen Dowd for what he considered unfair criticism of the pope, at another taking on the news editors for their approach to reporting on Benedict XVI's history on the sex-abuse scandals. While some Catholics cheered, others wondered if the tit-for-tat was slightly unbecoming for the archbishop of New York, and still others worried that Dolan risked seeming defensive and thin-skinned, a perception of the Church that New York Catholics felt they had only recently set aside with Egan's retirement.

Dolan also drew mixed reviews for his involvement in the controversy that erupted in 2010 over a proposed Muslim cultural center to be erected two blocks from the World Trade Center site in lower Manhattan. In effect, the experience was a crash course for Dolan in the high-octane, take-no-prisoners spirit of politics in the Big Apple. He tried to strike a balance, defending the right of Muslims to build such a center, but also acknowledging the sensitivities of 9/11 survivors and the families of victims. Dolan volunteered to act as a mediator, an invitation which was never really taken up. In the end, Dolan says, he wonders if he let down New York mayor Michael Bloomberg, who took a principled stand in favor of religious freedom: "One of these days I'm going to ask him about it," Dolan said, "because I feel comfortable enough to say, 'Mayor, did I let you down when you needed some help?'"

Dolan's role in the debate over gay marriage in New York, which ended with a historic vote in June 2011 to allow gays and lesbian couples to wed, also drew mixed reviews. His quip about "Orwellian social engineering," and a blog post in which he compared New York to China and North Korea for "redefining rights," was derided in some quarters as over-the-top and embarrassing, costing Dolan some of the political capital his gracious style had earned. Yet opponents of the law had the opposite beef, charging that at critical moments Dolan was missing in action. A June 25, 2011, article in the *New York Times* asserted that "the Catholic Church, arguably the only institution with the authority and reach to derail same-sex marriage, seemed to shrink from the fight." Reporter Michael Barbaro noted that Dolan "did not travel to Albany or deliver a major speech in the final days of the session," and that as the bill hurtled to a vote, Dolan was out of town at a bishops' meeting. To some, the suggestion was that Dolan had, in effect, blinked. Whatever one makes of those reactions, it illustrates that Dolan's charm hardly inoculates him against political criticism.

Finally, there's a root question about Dolan's tenure in New York that, so far, does not have a clear answer. New York is a behemoth, arguably one of the most complex ecclesiastical jurisdictions anywhere in the world, and it would therefore be a mammoth challenge for even the most adept nuts-and-bolts administrator, the wonkiest of all policy wonks, to get his hands around it. Dolan is such an extrovert, so thoroughly inclined both by temperament and conviction to focus on evangelizing the world outside the Church, one might legitimately wonder if his destiny in terms of internal Catholic life in New York is to be a beguiling and well-liked figurehead presiding over an essentially unchanged reality at the grass roots. A veteran New York priest put the point succinctly in December 2009: "There may be a new sheriff in town, but this is still Dodge City."

In the meantime, Dolan has been on the job long enough to form some early impressions of the unique opportunities serving as the archbishop of New York creates. For one thing, he says, he's come to see the transient, materialist, and ultrasecular elements of life in the city as an opportunity rather than a problem.

One of the things about New York is that you meet a lot of people who are "in between" in their lives. I meet a lot of women and men in their mid- to late twenties, who came to New York to have it all, and it's not working out. Sometimes it's working out economically, but often it's not working life-wise. The word I'm going to use, though sometimes I'm afraid it's a bromide, is nihilism. There is an atmosphere of nihilism, meaning that people are scared about the nothingness of what they have. Even though they might have a nice condo, even though they might have a nice salary—I know this sounds like the rich young man, or Francis of Assisi, or whatever, but so what? It's real. . . . What I have to offer them, what we together have to offer them, is a sense of a coherent and attractive worldview that helps make sense of their lives. I find one of the people who wrote most movingly about this to be Andrew Greeley. He borrows it from David Tracy, about the whole Catholic imagination. His point was that poetry always precedes prose, so first we absorb images, values, a worldview, a sense of dare and dreaming and hope. That's what the Church is best at.

Dolan also says he's made his peace with the fact that as archbishop of New York, inevitably everything he does has echoes around the country, and in some cases even around the world.

Since coming to New York, I'm much more aware of the didactic consequences of the things that I do because they're going to be quoted. So far, has that stopped me from doing anything? I don't think so. I also don't believe I've done anything thinking, "I'm going to do this because I want to shoot up a flare." But in a more general sense, I would hope that maybe I can offer a posture of availability, a sense of joy, a sense of fearlessness in not being afraid to go into the lion's den to talk about things . . . I hope that would set a tone in the archdiocese, and perhaps other places, that the Church is confident and unafraid. I think that's good for the Church, and if I can do that, maybe that's a contribution I can make.

The archbishop of New York is inevitably a national leader, but Dolan's role in that regard was set in cement by his election as president of the United States Conference of Catholic Bishops on November 16, 2010, by a vote of 128 to 111. As a technical matter, the result does not mean that Dolan is now the CEO of "American Catholicism Inc.," because in reality there's no such thing. Theologically, there's no layer of authority between an individual bishop and the pope, so that a bishops' conference is more akin to a gentleman's club or a trade association rather than a parliament for a national church. Nonetheless, the election means that Dolan will serve as the public voice of the American bishops in relations with the U.S. government, the Vatican, and the media. It also means that Dolan will lead the behind-closed-doors meetings of the conference's Administrative Committee, where most of the truly important decisions are made.

Dolan's election was an upset in at least two senses. First, the American bishops historically have been reluctant to elect archbishops and cardinals to head the conference, especially those who hail from major East Coast dioceses, on the grounds that those prelates already have plenty of power and influence. Second, there's a longstanding tradition in the conference that the sitting vice president automatically ascends to the top job. Heading into the November 2010 vote, the vice-president was Bishop Gerald Kicanas of Tucson, Arizona, and most observers assumed he would be elected to the presidency. When the bishops tapped Dolan instead, many observers styled it as an upset victory for the conservative "John Paul II" faction in the conference over the more moderate, social justice–oriented wing associated with the late Cardinal Joseph Bernardin of Chicago. Prominent Catholic commentator George Weigel, for instance, wrote an essay proclaiming "The End of the Bernardin Era."

Lending some credence to that ideological interpretation was the fact that just before the USCCB vote, some conservative Catholic media outlets dredged up old reports about the role Kicanas had played as rector of Chicago's Mundelein Seminary in the early 1990s in the case of Daniel McCormack, today an ex-priest and convicted sex offender. According to those reports, there were allegations against McCormack when he was a seminarian, and yet Kicanas approved him for ordination—the implied message being that if Kicanas were elected president of the USCCB, he would be hobbled from the outset by controversy related to the sexual-abuse crisis. Kicanas denied any wrongdoing, but the timing undoubtedly didn't help his chances of claiming the conference's top job.

Others, myself included, suggested that Dolan's election had less to do with the politics of left versus right and more with the most urgent perceived need facing the conference. It would take a particularly out-of-touch bishop not to realize that the Church has had a fairly disastrous PR run in recent years, especially due to the sexual-abuse crisis. In that context, I suggested, a majority of the U.S. bishops may have decided that now is not the time for a behind-the-scenes broker of compromise, but rather for their best "front man."

Dolan expressed shock at the result.

> *Number one, it was the third time I'd been nominated [as president of the conference], and I'd never been elected. Number two, when people would tease me about it or talk to me about it, I said no, the tradition of the conference is ingrained and there's no changing it. There's no way Gerry Kicanas will not be elected. Not only was I used to losing already, but I just didn't think it would happen.*

Dolan pointed to four reasons why he was elected, which seem to blend both the ideological and the public relations explanations sketched above.

> *First, I guess there was a feeling that it was time to break the inevitability of the vice-president becoming the president. Second, as much as I think it's inaccurate, in the minds of some bishops there was a sentiment that perhaps Gerry is to the left of center. Some people thought, "We're tired of that, we don't want to go in that direction." Third, as much as I hate to admit it, I think the revelations [about McCormack] did have an impact. I think the bishops may be so fatigued that they said, as unfair as it might be, we don't want to go through that again, and that's the first story that's going to be in the headlines. Fourth, some bishops said we need somewhat of a new image. Even the many who love [Cardinal Francis George of Chicago, the former president] and who admire him immensely for the cerebral, perceptive, theological approach he brought to it, apparently thought we might need more of a folksy, conciliatory presence. Perhaps they thought I was the guy and I hope I do not disappoint them.*

In the end, Dolan said, the fourth factor—the desire for someone who could project a different and more positive public face—may have been the most decisive. There are other American bishops just as conservative as he is, and who wouldn't be hamstrung by baggage on the sexual-abuse crisis. In reality, he argued, the decisive ideological shift in the USCCB had already occurred three years earlier, with the election of George of Chicago, which Dolan referred to as marking the closest thing to a "Reagan Revolution" in the conference.

Dolan insisted that he didn't campaign for the job, and seemed especially concerned that he not be seen as part of a behind-the-scenes effort to prevent the election of Kicanas, whom he regards as a friend.

I was a little fearful that some may have been maneuvering [to block Kicanas]. I let it be known, I don't want that to happen. I like Gerry Kicanas, he's great, he's a friend of mine, and I figure he'll get it, so don't let that happen. I don't know if it did or not. . . . I don't know if there were any smoke-filled rooms, but if there were, I wasn't in them. I was actually wondering if I'd be elected his vice-president.

Having now scaled the heights of ecclesiastical accomplishment, Dolan says in some ways arriving at the top is a "liberating" experience. Given that there's no higher job in the American church to which he could aspire, he says that at least no one can suggest that whatever he does now, or fails to do, is motivated by careerist calculations.

In a way, what else is there? Anybody who would have been tempted in the past to try to analyze things I was doing as posturing or self-interest, that's gone now. Like Francis George said, "What more are they going to do to me now? I've got Chicago!" Nobody can say Dolan is ambitious anymore. You might make that accusation in the past tense—and I hope this isn't true—but you might say Dolan was ambitious and he's been rewarded. But you can't say now that anything I do is out of a sense of ambition. Now I can just be myself, which is what I've tried to do all along.

In a similar vein, Dolan insists that he has no interest in ever taking up a senior post in the Vatican: "I found when I was rector of the North American College that even with the charm of Rome, and the fact that I'd never trade those seven years, I was always eager to get back home. I would never have wanted to work there."

Just to keep the record complete, there is one higher job in the Catholic system to which a prelate of Dolan's rank might theoretically aspire: the papacy. As I noted in the introduction, Dolan typically dismisses the question with a joke, and when I brought it up a second time, he didn't disappoint:

I can honestly tell you that it's not something I would ever even think about. That's so beyond anything I can imagine, that I wouldn't even fantasize about it. I mean, heck, the day before Saint Patrick's Day it was great that I was able to meet Sharon Stone. Talk about fantasies! Wow, there goes Lent! But what you're asking? Nope, it's not something I ever would, or could, contemplate in my wildest dreams.

SECTION TWO

~

CHALLENGES FACING
THE CHURCH

TWO

The Sexual-Abuse Crisis

Left to his own devices, Timothy Dolan would prefer to begin any conversation about the Catholic Church with the spiritual essentials: the person of Jesus Christ and his life, death, and resurrection; the community that extends the saving work of Christ in time, which is the Church; the basic questions that weigh on every human heart about the meaning of life, and the answers to those questions that can be found in a happy, healthy Catholic life. Yet Dolan also has his feet firmly planted on the ground, understanding that in the postmodern agora he'll be doing no more than preaching to the choir unless he first tackles the doubts and question marks that hang over the Catholic Church in the popular mind. These days, that means above all dealing with the sexual-abuse crisis.

Without any doubt, the various waves of sexual-abuse scandals that have washed over the Church since the mid-1980s collectively constitute the most serious crisis to face Catholicism in at least the last half century. To date, the Catholic Church in the United States alone has paid out an estimated $2.5 billion to settle sex-abuse litigation, and most experts believe that total could climb to $5 billion or more. Beyond dollars and cents, the damage to the Church's public image has been incalculable. A sort of popular math has taken hold in which a

Catholic priest equals a potential pedophile — a tremendous injustice to the vast majority of good priests who have never abused anyone but also an index of how seriously the Church's moral authority has been compromised. To be sure, a convincing case can be made that some of the criticism of the Church and its leaders has been exaggerated — driven in part by a secular media eager to cast the Church in a bad light, and in part by tort attorneys with clear financial incentives for poisoning public opinion against the Church. Yet there's also enough fire beneath the smoke that thoughtful Catholics realize the crisis can't simply be dismissed as media hysteria or a litigation strategy.

Debate continues on both how to explain what went wrong and what to do about it. More conservative Catholics often diagnose the crisis as a breakdown in discipline and fidelity, which crested in the "anything goes" era of the late 1960s through the early 1980s. Liberal Catholics are more inclined to read the crisis in terms of an unaccountable power structure in the Church, coupled with a repressive sexual morality and unrealistic expectations of celibacy for priests. Secular critics point to what they see as a pattern of secrecy and denial, along with charges that for too long the Catholic Church saw itself as "above the law." Whatever the merits of any of those positions, it's virtually impossible to have any public conversation about the Catholic Church in today's environment without grappling with the issues they raise and the courses of action to which they point.

Dolan is well aware of the passions surrounding the sexual-abuse crisis and the virtual impossibility of satisfying everyone. He became an auxiliary bishop in Saint Louis in June 2001, just before the crisis in the United States erupted, and Archbishop Justin Rigali made him his point man on the issue. When he became the archbishop of Milwaukee in June 2002 he immediately began meeting with victims and pledging to break with "business as usual." He got high marks for the sensitivity and honesty he tried to project, but the verdict about his policy choices was mixed. Upon his appointment to New York, the Survivors Network of Those Abused by Priests issued a statement calling his record on sex abuse "abysmal," charging that he did not reveal information about accused priests to the police and that he took no action against senior Church officials in Milwaukee who, in SNAP's eyes, were responsible for a decades-long cover-up, charges Dolan vigorously denies. However overheated some of that criticism may have been, it reflects the sort of questions many people are asking—not just about Dolan but about the Church's corporate response.

Dolan and I spoke at length about the crisis and its implications for the Church. He candidly acknowledges that he, too, struggles to understand how bishops and other Church officials could have allowed the problem of sexual abuse to fester for decades, while also insisting that bishops generally did their best by the standards of the time. He admits that an "old-boy network" in clerical culture was part of the problem and signals his willingness to consider new accountability measures for bishops, including checks and balances on their power in areas such as personnel and finance—such measures, Dolan argues, could actually strengthen the teaching authority of bishops by restoring public confidence. At the same time, Dolan also insists that the Church must not succumb to a climate of "viciousness" in seeking scapegoats for the crisis. He defends, for instance, the 2004 Vatican decision to allow Cardinal Bernard Law of Boston to end his career in Rome as the archpriest of the Basilica of Saint Mary Major.

Let's start with the simple question that the typical person in the street can't help but ask of the Church, and especially the bishops: How in God's name could you have let this happen?

I know saying this could get me into trouble, but I wonder the same thing. As I look back, when I was vicar for clergy in the Archdiocese of Saint Louis in the middle of all this, and then in Milwaukee . . . as I was reading those files, I wondered too. I asked myself, how could this have gone on? How could anybody have reassigned this guy? How could anybody have treated this with anything less than the rigor that we now know is essential? From a purely intellectual point of view, one can say, "Wait a minute. Nobody, nowhere, knew the gravity of this, in any discipline or any field." That includes jurisprudence, law officials, professionals, psychiatrists, doctors, other religions, you name it. Nobody understood clearly that this was a moral flaw that could not be cured or contained. This wasn't just a failure on the part of the Church.

That said, when you've got these serial offenders, when you've got this happening time after time after time, one just has to wonder what in the hell went on. I don't know the answer. I would have to say in the experience that I had in Milwaukee and Saint Louis, in the review of cases that I had to do, I never saw evidence that a bishop did not take it seriously. Whether it was any of the archbishops of Saint Louis, or Rembert Weakland, or William Cousins in Milwaukee, they did take it seriously. In other words, I don't think they just flippantly said, "Oh, that's just some parents squawking. So what?" No, they took it seriously.

Tragically, what they meant by taking it seriously now seems almost risible. Too often, what it meant is that the priest was called in for a good tongue-lashing. The bishop would say, "Go for a retreat, and if this ever happens again, you've had it. We're assigning you to a guy known as a good pastor, and he's going to make sure this doesn't happen again." Even much more reasonable things now seem completely inadequate. For example, somebody would tell the priest, "You're going away for a while. We're going to get a professional assessment of you, and the best we're going to do for you, buster, is to put you in limited ministry where you can be watched, whether that be at a convent or some health care institution, where the likelihood of your ever reverting to a predator status is negligible." Those are the kind of things that you saw. From a defensive point of view we could say, that's what everybody was doing. That's what every religion was doing, that's what the public schools were doing. Even so, it's still tough to bring any type of sense or consolation out of the way these things were handled decades ago.

Keep in mind, too, there were a good chunk of offenders who just left the priesthood. Bishops told them, "Get out of here." It wasn't that all the cases ended with reassignment. In general, however, it's not a pretty picture. In the end, I have to admit that it's beyond me how that could have happened.

We're eight years from the massive eruption of the crisis in the United States. How big a hit has the Church taken?

Incredibly big, and I don't think it's over yet. I'm a Church historian, but you don't need a degree in Church history to say this: This is the biggest crisis the Catholic Church in the United States has ever faced. At the beginning, I was stupidly saying that the sex-abuse crisis was comparable to the crisis over trusteeship in the early years of the American Church and the nativist controversies of the nineteenth century, but good God, who even knows what those were about today? The effects of this crisis have been monumental, and I don't say that with any fear of being contradicted.

What's dawned on me recently is that there's a two-tiered effect. There's the exterior effect on the Church's credibility, one subset of which would be the tremendous hit on finances. You know, there are quite a few dioceses these days that are close to financial collapse. This has just been a massive financial hit. On the money thing, I'm developing a theory that one of our major challenges today is that American Catholic leadership is being strangled by trying to maintain the behemoth of the institutional Catholicism that we inherited from the 1940s and 50s. But even deeper than the dollars and cents, there's the second hit in terms of the Church's moral voice. Many people cannot see a guy in a Roman collar without sexual abuse being the first thing that comes to mind. There's been a massive loss of credibility, and if you don't have credibility when you're preaching the Gospel, you don't have much. It's like a marriage: Once you lose that trust and credibility, it takes a long time to win it back.

What I've also wondered about recently, and I think a lot of brother bishops are going through this, is the interior horror of what it's done to us personally. I can only speak for myself, but it's tough for me not to second-guess myself. I think I'm a pretty confident fellow who's at peace with myself, and who doesn't sit around wringing my hands wondering what I should do. But I hope I am also a reflective person, and part of that reflection now always brings in the sex-abuse crisis. I always ask myself when I have a decision to make, how is this going to look to those who still have us under the magnifying glass of the sex-abuse crisis?

Do you find yourself pulling your punches?

I hope not, but I'm always conscious of the implications of anything I say or do. I would have to admit that rare would be the bishop these days, and I include myself, who is not tempted on occasion to be a bit more gun-shy than we know we should be when it comes to some tough moral issues, because we know what a beating we have taken.

Are you more conscious about the tonality of what you say?

Yes. I try to be much more patient and understanding of people who are just bitterly angry with the Church. Pre-2002, I might have been tempted to say, "Go someplace else if you don't like it," or "We're sick of your whining." I'm not talking about the professional victims.

I'm talking about people for whom this was a lance that allowed a lot of hurt and anger to come to the surface. I think we have to be patient and tender, sometimes to the point of heroism, in trying to listen to that and to help that play out. We must never give up listening and responding to those hurt. Just like Ronald Reagan succeeded in turning *liberal* into a bad word in American politics, I think this whole crisis has turned *bishop* and *priest* into bad words. We're aware of that. I don't want to reduce this just to a pastoral strategy, but I would say that a motive and inspiration for me, every morning when I get up and make my morning offering, is that in some way I hope I can help people rediscover some trust and appreciation for the Church. Believe me, I know that trust has been seriously damaged.

I do think there are some bishops and priests who get flustered. They say, "We're tired of this. We're tired of getting punched in the stomach, run over by dump trucks in the public square, only to stand up and have another one come at us. We've done the best we can. Nobody's made the progress we have. We've been contrite, we've got our house in order, so let's get back to doing the work of the Gospel." I worry that both strategically and in reality, if we give the impression that this was simply a temporary problem that we had to get over, that's not good. We're terribly naïve if we don't think there's something wrong with the Church's approach that would have allowed this to get so far away from us, and we have to be honest in facing up to that in whatever we say publicly.

If the outsider's question is "How could this happen?" the insider's question is "What about the bishops?" You've got tough policies now on priests who abuse, but where's the accountability for bishops who covered it up?

I can understand that criticism. Whether there's justice to it or not, I don't know. I can understand it particularly when it comes, as it does more often than not, from priests. They say, "Wait a minute. This has been hard for us to swallow. We've seen some of our best friends go. We know they probably have to go, we know what they did was disastrous and can never be reconciled, even if there are still enough cases that may be gray that we wonder if they've been thrown to the wolves. Why wasn't the same thing done to bishops?" I can understand that question. It's a legitimate question to ask. But what would have been the alternative? As a practical matter, most of the bishops who reassigned offenders are dead or retired.

Handling sex-abuse cases isn't the only management decision bishops have to make. The broader question is, is there a lack of meaningful measures of accountability for bishops in the Church?

De jure, I think there are important accountability measures, if you take the metropolitan structure seriously, if you look at the U.S. bishops' conference structure, if you look at the role of the nuncio. When somebody writes a history of this decade, they're going to find that the U.S. bishops' conference busted its chops trying to find ways to be internally accountable. Some of them were more successful than others. I'm not saying these all work, but de jure, there are structures that should work, including the roles of the papal nuncio, the Holy See, the conference, and the provincial structure of the Church. [Note: Catholic dioceses around the world are grouped into provinces, with an archdiocese usually at the center of the province. The archbishop plays a leadership role among the bishops of the province.]

De facto, have they worked? I don't know. I'm not trying to dodge the question, but I honestly don't know. I don't know, for example, if the Holy See, if the metropolitans, if provincial bishops have tried to say with respect to a particular bishop, "This guy needs to go. This isn't helping us." In the provinces that I've been in, that didn't happen. I'm not sure if people tried to get some of those mechanisms to click in, and they just didn't work. I hope it's clear that I don't tend to minimize this, but the bishops that I have seen who made flawed judgments, and there certainly were some, I don't think they ever made flippant judgments. I think they tried their best to judge cases with the science and the legal and psychological counsel available at the time. I didn't see any massive dereliction of duty in the cases I've had to review. They did try, in the vast majority of times, to treat this with the gravity it deserved. The dire mistake was eventually to allow some [abuser priests] back into ministry, even when "experts" advised them they could safely do so.

For the life of me, I'm still trying to figure out how this morphed from a problem about a little over 4 percent of American priests who abused kids under eighteen into an episcopal problem. Was there a big episcopal problem? You bet your bottom dollar there was. But that wasn't the major problem, if you ask me. The major problem was that priests were doing this. I think a lot of that is tort-attorney driven, because the money is in suing dioceses, not going after priests.

There's a perception that the problem with priests got fixed, but the problem with bishops didn't.

I could see why that would be out there. But historically, the problem was immoral, sinful predators among the priesthood.

Some would argue that part of the problem is that bishops were making these decisions in isolation. The instruments in the Code of Canon Law for including others in diocesan governance, such as a diocesan pastoral council, are mostly consultative. Is there something inherently flawed about that? Do we need a system of checks and balances that in some way would limit your power?

I'd be open to that. One would think, of course, that the Gospel alone would limit our power, because it calls us to be constantly humble and trying to examine our conscience with the help of other people to see if we're on the right path. Unfortunately, part of the Gospel is also original sin! That means that we who are supposed to do all that are also flawed. So, if you're asking, "Could a long-range effect of this mess be some accountability with teeth? That bishops would be held accountable?" Yes. I would welcome that. If you're asking me to go out on a limb, yes, I would welcome it. I don't think one has to say that would be tampering with the apostolic nature of the office. Lord knows we saw the apostles hold themselves to accountability in the Acts of the Apostles and the letters of Saint Paul.

For example, if in some future revision of the code you were required to have the approval of the pastoral council, or some other body, before you made certain kinds of personnel decisions, you would be okay with that?

Well, there'd be precedent for that, like we have now with the finance council. I can't sell a hospital, for example, or alienate other property without approval of a lay financial council. Would I be open to more of those kinds of things? I would. The other side of the coin, however, is that there's also a strong tendency to want to neuter the authority of the bishop, and to begin to wonder if the apostolic integrity [of the office] is essential to the Church. I believe it is, and we have to be very careful about tampering with that. You know, that's a strong, constant refrain from Cardinal Francis George.

These days, however, holding yourself accountable is actually a way to enhance the credibility of the apostolic office. I don't think we should be opposed to that. In fact, we have precedent for it. Look at what the Council of Trent did, in very practical ways. It limited, for instance, how often a bishop could be gone from his diocese.

That's pretty damned practical, isn't it? Or requiring a bishop to be in the diocese for certain feast days. We had an incident at one of the June meetings of the bishops a couple of years ago when one of the bishops stood up and said, "You know, we're in violation of the Council of Trent, because it says a bishop has to be in his diocese for Corpus Christi. That's today, folks!" Those are pretty practical ways of imposing accountability. Do we need that again? Yeah, I think we do.

On the subject of accountability, there are a lot of people who will not be convinced that the Catholic Church has learned its lesson because Cardinal Bernard Law was appointed archpriest of Saint Mary Major in Rome. Was that a mistake?

No, I don't think so. Maybe part of the way I look at it comes from having lived in Rome. For Bernie Law to have given up the archdiocese of Boston was a heavy penalty. For anybody to see in Saint Mary Major some type of compensation for losing the archdiocese of Boston, that's just ridiculous. Now, to an outsider, maybe it looks like he's still exercising some kind of prestige in Rome. I guess marketing-wise, somebody can say we should have thrown him to the dogs. But we're not just guided by PR!

I see Law as one of the great tragedies of this situation. In some ways, Bernie Law was a reforming bishop. I can remember when he was in Springfield-Cape Girardeau and [archbishop of Saint Louis] John Carberry was leery of him. He was suspicious of him, this kind of rebel down in the south of Missouri with these bold pastoral practices. [Law] took the tumble for this crisis. In the eyes of his critics, he became the Richard Nixon of the Catholic Church, didn't he? He became stereotyped as everything that's wrong with the Church, and those of us who know and respect him regard that as terribly unjust. Somewhere, too, we have to say that we cannot simply capitulate to a kind of viciousness, the insistence that this man needs to be drawn and quartered. It was a magnanimous gesture by Pope John Paul II to say that you're still welcome in the home of Peter, and you should be able to finish out your days with some trusted pastoral assignment, as minimal as it might be. As a factual matter, did it hurt us? I think in the court of public opinion, it did. Whether we should have capitulated to that public opinion, I don't think we should.

Let's talk about the basic lesson of the crisis. There's a left-wing diagnosis that says there's a deep corruption in clerical culture, combined with a fear of sexuality and therefore a repression of sexuality that explains the crisis. On the right, the theory goes that an atmosphere of dissent in the 1960s, a sort of anything-goes attitude, combined with a lack of firm governance from Church authority, was at the root of things. What's your view?

It won't surprise you to know that I think both of them are probably exaggerated. I would find myself more sympathetic to the second approach, and I think the research by the John Jay College of Criminal Justice shows there's something there. Look at how the numbers [of abuse cases] spiked around 1979. The clinicians who did the study don't know anything about internal Church politics, but their research shows that the time when the abuse became so pronounced was the same period when, for fear of generalization, what you might call the "wacky Left" had peaked. This was a time when everything was in flux. So I find myself much more in sympathy with the second way of looking at it, that so much of this was just a complete decimation of every type of structure, tradition, and discipline we had.

Part of how I think about all this is tied to my love of the priesthood. In many ways, I still have an altar-boy notion of the priesthood. To this day, I think of myself as a priest, not as a bishop or archbishop, and there's nothing else I ever wanted to be. Never, in any of the priests who have been normative in my life, was there any hint of predatory behavior. So for some to say that this terror came out of a system, or a culture, that was at its root terribly degraded, I find to be preposterous. Were there some things wrong with it? Yes. As with any culture, does it need some constant reformation, some constant looking at? Yes.

Looking back now, part of what went wrong was the assumption that the old-boy network could take care of this. I saw it in Milwaukee; I saw it in Saint Louis. A bishop, a vicar general, one or two other close people, took these cases very, very seriously, and they thought they were doing the best possible thing. They would have consulted, at a minimum, with a psychiatrist or a law enforcement professional about how this could be handled. But they would have more or less thought that it could be handled within the regular protocol of the Church's approach. That's where I think what's called "clerical culture" backfired. This failure — this scandal, sin, and crime — represents a terribly gross degradation of everything that that priesthood of Jesus Christ stands for. What I'm trying to say is that I don't think the priesthood, at its core, is somehow dysfunctional. Have there been dysfunctional priests? Yes. Are there some aspects of clerical culture that may have facilitated dysfunction in some people, someplace? I suppose so. I've never seen a culture where that wouldn't be true. Was that widespread, and did it flow from the very constitution of the culture? No.

Did the second round of the sexual-abuse crisis in 2010, which began in Ireland and Germany and eventually focused on the role of the Vatican and Pope Benedict, teach you anything you didn't already know?

From a negative point of view, it taught us that we are still rookies when it comes to getting our message out. We completely missed a chance to get any good news out, even though there's an important story to tell about the progress the Catholic Church has made in coming to grips with the crisis.

From a positive point of view, it taught me that for all the slaps and all the arrows we have borne in the last decade, the Church in the United States is now looked upon as the international paradigm for what to do. Back in 2002, we were blasted all over the place, including in Rome [for adopting a "zero tolerance" policy, or permanent removal from ministry for one substantiated charge of sexual abuse]. Now, [Rome] is sending study teams over here. These are the same guys who eight years ago were saying that the Americans have gone too far, this is an Anglo-Saxon problem, they're regaining credibility on the backs of their priests, and this is a blunt violation of canonical rights. All that has changed . . . I get letters from bishops in other parts of the world all the time, and other American bishops get them too, asking, "Can we come talk to you about what you did?"

I've also learned, and I hope this doesn't come off as paranoia, but I think there's a gross unfairness among some in the media profession who seem to have a fetish with only having the Catholic Church in the crosshairs on this issue. There's just a relentless drive to keep that story line alive.

You've challenged that bias publicly, in particular by taking on the *New York Times*. Do you think it's done any good?

I do, and I'm not just patting myself on the back. First of all, somebody needs to get that message out and question the impartiality of the media. Second, indirectly and personally, several journalists have spoken to me or written to me to say, elaborate a little bit more on why you feel this way. Give us some more proof, or some other episodes where you may have sensed this. That's happened enough that I think it's not bad for the beginning of some type of conversation.

Going forward, many observers have argued that one area that needs attention is false accusations. Real damage has been done to priests, many say, by an inability to cope with false accusations. Do you agree?

I do. Recently I was being interviewed by *60 Minutes,* and Morley Safer asked me, "Do you have any regrets about the way you handled the crisis in Saint Louis and Milwaukee?" I said there were three or four cases—thank God, there weren't many—of priests who were unjustly accused, and to this day they're living with that terrible burden. I said, in those instances we got it wrong.

Are those guys in ministry today?

The ones I know still are, but I don't think they've ever gotten over it. I can think of a particular priest in Saint Louis, and every time I see him I apologize. He's gracious enough to say, "It was the tenor of the times. There was nothing either of us could do." He's also kind enough to say, "Thank God you called it off at the last minute when you got the proper information." He said he went through hell but it came out okay in the long run, so don't worry about it. But I do worry about it, and I know he's not the same man.

Are the systems as they're functioning right now capable of preventing such harm?

I'm afraid not. The crux of the problem is at the initial report. As you know, most accusations are rarely about something happening now. It's very unusual for somebody to say, "Yesterday Father So-and-So did this." Instead, it's more likely to be something like, "It has come back to my memory that thirty years ago Father So-and-So did this." The first thing we tell them is that you need to report this to the D.A., because we'll report it too. What's the D.A. say? Nine times out of ten they're going to say, "We can't do anything about it" because of the statute of limitations and so on. "That means it's up to us to do something about it. Here's the tough question: While we're doing something, can the man stay in ministry? By the rules we have now, the answer is no. If the accusation is credible—and that's very different than substantiated, but if it seems like it could have happened—then we are obliged to remove the guy from ministry while we're investigating.

In the vast majority of instances, you can't remove a guy today without many people jumping to conclusions that he's guilty. In my time, a good number of those charges have been shown not to be substantiated. The guy goes back, but does he ever fully recover?

I honestly don't know what to do. If you didn't pull these priests, if you told them to stick around while we look into it and we'll come back to you in a month or two . . . if there was something to it, or if God forbid something happened in the meantime . . . This is what bishops lay awake at night worrying about. We'd never recover. People could say, "You mean you had a suspicion about this guy and you didn't do anything? He's still over teaching the first communicants? This can't go on!"

There, in a nutshell, is where I would say that our priests are in a tough situation.

Do you believe the percentage of false accusations is higher today?

I do. In the first two or three years of the crisis, when people would say, "What about false accusations against priests?" I would say, "I haven't seen any." In the first two or three years, that was my anecdotal experience. The stuff I was hearing was, unfortunately, pretty true. If you talk about my time in Saint Louis, there may have been ten to

twelve guys who had to be removed, and there was only one false accusation. The vast majority tragically were accurate. I wouldn't say that
anymore. Our evidence in New York, with the couple of cases we've
had, were both very scrupulously looked into and determined to be
completely incredible and unsubstantiated.

**Does that cause you to question the policy that many dioceses
still have of nearly automatic settlement of all these claims?**

I think so, although that's not to call into question the necessity of
doing that in the beginning. Now, I would question it. By the way,
what often happens if a charge turns out to be false is that the people
will say, "You ought to go after the person who brought this charge."
Most often, however, the priest involved will tell us, "Let it drop." It's
usually because they're so fatigued.

**Theologically, you're both a father and a brother to your priests.
Those are two things difficult to do at the same time. Are we
entering a period in which we're going to be emphasizing the
paternal dimension of the bishop's role more than the fraternal?**

Probably. Of course, the "paternal" role is much better than the
"boss" aspect of how we relate to our priests. "Fraternal" would be
the ideal model, "paternal" is acceptable, but "boss" . . . forget it.
Yet, of course, that is in some cases how our priests see us, and
it's also quite often how others regard us. I think what we're seeing today is an unfortunate move away from the fraternal dimension
of the relationship, to one that's at best paternal and at worst one
that becomes a boss/employee relationship. That's a problem many
bishops have.

Do you have sympathy for the view that widespread laicization as a result of the sexual-abuse crisis is eroding Catholic theology of the priesthood, which holds that ordination is for life?

Yes, I do. I have been constant in emphasizing that a major problem in postconciliar theology of the priesthood is that we have emphasized the function, the *doing* of the priesthood over the *being,* the identity. Thus, I proposed that we had to reemphasize the identity, the perpetual, life-changing essence of the priesthood. And now we're taking it away from men? It could hurt the Church's understanding of the nature of Holy Orders—although I still believe we must on occasion do it.

In two sentences, when a faithful Mass-going Catholic looks you in the eye and asks, "Archbishop, what should we make of all this?" what do you say?

The problem is, I'm not sure many people would even bother asking a bishop that question, or be inclined to trust the response. But what I would say is, ultimately this crisis is about the power of sin. We are sinful people, sin is alive, the effects of sin are with us, and that's what we're seeing. It's about sin in priests, sin in bishops, sinfulness perhaps in some structures. So come on aboard, because the job description of the Church is to be the extension in time and space of the One who came to conquer sin. Please, come on back, because we need you in that sacred endeavor we call the Church. Your faith is in Jesus, not in a priest or a bishop.

That implies that we have to respond not just in terms of policies and public relations, as important as those things are, but also on a spiritual level. Justin Rigali taught me this. While we were in the thick of it in Saint Louis in 2002, it had been suggested for maybe the third or fourth time that Rigali needed to sit down with his priests and go through all this again. I had advised him, "Yeah, you need to do it. I know we're sick of it, I know there's not much more to say, I know you're going to get the same hotheads yelling at you, but we probably should do it." He said, "No, we've had enough meetings. What we'll do now is have a holy hour with the priests." He was absolutely right. In the end, I think that accomplished far more than another bull session. That taught me something. Do we or do we not believe, with all our heart and soul, that the most efficacious thing we can do is to pray? I need to show to my priests and people that I believe that with all my heart and soul, and if we do that convincingly, there's always hope.

THREE

Women in the Church

Few complaints about the Catholic Church have more staying power than the charge that it has a women problem. The images are familiar: that Catholicism is the last bastion of patriarchy, that it's a "boys' club," and that its celebration of traditional roles for women as wives and mothers amounts to a pious smokescreen for denying women access to the halls of power in the real world and in the Church. It's easy enough to understand where those impressions come from, starting with the obvious fact that the Catholic Church denies women the possibility of being ordained as priests or bishops. Church spokespersons can insist until they're blue in the face that the priesthood is about service rather than power, and therefore that reserving the priesthood for men is not about defending male privilege, but since in practice the highest leadership ranks of the Church are composed exclusively of men, many people are going to find that a tough argument to swallow.

The debate over women priests is merely the most symbolic instance of what critics see as a deeper problem. Popes and other Catholic leaders have denounced "radical feminism" so often in recent decades that it almost seems to loom as a special bête noir for the Catholic Church. Naturally, many feminists both inside and outside the Church, who associate women's rights with liberal positions on sexual and reproductive matters, especially abortion, tend to return the favor, seeing the Church's hierarchy as a primary cultural foe. Over the last couple of decades, the Catholic Church has effectively squelched a trend toward gender-neutral language in its prayer and worship, for example, insisting that God must remain "he" and "him," that the Holy Spirit is not a "she," and that the term "men" can and should still be used to denote all members of the human race. As of this writing, a Vatican-sponsored investigation of American nuns (the technical term for which is a "visitation") is still under way—another instance, in the eyes of critics, of Catholic officialdom being uncomfortable with strong, independent-minded women.

Defenders of the Church will often point to veneration of the Blessed Virgin Mary to insist that feminine symbolism plays a defining role in Catholic spirituality, but even Mary has become a bone of contention for feminist critics. As both Virgin and Mother, they argue, the figure of Mary sets an impossible standard for any real woman to actually meet. Moreover, the critics suggest, the cult of chivalrous devotion to Mary simply reinforces antique stereotypes of women as essentially passive, objects of veneration rather than protagonists and architects of history.

In response to all this, Catholic spokespersons will generally offer some version of three basic arguments.

First, they say, the Church's problem is not with the emancipation of women, meaning a legitimate insistence on the full equality of women in the social, occupational, cultural, and political spheres, or even for that matter inside the Church. Rather, they say, what the Church objects to is an ideological version of feminism that posits a sort of class struggle between men and women, or that fosters the idea that there's a tension between being a fully emancipated woman and also playing the traditional roles of wife and mother. In fact, they point out, Pope John Paul II pioneered what is today usually called the New Feminism, premised on the idea of "complementarity"—the notion that men and women are fully equal but destined both by God and by human biology to play distinct roles that complement each other. This Catholic version of feminism is actually more "feminist" than the old version, its defenders argue, because it rejects the idea of a power struggle between the sexes—a notion that New Feminists see as a classically masculine construct that "first-wave" feminists uncritically adopted.

Second, at a more commonsense level, Catholics will often argue that regarding the Church as a "boys' club" has things the wrong way around, because it focuses only on life inside the sanctuary. Everywhere else, they insist—in families, in neighborhoods, in schools and virtually every other venue in which real life unfolds—women are, and always have been, the real carriers of Catholic culture. It's women who educate children in the faith, women who sustain the networks of care that shape parish life, and women who turn out in substantially larger numbers than men for most Church activities. In that sense, defenders of the Church say, nothing could be sillier than suggesting that Catholicism needs to "empower" women, since everyone knows that the real power in the Church, meaning the power to transmit the faith to the next generation and to nurture and sustain it over a lifetime, has always belonged primarily to women.

Third, Catholic leaders insist that an exclusive focus on the ordination question misses the bigger picture, which is that in every job category in the Church that does not require a Roman collar, Catholicism typically outperforms other social institutions in terms of promoting leadership by women. In diocesan-level administration in the United States, 48.4 percent of all positions today are held by women. At the most senior levels in dioceses, 26.8 percent of executive positions are held by women. By way of comparison, a 2005 study of Fortune 500 companies found that women held only 16.4 percent of corporate officer positions. Women occupied only 6.4 percent of the top earner positions. Similarly, a 2007 study by the American Bar Association found that just 16 percent of the members of the top law firms' governing committees were women, and only 5 percent of managing partners were female. According to a 2004 report from the Department of Defense, women held just 12.7 percent of positions at the grade of major or above. Such data, some Catholics suggest, points to an obvious question: Who's got the real problem with empowering women?

Dolan is well aware of perceptions of Catholicism as a boys' club, and he sees them largely as "malarkey." He says that his own formative experiences in the Church reflect the imprint of strong, independent women, especially the Sisters of Mercy, and that he's fully supportive of seeing more women in positions of leadership in the Church in all those ways that don't require sacramental ordination. Yet Dolan insists that women have always been the real architects of Catholic culture, both in families and in parish life, and hence talk about the need to "empower" women in the Church is based on a fundamentally inaccurate reading of how the Church actually works. Dolan also speaks candidly about the Vatican-sponsored investigation of American nuns, saying he believes the underlying concerns are justified, but worries that it could "blow up" because of perceptions that it's a punitive exercise rather than something constructive.

Aside from your own family, what were your early experiences of women in the Church?

It would have been primarily with the Sisters of Mercy from Drogheda, Ireland, who sent four sisters over to Holy Infant Parish in 1957. One of them would teach me in second, fourth, and fifth grade, Sister Mary Bosco, who had a towering impact on my life and to this day is a spiritual mother to me. The sisters were loving, warm women but also strong and independent women. I would say, looking back, that they instilled in me a Catholic ethos, a sense of a Catholic identity in the world. It's what Andrew Greeley calls a "Catholic imagination." They played a key role in fostering a sense of warmth and belonging in the Church. That meant the liturgy, prayer, the Blessed Mother, the Eucharist, the pope, song, poetry, history—it was all part of a Catholic worldview. The sisters also helped kindle my passion for history. Being Irish, I suppose, they had a special flair for history . . . telling stories about the history of the Church, Bible history, stories about European and Irish history. They were dynamite teachers. Sister Gemma, who taught me in sixth and seventh grade, was just fantastic.

I'm honest enough to admit, because I keep in touch with other kids who also went through those same experiences, that a good number of them did not find it as consoling and exciting as I did. I know there are people, because I meet them, who do not have fond memories of the sisters. They were very strict, sometimes even using the ruler! In general there was a great love, but I know there are people who look back on that as something they're fleeing. Naturally, that gives rise to a kind of person who has big anger issues with the Church, but that wasn't how I experienced it at all. For me, growing up in that environment meant Sister Gemma teaching us about art and poetry. . . . It was almost a John Paul II approach to culture, that culture is the engine that drives your faith.

During the turbulence of the late 1960s and early 1970s, when I was in seminary and watched a number of good guys walk away from the priesthood, the sisters also helped me enormously. By now the sisters were no longer just matriarchs to me but also friends—Sister Mary Bosco, for example. Sister Rosario, who's still one of my best friends, is now the principal of my home grade school. Back in those days, I was talking to the sisters a great deal. They were all saying, "Well, you know, Tim, we ride through it. The Church has been through it before." It was almost like New Testament stuff: Hold on to what you received, and we'll get through it. They were never reactionaries, but they had a deep calm about them, a sense of, "Things will work out."

In the court of public opinion, there's a common feeling that the Catholic Church is antiwoman. What do you say to that?

Malarkey. I agree with the British poet John Ruskin, who said that the Catholic Church has been the greatest ally women have had as far as extolling the dignity of women. Some of this is just the culture in which I was raised, because some of the most normative people in my life were women: obviously my own mother, my two grandmothers, the sisters in the school. It was a culture where everybody knew that the real power in the parish, the real power in Catholic culture, by which I guess I mean the chemistry of family life, were the women. Governmentally, we're priests and bishops, but did I ever sense any injustice toward women? No.

You can appreciate, however, that the typical person looking at a papal event

Where the only woman you see is the one who jumps the barricades and goes after the pope?

Right, where you have rows of men in crimson and purple and black before you ever get to a woman, except for the elderly nuns in the wheelchairs in the front row. The obvious temptation is to say, "That's a boys' club."

However, if what you're watching is a beatification or canonization ceremony, the odds are fairly high that the tapestries hanging from Saint Peter's Basilica will be women, because more often than not we're beatifying and canonizing women! Externally, sure, the perception [of Catholicism as a boys' club] is there. One might just as well say that because only men play football, therefore we have a male-dominated society in the United States. In the last fifty years or so, women have made great gains in this society, and yet it's still just men on the football field. In other words, external perceptions don't always accurately reflect what's really happening.

If you and I walked out onto Fifth Ave right now and stopped ten people at random, don't you suspect that five of them will say the Catholic Church is antiwoman because it won't allow women priests?

Probably. I would say that's probably a perception, but an unjust perception in my book, which we're stuck with. But I would say that people in the know—and by that, I don't mean they have academic credentials, but people who just live and breathe Catholicism—they know that's not accurate. On the other hand, I have to say that at least inside the Church itself, I actually don't see the ordination issue flaring up as much these days. During my first ten months in New York, I've met with a lot of folks, I sat at tables up and down the archdiocese, and I didn't hear one person bring up women's ordination.

Five or six years ago, on the other hand, you could always count on somebody to say, "Why are you bishops afraid to talk about women's ordination?" I would reply, "What do you mean, afraid? I'm more than happy to talk about it. Heck, my barber asks me about it!" I can remember that a reporter asked me on a radio show in Milwaukee, "Why are you bishops afraid to talk about this?" I said that I'm not afraid to talk about it at all. She wanted me to talk about how I feel about it, and I said I'm happy to do that, as long as you know that in the long run what I feel about it doesn't amount to a hill of beans. As bishop, my role is to try my best to present the teaching of the Church. I'll do that, and then I'll tell you how I feel about it—which, it won't surprise you, happens to be consonant with the teaching of the Church!

When it comes to women in the Church, a key difference between the dissidents and those who want to stay inside the Church is that dissidents push the ordination question, while the others want to promote women in every way short of sacramental ordination. On that second front, do you think there are some things we can do?

Yes, and I think we are doing it. Look, if you asked people what would be the boast of the Catholic Church in the United States, odds are that most of them would say health care, education, and charities, correct? You and I both know that those are women-led and women-driven. That's certainly true in this archdiocese. I was in a few schools recently for Catholic Schools Week, and women are running that enterprise. When I go to visit our Catholic Charities, which has a massive organization and infrastructure in this archdiocese, you see women. You don't see bitter or angry women, women who are grinding their teeth saying, "Why can't we be priests?" You see women who put me to shame in the way they've digested the Gospel, and they're happy to be part of the Church's good work.

Would you be comfortable with a woman as a chancellor of your archdiocese?

Yes, absolutely. I had a woman as chancellor, a great one, in Milwaukee, Barbara Anne Cusack.

How about a woman as general secretary of the United States Conference of Catholic Bishops?

The job of general secretary is part of the conference's episcopal infrastructure to such an extent that it probably still should be a priest. That said, am I glad that we have women as associate directors of the conference? You bet, and they've been exceptional. As a historical matter, when people look back they'll probably say that one of the smartest things the bishops of the United States ever did was to name Helen Alvaré the director of the Office for Pro-Life Activities. She was dynamite—an attractive, articulate, credible woman.

Do you think it was a mistake that during the peak period of the sexual-abuse crisis in the States in 2002 and 2003, Catholic women, especially those who were parents, weren't more visible?

Yes, I do. Women were, of course, original members of our National Review Board. Tactically, strategically, bishops probably should have been talking less and parents, especially women, more. Of course, the media wanted to hear from the bishops, and we bishops had some hard questions to answer that we couldn't duck. But if you want to know about the overall approach of the Church to caring for children, including its efforts to promote a safe environment for children, obviously the best people to speak to that would be parents, especially women. We need to think about ways to hear their voice more—first of all in our own internal reflections, but also in terms of shaping the Church's public message.

What about a woman heading a Vatican congregation?

I would think that the prefect in the congregation probably needs to be in holy orders, again because that job is part of the episcopal infrastructure of the Church, but at levels below that, by all means. For example, what about a woman running the Vatican Press Office, so that she would be the primary spokesperson for the pope? I would say bring it on, and may their numbers multiply!

What do you make of the current Vatican-sponsored visitation of American nuns?

Had anybody asked me, which they didn't, I would have advised against it. Do I think it's justified, that there are legitimate worries about women religious? You bet I do. But should we do it? Probably not, at least not in this way, because the danger is that it may be seen as something heavy-handed and punitive, and therefore it risks being counterproductive. You know what drives that worry for me? It's my desire to protect the Holy See. I so value Rome that I don't want it to use its trump cards on issues that could backfire. When you're collecting baseball cards, you only have so many Stan Musial cards to trade. You don't use them to get some silly things—you save them for Mickey Mantle. Procedurally, strategically, the Holy See is at its best when it says to us, "We're worried about this. Could you bishops tell us what you think?" A visitation from the Vatican risks being seen as overkill.

I'll give you another example of how I think about that. You probably know that two or three years ago, at an executive session of the bishops' conference, we hotly debated whether or not we should ask the Congregation for the Doctrine of the Faith for a clarification about the issue of giving Communion to politicians who have a pro-choice voting record. I argued against it. I can remember thinking, "Let's trust the principle of subsidiarity, a genuine Catholic value: Let things be settled at the local level."

I suspect a lot of Catholics look at the visitation and think, to put it bluntly: "If even the nuns are in trouble, what hope is there for the rest of us?"

Sure. Or a lot of people will probably say, and actually are saying, "Why doesn't the Vatican investigate the bishops?" But let's try to understand that a visitation is not intended to be punitive. It's not necessarily negative.

You know a lot of nuns are experiencing it as punitive.

I understand that. I encourage them to keep in mind, too, that we try our best to have some type of accountability at all levels in the Church. We bishops go every five years for these *ad limina* visits, where we give a report on what's happened in our diocese for the last five years. There have been dioceses that have had visitations, seminaries that have had visitations. I try to say, "Keep an open mind, sisters, which is a virtue that you all have had in spades the last forty years." Perhaps this could be some type, even if awkwardly expressed, of an offer of help from the Holy See. They hear you're in turmoil, they hear you're worried about the future; they hear you're very concerned about the lack of vocations, your property, and caring for your elders. This is sort of like them saying, "Sisters, could we be of help? Let's try to gather some data and see what's going on here."

Now, a lot of sisters will say, "Would that it were that way, but we know they have listened to these right-wing bloggers who say we're all heretics." I don't take that extreme view. Is Rome worried that there are some elements of women religious who have perhaps dangerously drifted from the heart of the Church? I think they may be worried about that. I'm not an alarmist, but I do think there might be some basis for concern. On the other hand, I'm certainly not one of these who believe they've gone completely haywire, or that they're scandalous heretics. I don't know what we'd do without the sisters, and the vast majority of ones I know are very effective, loyal members of the Church. Are there examples of some who may be skating on thin ice when it comes to issues of faith? Maybe. Is this the major reason for the visitation? I don't think so. I think Rome is being practical in saying, "Something has gone wrong. There are some problems there, and we don't exactly know what they are, but we hear from enough people that there are difficulties."

We can't have our head in the sand. As a historian, I can't help thinking that when somebody looks back at postconciliar American Catholicism, the two things that changed the most radically after 1965 would be the dwindling of the religious life of women and the virtual disappearance of the sacrament of penance. These are two things that were standard, celebrated, dramatically obvious features of vibrant Catholic life pre-1965, which today are no longer there. We don't talk about it very much. A lot of things we do talk about, I think, can be traced back to these two—vocations, Catholic education, our whole notion of right and wrong in terms of moral consciousness. Now, does the Holy See want to talk about what's going on with consecrated religious in the United States? I think they do, and I think they've got a good point in wanting to.

Is the visitation the right instrument?

Could it have been done better, with more preparation? Could it have been done with the Vatican inviting some of the sisters over to say, "We're worried, we want to be of assistance, do you think a visitation would help?" Yes. In retrospect, one could probably say, "This could have been approached in a better way." But we've got it now. I met with the sisters of the archdiocese a few months into the process, and most of them were saying, "We were kind of livid about it at the beginning, but now that it's going on, it's not too bad. Some of our houses are even saying this is kind of helpful." So I'm hoping that something good, something constructive, will come out of it.

One point that frustrates me is that by talking so much about the visitation, or more generally about problems in women's religious life, the big picture tends to get lost. Women religious are the face of the Church in so many ways, and yet when I meet with them, the discussion so often focuses on nitty-gritty details—not just the visitation but also practical problems like whether the archdiocese can help out in terms of creating a common center for the care of their elder sisters. Those are all important things to talk about, of course, but where do we step back and focus on all the ways that women religious help us to capture the soul and the heart of our people? If we've just become another hobby, or a project, or a political party, we're duds. Maybe we should talk less about externals and more about the soul of our faith and vocation.

Suppose you walked into such a meeting and said, "I know you want to talk about the visitation, and I do too. But I also want to talk about how to put a spotlight on all the good things you're doing, because I don't want the visitation to be the only story about nuns in the United States. I know what you do is precious and it makes the Church come alive. Let's brainstorm about how to lift all that up."

That's a terrific approach. Of course, they would probably say, "Not bad, but we are upset because we don't get the coverage in your paper, or the only pictures in there are with nuns in veils, or you've been here for ten months and haven't even visited our motherhouse yet." Those are perfectly understandable criticisms in themselves, but they also come out of this small view we've been talking about—and I don't mean that critically, because I love our sisters. Actually, thanks, you've given me an entrée for the next meeting. In some way we bishops, we pastors, we teachers, we shepherds, have got to reclaim the dream. We've got to shift the agenda, and I believe firmly that our Catholic women, perhaps especially our women religious, can be our partners in doing so. We're not enemies, we're allies! Cardinal George is right: Too often we stupidly think in political terms, with the bishops cast as bullies and power-hungry conservatives, while the sisters are progressive reformers. Such a vocabulary and mentality is harmful.

FOUR

Pelvic Issues

In popular discussions of Catholicism, there's a fairly narrow canon of issues that always seem to surface. At the top of that list would be matters related to sexuality, including abortion, gay rights, birth control, marriage and divorce, and priestly celibacy. Collectively, wags sometimes refer to this cocktail of concerns as the "pelvic issues," and any media analysis of coverage of the Catholic Church over the last fifty years would undoubtedly conclude that these issues have loomed extraordinarily large. Case in point: Pope Paul VI reigned over the Catholic Church for fifteen years, from 1963 to 1978, guiding it through the turbulent years after the Second Vatican Council. He left his imprint on virtually every zone of Catholic life, from liturgical practice to social teaching, and is widely credited with holding the Church together when there was a real danger of it splitting apart. Yet today, virtually the only thing most people associate with Paul VI is his 1968 encyclical letter *Humanae Vitae* ("Of Human Life"), which reiterated the Church's traditional ban on contraception.

Catholic insiders who have been around for a while often become frustrated when these subjects surface, because it can feel like they've been talking about almost nothing else for at least the last three decades. It's not as if there aren't other compelling story lines about the Catholic Church, from the phenomenal growth of the faith in the global South, to developments in Catholic/Muslim and Catholic/Jewish dialogue, to the sprawling galaxy of new lay movements and new religious orders that dot the Catholic landscape. All those developments are arguably more consequential for the future of Catholicism than stale debates over birth control or celibacy, but they rarely seem to get the same traction either in the media or in popular water-cooler conversation.

Those frustrations aside, thoughtful Catholics nevertheless recognize that matters of women and sex remain sticking points for a broad swath of humanity in thinking about Catholicism, and therefore they're un-avoidable. Given today's rising sensitivity to gay rights, the perception that Catholicism fosters a form of theologically sanctioned homopho-bia is enough, all by itself, to alienate important sectors of opinion. The sexual-abuse crisis has turbocharged debates over priestly celibacy, with a growing chorus of critics suggesting that a repressive approach to sexuality may lurk in the background to the scandals of recent decades. The fact that polls in the developed West show that overwhelming majorities of Catholics reject the official teaching on birth control is also routinely touted as evidence of a collapse in the moral authority of the Church, as well as the hold that the pope and the bishops have over their own flock. Whether any or all of those charges have merit is be-side the point; as long as they cloud perceptions of the Church, efforts to evangelize the world and express what Dolan calls the "romance" of Catholicism will be significantly hindered.

Unsurprisingly, Dolan declares himself in complete agreement with the official position of the Catholic Church on all these matters. The drama of listening to Dolan talk about them, therefore, lies not in the conclusions he will eventually reach but in how he gets there. His ef-fort is to apply an "affirmative orthodoxy" twist, which means he'll take any question phrased as a negative—why does Catholicism reject birth control? for example—and attempt to turn it into a positive, stressing what it is in each case that Catholicism actually affirms and embraces. Whether that will be enough to satisfy the Church's critics on the "pelvic issues" is a long shot, but at least with Dolan leading the conversation, it's more difficult to get the idea that what lies beneath the Church's positions boils down to fear, anger, and the raw drive to protect male privilege.

Those who embrace Church teaching on these points may find in Dolan's approach a new vocabulary, and a new tone, with which to explain and defend those teachings in the postmodern marketplace of ideas. Those who decided long ago that the Church is full of it, on the other hand, may at least be more inclined to conclude that Catholicism is wrong but well intentioned, as opposed to wrong and malevolent. For anyone who knows the recent history of public perceptions of the Catholic Church when it comes to sex, that alone would probably seem like progress.

Just as with women, there's a perception that the Catholic Church is anti-gay. How do you react to that?

Is the perception out there? Sure, but I don't think it's correct. I like to deal in examples, so let me tell you this story. We were in Washington, D.C., for a bishops' meeting maybe four years ago, and as we processed into the Basilica of the Immaculate Conception, we were met by taunts and protests that the bishops of the United States are homophobic, that we hate gays. The demonstrators were asking, "How dare you call us disordered and intrinsically evil?" and so on. I got home on Sunday, for Mass at the Cathedral of Saint John the Evangelist [in Milwaukee]. There I've got protestors outside the cathedral saying the exact opposite thing, that Catholic bishops love gays. "How dare you? They're perverts." These protestors were quoting the catechism, where it says people with a same-sex attraction are still made in the image and likeness of God. In other words, they hated our guts because we defend the inherent dignity of gay men and women. My communications director said, "Let's go out the side door. You don't want to meet these people." I said, "The hell I don't! This is too good to pass up." I wanted to be out there and shouted at by people saying we're too pro-gay. I said, "Let's go out the front door," and that's exactly what we did.

That's where we're at, see? One camp seems to feel that if we don't let people do whatever they want, wherever and with whomever, somehow we don't like them or we feel they're not equal. That's not it at all, and in some ways those protestors in Milwaukee understood more clearly what the Church is actually saying than many of our critics on the other side seem to. We may balk at certain behaviors, but we are unflagging defenders of the rights and human dignity of all men and women.

What is the Church actually saying to homosexuals?

First of all, we're saying that it's absurd to identify yourself with your sexual urges. When somebody comes to me, as people often do, and says, "I must tell you, I am a homosexual," or "I am gay," I say, "Well, thanks for your confidence. Nice to meet you, sit down, you're welcome here, but as a matter of fact, no you're not. You happen to be John Jones, who is a child of God and redeemed by the blood of his only begotten Son, destined to spend eternity with him. When God looks at you, he sees a work of art. That's who you are. You happen to be sexually attracted to men, but that doesn't define who you are." Now, I happen to think that's rather liberating, it's ennobling, but our culture doesn't see that. There's the great challenge, to make people see that we are not our sexual urges.

A church, or any authority, like a parent, who would stand up and say this is who you are, this is your birthright, and there are certain things you can and can't do because it detracts from who you are, this is thought to be verboten today. For some reason, we have put our foot in our mouth when we have tried to say these things, and I don't know how we get out from that. I'd like to think we're the best friend of humanity, no matter what their urges might be or what their inclinations might be, because for us all that is secondary to who we are: children of God, made in his image and likeness.

Is this not the great treasure, in the long run, of the pontificate of John Paul II, that who we are is defining, not what we do? There's that wonderful line from *Pastores Dabo Vobis*, that the great temptation today is to define our worth by having and doing, not being. It all comes down to that, doesn't it? Seen through the eyes of God, whatever your sexual attraction is, I don't really care too much about. If you act on this attraction, it might diminish who you are, but I'm dealing with who you are and the way God sees you. If you see yourself as God sees you, well, you will act virtuously.

How to sell that, how to market that? That's a key question, and one to which I'm not sure I yet have the answer. How do we as a church find a way to come across as what we truly are, which is the best friend of everything that is most noble, virtuous, liberating, warm, and tender in humanity?

If somebody comes to you and says, my attraction is same-sex but I want to be a faithful Catholic, the only thing you can say is that they're called to a life of chastity. You can understand how that's a tough sell.

It is, but chastity is not just an expectation of people with a same-sex attraction. I can tell story after story from being a parish priest. I once had a man in his mid-thirties, at the peak of everything, with a wife who had become an invalid, and he's going to have to be a celibate the rest of his life as far as sexual urges go, because she cannot engage in sex. Does he live a faithful, happy, whole life? You bet he does. Would he change it for anything in the world? No. He, a married man, is called to heroic chastity for the rest of his life. It goes back to our pivotal teaching on sexuality, which is that sexuality mirrors the love God has for us, so it has to have those same characteristics, meaning lifelong, life-giving, and faithful. Anything outside of that can't do. I understand that's a very tough sell, but fundamentally it's a very positive, beautiful vision of human love. A lifelong, life-giving, faithful marriage between a man and a woman, open to children, is, simply put, the only way God intends sexual love to be expressed.

Again, the point doesn't just apply to people with a same-sex attraction. If you've got a husband who comes to you and says, "It's really not working out too well. I love my wife and wouldn't want to leave her, but sexually it's less than fulfilling. I'm on the road quite a bit, and couldn't a case be made that it's not really just for me to live a chaste, celibate life?" The Church would say, yes it is just, and for the same reasons. Ultimately, this is not about trying to control people's lives by telling them what they can't do. It's about trying to guide them, walk with them, along the path to true happiness and fulfillment, the kind of happiness that lasts a lifetime and extends into eternity. Somehow we've got to find a way to broadcast the idea that the Catholic Church is in the happiness business!

I know this may be difficult to talk about, but you had a priest friend, someone you knew from your student days in Rome, who died of AIDS. Can you say more about that?

He was a dear friend, probably my best friend at the North American College. It gets a little delicate, because as close as I was to him, I had no idea of his struggles in this area. I have absolutely no evidence that he was leading anything but a virtuous life in Rome, but apparently, a couple of years after ordination he took a leave of absence, and I lost touch with him. I didn't know where he was, and nor did his bishop, who was awfully good to him. I would call the bishop and write him, and he would say, "Tim, I wish I could help you, but I don't know where he is either." All I know is that he asked for some time away, and it was a pretty considerable length of time. We're talking about five or six years away from the priesthood. He then came back, thanks be to God, and he was a great priest for the rest of his life. He ended up as a chaplain at a Catholic hospital. I visited him quite a few times there, but we never talked [about his time away]. He and I knew each other pretty well, but there were some areas in his life that I just knew weren't going to be open.

Eventually, the day came when he called to say, "Tim, I've been diagnosed with HIV/AIDS." This would have been in the late eighties, so it was before any hope of treatment. He never told me how he got the disease, but that didn't diminish our friendship. I was with him the week before he died, and we concelebrated Mass on what turned out to be his deathbed. He said to me, "Tim, you know I'm dying. When I do, would you bring my remains over to Rome? I'd love to be buried in the Campo Verano [a famous cemetery in Rome]." I said, "You bet I will, although I'm not even sure how we'd do it." He said, "I couldn't care less. You could bring me over in your carry-on bag, for all I care, as long as there's a bottle of Sambuca by the remains!" So I did, and he's at Campo Verano. When I'm in Rome, I make a point of visiting his grave.

Has that experience given you a special sensitivity to people struggling with AIDS?

I hope that it adds to it, but I don't think it's all based on my experience with my friend. I can't understand why anyone would think treating people with compassion, even people who may have fallen short in one way or another in their lives, requires some kind of explanation. As I said, I don't know what happened with him during the years he was away from the priesthood, but let's say he was engaged in behavior that, objectively speaking, the Church would consider sinful. So what? He obviously repented and returned to his vocation. We priests should be entirely conversant with, even in a certain sense comfortable with, sinners. In spiritual direction or confession, when people talk to me about the various sins in their lives, I usually say, "You've sinned. You've confessed something that, as a Catholic, you're honest enough to say is less than consistent with what you believe your God and your Church call you to. You're sorry, right, and you're going to try with God's grace to do better? Well, fine. Nice to be with you. God forgives you, and God bless you. Go and sin no more!"

I don't know where this idea of an outcast status imposed by the Church upon sinners comes from. I don't know why anybody would feel we would look upon homosexuals who fall, for example, any differently than I would somebody on the other side of the confessional who said he had just lost his temper again with his kids, and knew that he had hurt them bad. I hope I could say to both, "You're right, I'm glad you're sorry about that. Let's work on it." Yes, a homosexual act is objectively sinful; so is a heterosexual act, apart from marriage; so is losing your temper. We repent. We make a firm purpose of amendment. We ask God's mercy and grace to do better.

I sometimes wonder, am I too simple about this stuff?

Let's take a practical question. Say you're back in a parish, and you've got somebody you know is in a homosexual relationship, and they're not coming forward for Communion, but they come to Mass every Sunday and otherwise take part in the life of the parish. Are you comfortable with that?

Sure, I'd be glad they were there. I'd welcome them. Of course, there's a didactic character of the Church that we can never overlook, because the Church is a teacher at her core. If other people knew about it and were scandalized by it, or if the person was leading that kind of life and bragging about it, holding it up as an example, contradicting Church teaching, then we'd have a problem. But if somebody that I know privately is in that kind of relationship wants to be part of the parish? Not only do I not see it as a problem, I'd welcome them to the Church. And I would affirm their honest decision not to receive Holy Communion.

What about this case? Two men are in a same-sex union who have adopted a child and want that child to attend a Catholic school. We just had a case like that, and I replied, sure, that child is very welcome, as long as there is a certain understanding. In justice, we need to acquaint the "parents," I suppose in quotation marks, with some of the implications of this decision. In justice to them, we need to be up-front from the beginning. We need to say, "You want your child in a Catholic school, and your child is welcome. But you do realize there might be some discomfort insofar as that at a certain point in their catechesis, the child might learn that the kind of life you are leading is contrary to the teaching of the Church. You may also want to know that if it becomes public you're leading this kind of life, there may be some discomfort for your child and for you." We have to be pretty blunt from the beginning about some of these things. We also need to say, "When it comes time for your child's First Communion, you would be unable to receive Holy Communion with your child. If you're accepting of all that, then I would be open to accepting the child."

Aren't there analogous situations with parents who are married outside the Church? Or, to take another example, when you have a teacher in a Catholic school who's talking about the sinfulness of the abuse of alcohol, there may be a fair number of kids sitting there thinking, "Wow, she's talking about my dad." In other words, I think it's a mistake to treat homosexuals as a special case. There are all kinds of situations in which people may fall short of what the Church would see as the ideal, and I would hope that in all those cases we can find ways to balance the need to be clear about our teaching with being pastoral and loving in the way we relate to people. If we only took the children of saints in our schools, our classrooms would be empty!

Do you think it's important for bishops to listen to the experiences of gay Catholics?

I think it's important to listen to everybody. Not long ago, a group of self-described "gay Catholics" asked if they could see me. They were very surprised when I said, "Sure." We ended up starting at four P.M. and going until about six-fifteen, which was far longer than either of us expected. At the end of it, they reported they were utterly amazed that it had been an enjoyable, productive encounter. They kept saying to me, "You didn't seem threatened." I replied, "Why would you threaten me? You tell me you're believing Catholics, and I trust you, I respect you. We had a candid exchange. There are some things I said that you probably found difficult to hear, and there are some things you said that I'm not able to accept, but boy oh boy, has this been enlightening and productive."

What were the sticking points?

Obviously, the primary one is how you blend the spirit of "All are welcome" with the "No, you're not!" Meaning, everyone is welcome, so if you just told me that you're a man with same-sex attraction, you need to hear me say that you are as welcome at Sunday Mass as my mother is. I love it when you're there, and it hurts me when you're not. You also need to hear me say, and I trust that you believe, that part of Sunday Mass is going to be a clear exposition of the teaching of Jesus as understood by his church for two thousand years, which periodically is going to say that sexual love is such a reflection of the way God loves us that it's intended to have the same three characteristics: It's faithful, it's forever, and it's life-giving. Ergo, it can only be experienced by a man and a woman in a lifelong faithful relationship of marriage, and any type of sexual pleasure outside of that is something less than God intended. We will challenge you, and everybody else, to accept that, and to go through an interior conversion that would allow you to be at peace with that, as we would in other areas.

My bottom line was something like this: You'll be happy to hear me say that everybody here is welcome, no matter their language, color, or sexual preference, and we owe each other dignity and respect. You're going to cheer me on when I say that, because you know that some other people in the Church may be bristling. But be prepared to bristle yourself when I talk about God's plan for sexual love, because that's part of the Gospel too, and you may not be comfortable hearing that.

Were they worried about anything in particular?

There are three or four parishes in the archdiocese of New York, mostly in Manhattan, that would have the reputation of being "gay-friendly." I think they were worried that I might clamp down on them.

Were you able to reassure them?

I hope so. Among them were two priests, who did not identify themselves as gay priests, but who simply said we cherish the opportunity to minister to these people and we do everything we can to cultivate a spirit of welcome. I said, "Good, I'm glad you do. Keep it up. Be faithful to the virtue of hospitality, and be faithful to preaching the virtue of chastity."

Let's shift gears to celibacy. Give me the affirmative-orthodoxy argument for celibacy.

The best anecdote for me is from my friend Sister Rosario. Forty years ago, if not longer, I was in college seminary and probably questioning celibacy. She was a young sister at Holy Infant at the time. She was an excellent first-grade teacher, very effective. One day she kept a little girl after school to help her with her reading, knowing that the girl came from a very troubled and dysfunctional family. She noticed that the girl kept looking at her, and so finally she asked, "Haley, why do you keep looking at me?" The girl said, "Sister, are you married?" This is a little first-grader, and Sister Rosario replied, "No, I'm not married." The girl said, "Oh, good, then you belong to all of us." I have never forgotten that story. In a very beautiful way, the story offers an icon of what celibacy is all about. It's a liberating ability to belong to everybody.

I've never been much for the pragmatic arguments, and I think we make a big mistake when we go there immediately—you know, that celibacy allows you more time, it frees you up. First of all, I think that's an insult to marriage, and second, God knows we've got enough examples of celibates who aren't freed up. I know some theologians think it's very outdated, but for me the spousal imagery says everything. Celibacy allows us to have a passionate, personal, unfettered commitment to Jesus Christ and his church, which perhaps might not be as evident or as easy if we were married. I sometimes think, too, that we do not give enough credit, although this is not a phrase you'd want to use publicly, to the whole eschatological dimension of celibacy. There is a certain amount of mystique, otherness, transcendental characteristic of the priesthood because of celibacy, which I think is very didactic and has tremendous positive repercussions. There's a sense of belonging somewhere else that I think is very powerful and cannot be underestimated. I think Catholic people sense that in their gut, even if they're unable to articulate it.

Of course, the Catholic Church already has married priests, both in the Eastern rite churches and by way of converts from some Protestant traditions. Would you be open to further experiments along those lines?

Theoretically, would I be open to a discussion about a more expansive welcome for married clergy? Theoretically, yes. Strategically, I worry about the timeliness of it. At a time when priestly identity, priestly values, are under siege, I wonder if this is the time to sell the store. In other words, I worry about the strategic prudence. I don't buy the argument, by the way, that getting rid of celibacy is the answer to the priest shortage. That hasn't been the experience of the Anglicans, or the Orthodox. I could see, however, that in some specific situations, the ability to ordain the *viri probati* [married men known to be solid, faithful Catholics] might make sense. Haiti in the aftermath of the earthquake might be a good example. Two or three bishops could go to the Holy Father and say, "Our clergy, the few that we did have, are now gone. We have absolutely nobody here. Would you give us permission to ordain these six men, who happen to be married?" I could see that happening.

Let's talk about the recent controversy in the Diocese of Phoenix, where Bishop Thomas Olmsted decreed that a hospital is no longer Catholic because, in his view, it permitted a direct abortion. The hospital insists that's not the case, that it saved the only life it could, which was that of the mother. What did you make of that case?

I honestly don't feel that I knew the details well enough to pass judgment. I have absolutely no embarrassment about admitting that I need help when it comes to delicate matters of moral theology. The caricature of some bishop sitting in his study making these split-second decisions about complex questions is crazy. I'm sure Bishop Tom Olmsted did endless study and thinking and praying and consulting about this.

Critics say that if what happened in Phoenix were to become national policy, it could mean the end of Ob/Gyn in every Catholic hospital in America, because medical and governmental regulators would take away their licenses.

That might be overly dramatic. What I wonder about is this: There are always people eager to say that a bishop has overstepped his bounds, but where are those same people when the government oversteps its bounds and threatens to close us down? Surely interference by the state is at least as worrisome as alleged interference by a bishop.

You know that I wrote a book on [Archbishop] Edwin O'Hara [of Kansas City, from 1939 to 1956]. After the Second World War, at Queen of Heaven Hospital in Kansas City, Edwin O'Hara with the brave Maryknoll Sisters decided that we will begin to hire black physicians, train black physicians, and accept black patients. We will not have segregated hospitals. The government, local rather than federal in his case, said no, you can't, we'll close you down. O'Hara and the sisters said, "Try it. We dare you. Drop dead." They were prophetic, and thank God they were. Is there not an equally compelling issue here? If the government is forcing us to do something contrary to what we believe, should we just take it, just lay down? I think we should say you're not going to close us down, and if you try, you're going to have a big fight on your hands.

Some have suggested the fall-out might be that Catholic hospitals might just walk away, cutting their ties to the institutional Church and incorporating under civil law as a hospital "in the Catholic tradition." Are you worried about that?

That's a concern, yes. It would be a lessening of the bond, moving outside the traditional orbit of Catholic health care. Of course, there are realists who would say, "Isn't that what's already happening?" They would say, this is what we've already got, and it's time for some truth in advertising. Do we just come out and say this isn't a Catholic hospital, or do we go ahead with the charade that everything is fine and these places are really Catholic? There are many bishops, and many Catholic laypeople, who ask what's the difference between walking into a Catholic hospital these days and a secular hospital, other than maybe crucifixes on the wall? I'd like to think that there are some differences. I think it's hyperbole to say we've gone to such an extreme that there aren't. But I do think those who say, hey, let's just admit reality here, may have a point.

The worry is that our Catholic hospitals are now where our universities were back in the 1980s, slowly drifting out of the Catholic orbit. Is it time to call the question? A historian fifty years from now who does a master's thesis on this issue will either say that Bishop Olmsted was prophetic in calling a question that's been buzzing around in our bonnet for a long time, or that the very calling of it provoked something that now we regret. I honestly don't know which way things will go.

I do know, and I don't just feel obliged to say this, that I know and respect Tom Olmsted very much. It would be tough to find a more sincere, gentle, humble, thoughtful guy, and a more pastoral guy in the best sense of the word. To caricature him as some sort of arbitrary bully is just false.

Would you be willing to see some Catholic hospitals cut their ties with the Church if it meant defending the genuine Catholicity of those that remain?

I would regret that, and I would worry that in the future we might be sorry that we did it. Fundamentally, however, I think it would be worth taking that risk to defend the integrity of Catholic hospitals.

I understand, however, that doing so would come at a price. One of my pet theories is that the diminishing institutional presence of the Church today constitutes a real crisis. I worry that the downsizing we're experiencing, because we don't have the money or the manpower anymore to keep up that institutional presence, is being milked by our enemies to neuter the voice of the Church in the public square. When I go to Albany, the reason that doors open is not because of what the Church teaches. It's because of soup kitchens, and adoption, and health care, and nursing homes, and inner-city schools. As those decline, I'm going to be about as welcome in Albany as the Greek Patriarch. Why do people listen to the pope? Why do countries have diplomatic relations with him? It's because he—not he, but the Church he represents—runs the largest nongovernmental system of health care, education, feeding of the poor, and so on. If that begins to splinter, I'm worried about what it might mean in terms of our effectiveness in public affairs.

The other reason to regret any move toward weakened ties with Catholic institutions, such as the hospitals, is that it says something about our ecclesiology. We are an incarnational, sacramental Church. We're on city blocks. That's where we're enfleshed. That incarnational persona of the Church is gradually melting away, isn't it? That's something we have to be worried about.

Finally, you're well aware that polls show substantial majorities of Catholics, at least in North America and Europe, reject official Church teaching on birth control. Where do those Catholics stand vis-à-vis the Church?

If what you're asking is, would I be one of those who's quick in telling people that they're out of the Church? No, I would not, and I wouldn't want to be. People who are struggling to understand, accept, and live the teachings of Jesus and his church need the Church more than anybody.

If you've got somebody who's got trouble with the creed that we recite on Sunday, I think he or she ought to ask, "Am I still at home in the Catholic faith?" If I cannot profess the divinity of Jesus, the real presence of Christ in the Eucharist, the Blessed Trinity, the salvific nature of our Lord's dying and rising, if one can't profess faith in that, one should personally ask, "Am I still at home in the Catholic faith?" But are there other issues where we can kind of banter back and forth? Yeah, probably, and especially about the way these things are expressed. You and I both know that most Catholics don't talk about these kinds of things anyway. The press, not the Catholic people, keeps chattering about birth control. I actually wish people would argue with me on that issue, because we've got a compelling message.

There's sort of a Catholic mind-set that people basically know we've got a God who loves us, who sent his only Son to save us from our sins, who wants us to live forever with him in heaven, who answers prayers, who's given us some expectations for life, who's given us the gift of the Church as a family here on earth to support that. That's the Catholic mind-set that we all agree upon, that we love and want to pass along to our kids. I also think people can kind of come and go in their faith, can't they? It's similar to what happens in our biological life. There are certain things I believed when I was eighteen I wouldn't be caught dead believing today. I'm not talking just about theological things but about political ideas, things I may have done healthwise, or whatever. That's true with the faith too. At various points in our lives there may be aspects of the Church's teaching with which we struggle, and that's a perfectly normal progression. We need to be clear in presenting the Church's teaching but patient with the struggle to live it. After all, that's how God is with us.

FIVE

Faith and Politics

Aside from the sexual-abuse crisis, probably no story line about the Catholic Church in the United States has generated headlines more consistently over the last several decades than that of the role of the American bishops in national politics. In part, that's because routine religious activity doesn't count as news for most mainstream media outlets, so it's only when religious leaders intersect with the sort of things that secular observers consider important—chiefly politics but also, say, finance or entertainment—that they tend to get noticed. A bishop could produce an erudite five-thousand-word pastoral letter on sin and redemption, and precious few would take notice. If he delivers an offhand, thirty-second remark about Obama and abortion, however, it'll capture the attention of reporters and pundits everywhere. In part, too, the attention to faith and politics reflects a widespread belief that the bishops' political role in the United States has shifted in important ways in recent years, away from a peace-and-justice emphasis toward acting as the new voice of the religious Right.

In the 1980s, the U.S. bishops were often styled as allies of the political Left because of high-profile documents from the bishops' conference on war and peace and on economic justice. More recently, the bishops have been seen as fairly reliable partners of the political Right because of their emphasis on the "life issues," principally abortion but also homosexuality and gay marriage, embryonic stem-cell research, euthanasia, and a number of other debates—all areas where the bishops usually have more in common with Republicans than Democrats. Another issue where the American bishops increasingly play a lead role in politics is immigration reform, partly as a matter of social justice and partly as a reflection of the changing demographics of the American Church. By 2030, the Pew Forum projects that more than 40 percent of the Catholic population in the United States will be Hispanic, which suggests that immigrant rights will be a top-shelf concern of the American hierarchy well into the twenty-first century.

To some extent, whether one sees the bishops as "liberal" or "conservative" depends more on perceptions of where they invest their time and treasure rather than on their official positions. A face-value reading of the positions expressed in the catechism and other Church statements clearly defies such pigeonholing. Officially speaking, the Catholic Church, including the bishops of the United States, are anti-abortion, antiwar, pro-environment, anti-death penalty, pro-immigrant, anti-gay marriage, and in favor of strong social measures to protect the poor. As John Carr, a longtime policy adviser to the U.S. bishops, puts it, anyone who takes the full range of Catholic social teaching seriously is destined to end up "politically homeless" in America.

The bipartisan nature of politics in the United States, where Republicans often seem more sympathetic to Catholic positions on life issues and Democrats more receptive to Church concerns on economic justice and other matters of social policy, tends to put American Catholics in the position of forever making Faustian choices between the lesser of two evils. The debate over health care reform that unfolded in early 2010 offered a classic example. The Catholic Church teaches that access to health care is a universal human right, and the U.S. bishops have been on record in support of health care reform since the early twentieth century. Yet the Church also teaches that the cornerstone human

right is the right to life, and pro-life critics saw the final health care reform package promoted by the Obama administration and Democratic
leadership as opening the door to wider federal funding of abortion. In
the end, the U.S. bishops opposed the measure, while other important
Catholic voices, including the Catholic Health Association, supported
it. Many were dismayed by the appearance of a divided Catholic voice,
but given the way the American political system constantly seems to pit
one set of Catholic values against another, such division was probably
inevitable.

Whenever bishops speak out on political questions, they court a
multitude of headaches. Some critics charge that they shouldn't be
doing it at all, insisting that separation of church and state in America
implies that politics must be an entirely secular enterprise free of "sectarian" or "confessional" influence. Even those who in principle support the idea of a moral voice in political debates often recoil when
that voice cuts in a direction they don't support. Bishops also have to
worry about dividing their own flock when they take political stands.
Any pastor will tell you that when he preaches on God's love or the
importance of forgiveness, most people nod approvingly, but if he starts
talking about abortion or the death penalty, some of them head for the
exits. If that's true of ordinary parish priests, it's all the more the case for
bishops, who face push-back not merely on the steps outside church
but on opinion pages, talk-radio outlets, and prime-time cable-TV
news shows.

All that, however, rarely seems to stop bishops from wading into
political debates, and for better or worse, what the bishops say on politics has an enormous influence on shaping public perceptions of the
Catholic Church. Dolan certainly is not gun-shy about taking political
stands himself, though in characteristic fashion, what's striking is not
so much his message as his tone. He'll take clear positions, but he's also
committed to generosity toward those with whom he disagrees—one
classic example of which is his unwavering conviction that abortion
is the paramount human rights and civil rights issue of the day, com-

bined with a general reluctance about punitive measures such as denying Communion to Catholic politicians who don't support greater restrictions on abortion. In that and many other ways, Dolan is likely to play a key role in shaping the political role of the Catholic Church in America for some time to come.

There's a fairly wide perception that in recent years the Catholic bishops of the United States have entered into a de facto alliance with the Republican Party. What do you make of that?

I know some people have that perception, and I can understand why people might think that way because of the dominance of the pro-life issue. The Republicans, at least on the surface, are much more aligned with our pro-life stand, especially when it comes to the anti-abortion part of it, than the Democrats. So certainly there is that perception, but I don't think it's always accurate. To tell the truth, I get far more criticism from people who feel that we bishops are much too soft on the Democrats, who feel that we are actually in the pocket of the Democrats, especially our infrastructure at the bishops' conference in Washington.

I hate this word, but the situation is much more "nuanced" than simply saying we're in bed with one party or the other. My experience is that we bishops are actually fairly scrupulous in wanting to avoid any partisan flavor. Are there exceptions? Sure there are. But in general, I find bishops almost bend over backward trying to make sure that we don't seem to favor one party over the other. That said, it's true that most of our headline-grabbing conflicts in recent years have been with Democrats. As an American historian, I could go on at length about what I see as the tragic turning away by the Democrats from the pro-life issue. In fairness, however, the Republicans have not always been as aggressive on the issue as we might hope they would have been. In some ways, both parties have let us down.

On the so-called "faith and values" issues, does the Democratic leadership often seem more antagonistic to what you might call Catholic concerns? Yeah, I'm afraid there's no denying that. I find, however, that when I talk to many Democratic leaders, they often shy away from some of the ideology—again, with some exceptions. There are some die-hard pro-abortionists, but in general Democrats seem to be realistic people who simply want to make things work. Of course, what politicians say on the campaign trail is one thing, and what they say and do behind closed doors can sometimes be another.

I know there's a perception in some quarters that Catholic bishops in America are somehow political bulldogs, but frankly, if you take an honest look around, you'll see that other religious leaders often can get away with things that we never could. For example, I've been very careful about meeting candidates in New York, for fear that someone might construe the meeting as an endorsement. If I feel like I have to take the meeting for one reason or another, I'll do it away from the cameras and off the record. But the very next day, you could easily see that a black minister not only met with the candidate but had him speaking from the pulpit! There's absolutely no timidity there, and no one criticizes them. I know that some people think we're too political, but I wonder sometimes if we bishops have bought into that a little too much. Are we scared because we know we're held to a different standard?

Some people have the impression that the Catholic bishops in America have become more sharply defined ideologically in recent election cycles. With the death of Jerry Falwell and with Pat Robertson withdrawing somewhat from national politics, some observers would say you've become the new voice of the religious Right. Is that accurate?

I don't think so, but if the point is that our message has become more sharply focused, I would agree, and I think it's because of the towering nature of the abortion issue. Even though I'm not among those who feel we should exclude people from the big tent, I do feel that it's to our everlasting credit that we've been prophetic on abortion. When the history of this era is eventually written, the fact that the American bishops have stood out on that issue will certainly be to our credit.

Historically, I think it's entirely valid to make a comparison between the pro-life issue and the slavery issue. Today we look back at the American bishops on slavery and we blush, because we were far from prophetic. With one or two exceptions, there were no American bishops in the nineteenth century who stood up and said, "This is intrinsically evil and we must put an end to it now." Most bishops believed the issue to be too controversial, so we're not going to talk about it. We have to save the internal unity and cohesion of the house. At one point, the bishops actually wrote, "We leave this issue up to worldlings." Like we're on Mars or something! We look back with embarrassment on that sort of thing, and rightly so, but we won't on the abortion issue.

Are you saying that the perception of being in bed with the Republicans, or the political Right, is the PR price that has to be paid for taking a strong stance on abortion?

Yes, that's exactly right. Most bishops are politically sophisticated enough to realize that this isn't really a Republican/Democrat issue. They know that our pro-life credentials do not depend on being partners with either the Republicans or the Democrats.

Why do you think abortion has become the litmus test for Catholic fidelity in the United States in a way that it hasn't in other parts of the world?

I don't know, but I'm glad it has. I don't think that on most political issues I'm particularly simplistic, but this one does seem pretty black-and-white. We're talking about human life, an innocent fragile baby, who deserves the full protection of the law. It's to the credit of the Church that we've made this the dominant social justice issue, the number one human rights issue, of the day. As much as enlightened society would like to say that this issue is going away and it's no longer considered a major concern, it still is. We all know that. It's the issue that just will not go away.

Why isn't this true elsewhere? I don't know. Is it the case that Europe gave up years ago on thinking that morality should have anything to do with politics? Perhaps we American Catholics, funny enough, have imbibed some of the Calvinist or Puritanical cast to things. America at its origins reflected a Calvinistic undercurrent, that in some way Geneva should reflect the Heavenly Kingdom, and that politics should reflect what is most moral and ethical. That may not be what you might call the most Catholic way of putting things, but it would be part of what scholars call "American exceptionalism," the American Puritanical-Calvinistic ethos, which in some ways dovetails with the Catholic approach to the pro-life cause.

What do you think?

If you want a more immediate explanation, to me it's this: In Europe, abortion is a settled question. Take Italy. There were two referenda on abortion, in 1974 and 1981, and the Church lost both. In America, that's not the case. It's a live issue for us in a way that's not true for much of Europe.

You're probably right, that many European Catholics believe that not putting the same emphasis on abortion as we do is simply realism. That reminds me of a story from the 2004 *ad limina* visits of American bishops. [All bishops are required to make a trip to Rome to see the pope and other Vatican officials every five years. They're called *ad limina* visits, meaning "to the threshold" of the apostles.] The story involves a bishop from our region.

When Pope Benedict XVI was still Cardinal Ratzinger, everybody always reported that their best meeting on these *ad limina* visits was with Ratzinger in the Congregation for the Doctrine of the Faith. Sure enough, we had an hour with him, and the meeting was completely disciplined and right on target. At the outset, we were all moved by the fact that he walked in right on time, because other Vatican officials sometimes kept us waiting awhile. He opened the meeting by saying, "My brothers, these are the issues I would like to discuss," and he laid out five concerns. One of them was hospitals, I think one of them was Catholic higher education, and one of them was politicians and Communion. Remember, this was right around the 2004 elections. He said, "I hear this is controversial." Then he stopped, and we all thought he would start talking again, but he said, "No, I want to hear you. Tell me about these things." So we all gave him our views.

When it was this bishop's turn, he said: "Your Eminence, it seems sometimes that the Holy See expects bishops in the United States to be much more definitive on the issue of pro-abortion politicians, and much stricter, than you bishops are in Europe. We've been riding up and down the streets of Rome this week, and we see placards of the mayor of Rome supporting gay marriage. We also see placards for different political leaders here, known to be Catholic, who are pro-abortion. We've never heard the bishop of Rome asking to dialogue with the mayor about this particular problem, or threatening to deny him Communion. Why is that never brought up here, but we get instructions all the time on this issue?"

That was obviously a pretty direct question, but Ratzinger didn't get flustered at all. Instead, he simply turned and said, "Perhaps my Italian secretary would be able to shed some light on that!"

As I recall, the secretary said something like, "Well, it's because here in Europe, unfortunately, we believe there's a strict cleavage between one's political views and one's deeply held religious views."

This bishop said, "You know that's precisely what John Kerry says, that his deeply held religious conviction is against abortion, but there's a difference on the political plane. So why are some of us getting the hint that maybe we should not give John Kerry Holy Communion, when that wouldn't be a question here?" The long and the short of it is, there was really no answer given.

In retrospect, the documents from the Holy See on this issue generally have been very clear and enlightening in terms of principles, but there still seem to be some questions on implementation.

Where do you stand on denying Communion to Catholic politicians who have a pro-choice voting record?

I always say that I don't know why this topic only seems to come up with regard to abortion, and I don't know why it's only directed at politicians. I give the example, which tends to mute liberal audiences, of when I was in Milwaukee and the Ku Klux Klan showed up at the courthouse to demonstrate. They did it on a Friday, and on Saturday we had an ecumenical cleansing of the courthouse steps. I helped lead the ceremony, so I brought holy water and the *Book of Blessings.* At one point a reporter said to me, "Archbishop Dolan, if any of these Klan members were to show up at the cathedral tomorrow for Holy Communion, would you give it to them?" I said, "No, I wouldn't." Of course the liberals applauded that—"How prophetic, how bold!" Yet they wouldn't apply the same logic to the abortion question.

That said, in general I think Communion bans are counterproductive. Unless the defiance of Church teaching is extraordinarily blatant, unless it's really scandalous, then I would be very reluctant to turn anyone away. I suppose if you had a Catholic legislator who's almost saying, "I don't regret abortion, and I'm not working to control it. I'm actually going to promote it and expand it and try to make it virtuous. I think it's a great thing," then I would probably feel obligated to step in. That's quite different, however, than a politician who is honestly struggling with the issue. For that reason and many others, imposing Communion bans would not be my ordinary modus operandi.

Some who are opposed to Communion bans say they're counterproductive. The argument is that as long as the public focus is on the merits of the pro-life argument, the pro-life side does well. But when the focus shifts to the bishops' exercise of power, then you lose sympathy.

There's some truth there. Strategically, we play into the hands of our enemies when we do things that in the public mind seem to reduce abortion to an intramural Catholic issue. When we start talking and acting in a disciplinary way, we have given aid and comfort to the enemy. This is actually a bit of a corollary to the tsunami of the sex-abuse crisis, because if you can play into perceptions that this is some strategy by these bullying, unreliable bishops, boy, you've really hurt the cause. Once you make the bishops the issue, at least in some circles the battle is already over, because people will say that the bishops can't even keep their own house together.

I don't want to play into perceptions that the abortion debate is essentially about Catholics, or Catholic bishops, trying to ram their sectarian morality down everyone else's throat. I think the abortion issue keeps its traction at the American table because we have not allowed it to become exclusively a Catholic or confessional issue. It's now a human rights issue, it's a civil rights issue, it's a social justice issue. It's something that goes back to the fundamental principles upon which this republic was founded. Anything that we do to make it [look like] a "Catholic issue" only means that they're going to print up more KEEP YOUR ROSARIES OFF MY OVARIES signs!

There are some who will say, "We'll listen to you bishops about the unborn child once we're convinced that you have the same concern for the child after it's born." That is, some believe your concern for human life stops at the womb, and that your emphasis on abortion has come at the expense of defense of the poor, the environment, war, and other issues.

Again, I know that perception exists, but I don't think it holds much water. In general, I think we do a laudable job of keeping before us the whole array of issues. Is the protection of the life of the baby in the womb the top priority at this moment in cultural history? Yes, but that doesn't mean we're not savvy enough to know that one of the ways you defend unborn life is to make sure that after its birth, the baby is also protected, and that it can take its place in a society that welcomes and nurtures life at every stage. Here in New York State, the Catholic Conference recently noticed that there was going to be a big slash in the state budget in funding for neonatal care, to help poor mothers with their children — to give them a little more time off work to stay at home, special consideration for food and clothing, and other measures to support newborns and their mothers. We argued for keeping the funding, knowing that we have to take a strong stand on this. I know that's just one instance, but it illustrates the point: I don't believe our emphasis on abortion has come at the expense of other social justice concerns.

You know, they say all politics is local, but all politics is about timing as well. In different eras in our history, there are certain issues that rise to the top. In the 1960s and '70s, I guess it was civil rights and the war. In the eighties, it was the nuclear-arms race. Now it's the pro-life issue. So do we bishops highlight certain issues in different historical moments? Yes, we do, and in the era we're in right now, that priority has to be protection of the baby in the womb. Does that mean we ignore the others? No, it's just that strategically this is the one grabbing headlines right now, and this is the one on which we better be out front.

Let me ask you directly: Is there room for a political liberal in the Catholic Church?

Of course there is, and there always has been. In my study of Church history, I was always a fan of figures such as Giuseppe Toniolo and Ludwig Windthorst, of all the European center parties, where you saw the Church in the nineteenth century trying to reconcile itself to democracy. I'm talking about people like Lacordaire, Montalembert, Lamennais, all of whom would probably have been regarded as liberals in their day. I always thought these were brave souls who were trying their best to bridge the gap between Catholic tradition and the new world being born. Catholicism will always have its progressive wing and its more traditional wing, and as long as we stay together on the core principles of the faith, I think that diversity is a very healthy thing. We need people pointing the way forward, just as we need people to remind us of our roots and our past.

Further, it's also worth saying that there are issues where the conservatives in the Church feel just as uncomfortable with what the bishops are saying or doing as the liberals sometimes do on other matters. It's a bit of a secular, left-wing bias to believe that it's only the liberals in the Church who are dissatisfied! Those who know it from the inside know it's much more complicated. Don't forget that the only formal schism after Vatican II, the Lefebvrites, actually came from the Catholic Right, not the Left.

When the bishops, when the Church, take a position against abortion or same-sex marriage, one frequent accusation is that you're trying to turn this into a confessional state. How do you respond?

I would say that America is at its best when religion has a place at the table. The genius of American democracy is when people of different moral tongues speak up, and that's what we're doing. On these cases, too, I think we need to be much more credible and try to get our act together in stating: Is it true that the Catholic Church is against same-sex marriage? Yes. Is it true that the Catholic Church is against abortion? Yes. But that's not the reason that we're trying to be so forceful here. We're also saying that these are issues of human rights, these are issues of natural law. In other words, this isn't about trying to impose specifically religious convictions on the entire country.

If I were calling for a constitutional amendment trying to outlaw hamburgers on Fridays during Lent, you would have every right in the world to say I'm trying to impose Catholic teaching and discipline on American society. As a matter of fact, we're not. We're speaking about issues here that are at the core of what we are as a republic. One does not have to be a person of faith, whether that faith be Catholic, Jewish, or Baptist, to hold these views. We're more speaking as Americans, as people of faith certainly, but we're making the argument on the basis of fundamental American values. I think we can probably be a little better about making that clear.

I recently spoke to a politician who had just lost an election. He's a good Catholic, and he was trying to understand all this. He had been at odds with the bishop on the "gay marriage" issue. He asked me how he could "impose" his Catholic values on others. I said to him, "You know, we happen to be against robbery too, and it's not just because it's against the seventh commandment. In a civil, responsible society, one has to protect the property of others. If you as a Catholic political leader support laws against robbery, are you trying to impose your Catholic values on the rest of the country? No, you're not. It's the same thing on the abortion issue."

Let's say you have a Catholic who's sincerely pro-life but who believes that America right now isn't ready to overturn *Roe v. Wade*. They argue that you have to prepare the culture before you can impose a law. Where is that person vis-à-vis the Church?

I think it would depend on if one has given up on the final goal of eliminating abortion. You do have some Catholic politicians who will say, "I'm with you all the way. I will never give up on working toward overturning *Roe* v. *Wade*. I will never give up on promoting a society free of the radical abortion license. That having been said, right now I'm probably unable to do that with the vigor I might wish, and I'm probably going to have to take some stands that seem less than rigorous, but I will never give up that goal." I could live with that. For somebody who just says, "Archbishop, I'm with you all the way, but believe me, it's a losing battle. We might as well wave the white flag, and maybe try to get some cutbacks, but in general we just better live with it." That I couldn't accept, because they've given up the fight. I think we've got to persevere in the goal. Remember that John Paul II in *Evangelium Vitae* did seem to give a nod and a wink to a gradualism, that sometimes we have to be patient, and sometimes we have to live with imperfect legislation that helps us achieve the goal even if it's not totally doing away with the evil that we oppose.

Could a Catholic, in principle, be faithful to Church teaching on abortion and nevertheless say that as a matter of civil law in the here and now, this is not the right strategic move?

This could be analogous to the ameliorist position on the slavery issue. You know, there weren't too many Catholic abolitionists. There were, unfortunately, quite a few Catholic defenders of slavery. But there were also quite a few Catholics who felt, let's work gradually to try to get it over with. Let's take our time and gradually get there. I think that was morally acceptable, although as we look back now, it seems embarrassing, because this was the kind of thing where we should have just said, "No, we can't tolerate this. This has got to change, now. This is a blotch on our national complexion."

Among the ameliorists, there were two ways. One wing would say, "We're not going to rest until this is done away with, but we're probably going to have to take our time." There were others who said, "No, we're going to keep trying to chip away at it, but darn it, slavery's here to stay. We might as well just learn to live with it." Number one I could live with, number two I couldn't. The same would apply to abortion today.

In other words, mistaken political judgment and heresy are not the same thing.

That's true. The late Cardinal Avery Dulles raised some of the questions you're talking about. He often asked about the ability to enforce a sweeping law against abortion, and he would quote Saint Thomas Aquinas to say that we shouldn't pursue an unenforceable law. Dulles was certainly not what you would call "soft" on abortion, but he recognized the legitimacy of the question about how you translate Church teaching into public policy.

There is space in Catholic conversation for somebody to raise those questions?

Oh, of course. If somebody asked me what you just did, would I have a fit? Not at all. I would probably give the same answer, which is that we can't ever give up on the goal of eliminating abortion, but are you asking something that I think deserves a hearing? Yes, you bet.

Let's talk for a moment about the Obama/Notre Dame controversy in 2009. You were among the bishops critical of Notre Dame for inviting Obama to deliver the commencement address and for giving him an honorary doctorate. What went wrong there, in your eyes?

This was a time when the Catholic voice in the United States needed to be united, when we were in a wait-and-see attitude about a president who both inspires us and scares us. It was a time when we had articulated some very legitimate fears about past statements of Obama on abortion, some of which were even antithetical to one of the core messages of the Church. We needed a coherent voice, and yet Notre Dame, which is arguably one of the most symbolic Catholic voices in the United States, instead said it's time to canonize this guy. I don't know if that served the Church well. To use the language of Bishop John D'Arcy [of South Bend, Indiana] and the Notre Dame theologian John Cavadini, I don't know if that was "ecclesially responsible."

Now, I'm not one of these who would then say, "It's all over with Notre Dame. That door is closed, that's gone. We do not want them at our bishops' conference, we are not going to go to their campus anymore, they must pay a price." That's where I find myself backing off. My feeling is, state your case, be firm about it, and then work at it. Will there come a time, because I have so much love and respect for Notre Dame, that we're probably going to have a pretty heated discussion? Yes, I imagine that time will come. But does that mean we should say to Notre Dame, "Get lost, you're outside of the camp now"? No, it doesn't.

Some said the problem wasn't so much inviting Obama to speak as giving him the honorary doctorate. Do you agree?

I'd say that would have softened it. For instance, there didn't seem to be much controversy about Obama going to Georgetown, except for that unfortunate drape in front of the crucifix, and who knows if that was even intentional? Other than that, you didn't hear too many people say he should not be invited. One could say the whole purpose of a university is to have a fair, civil exchange of ideas, and the president of the United States, whether we like him or not, obviously has something to say. Giving him a chance to say it on a Catholic college campus is pretty much a part of our mission.

Now, others might say, "Come on, Dolan, there's a big difference between Georgetown and Notre Dame." The reason nobody complained about Georgetown is that by now, people aren't surprised by anything they do. But with Notre Dame, we thought these are folks who get it and who take their Catholic identity seriously. When they do something like this, it hurts. I said that to the president of Notre Dame [Father John Jenkins]. I said, "John, in some ways you should take it as a compliment. We love Notre Dame so much that when you did this, it really hurt and disappointed us."

Let's say Fordham, which is in the Archdiocese of New York, wants to invite Obama to speak. Are you comfortable with that?

If Father Joseph McShane [president of Fordham University], with whom I get along really well, were to tell me that Fordham is having a forum on foreign policy, on some issue in the Middle East or something, and we're going to invite the president of the United States, I'd say great, I'd like to be there. If they want to give him the founder's medal or another honor, I would have reservations.

I know you've had the opportunity to meet President Obama. Are you impressed with him?

Yes. He's very shrewd, including his approach to religion. One of my fellow bishops worries that in Obama we now have a "theologian-in-chief, a new national pastor, and the new patriarch of the Catholic Church in America. He's deciding Catholic teaching, rather than the bishops." Obviously, for the bishop who was telling me this, it wasn't intended as a compliment, but more as a complaint that Obama has managed very successfully to divide the Catholic voice in America. That may be pushing it a little bit, but I do think we have a very clever president.

I've been impressed with Obama's sincerity. On the day of the vote on health care, which was a tough day for us, I was talking to Patrick Gaspard [director of the Office of Political Affairs at the White House]. He said that some of the things [Michigan congressman] Bart Stupak had said about a group of sisters who came out in favor of the legislation were very uncivil. I said, "Patrick, there's been a lack of civility on both sides. Have you read Maureen Dowd this morning? For anybody you can bring up on the pro-life side who's been uncivil, I can match it." He said, "Point well taken." I then remarked, "Having said that, I think the man you work for, the president, has been a model of civility." I do admire that.

Where do things stand in terms of the dialogue between Notre Dame and the bishops?

I think in the long run the controversy may have been a positive moment in the life of the Church, in that it front-burnered several issues such as Catholic identity, getting along with the bishops, and the pro-life cause. I've met with Father Jenkins [president of the University of Notre Dame] a number of times. Although I don't think he's contrite about his decision, he does sincerely recognize that this ruptured his relationship with many bishops, and he's not comfortable with that. He recognizes that any Catholic university has to take seriously its cooperation with the bishop, and needs to recognize the authority of the bishop. I think he's asking, how can we do that, and how can we correct what's happened? Personally he's met with me a time or two, once since my election [as president of the bishops' conference], simply to ask, "What do you advise? How can I repair this breach?" He's very candid in saying, "I still don't know why they're so upset. I still think what I did was defensible." But he's also realistic in saying, "I don't like what's happened because of it. I prize Notre Dame's stature as the iconic Catholic university in the United States. Not only do I prize it, I want to defend it, I want to strengthen it, so how can I?"

If you were invited to deliver the commencement address at Notre Dame, would you accept?

Maybe not right now, but in the future I probably could. It might still be a little too neuralgic right now. Something might be read into it, like a *sanatio in radice* [a canonical term for correcting legal defects, which colloquially means "to make a problem go away"] and I don't know if I would have the right to allow it to be interpreted that way. But in the future, it could happen. This goes back to something I've said before: I might disagree with what people do, but I don't like questioning motives.

Concretely, is there something Notre Dame, or any other Catholic university, could do that would signal its desire for good relations with the bishops?

A Catholic university needs to be of service to the bishops. I'm not talking about admissions or scholarships, but if a bishop needs something—perhaps some advice legally, for instance in governance of schools matters, or even such strategic issues as whether it's better to merge schools or get a new one—the first place he should go is to a Catholic university. That's something Notre Dame could do ... asking bishops, "What do you need? You're facing some pretty sharp religious liberty issues coming up, you're facing a lot of educational issues. How can we help?" Think of what we're all going through on the question of charter schools, yes or no? Are they worth working for, or is that just another nail in the coffin of our Catholic schools if we buy into them? These are areas where our Catholic universities ought to be helping us. They ought to have some data, some studies here, and that's where I think a Catholic university can reclaim a sense of ecclesial service. I think they want to, because they've asked me some areas where they could.

I also think sometimes universities can also make a mistake that we bishops have made in the past, of being a tad arrogant. They'll sometimes come out and say, "The universities are where the Church does its thinking." Like thinking doesn't happen anywhere else? Like we bishops don't think? That's not good. For sure, the university is one of the places where a safe and secure arena is created so that leadership in the Church can do its thinking. We can live with putting it that way. But don't tell me that we're the slobs who are worried about turning on the lights and fixing the boilers, while you all are wrestling with these real cerebral issues. That's not it. We want to think along with you. We don't contract you to do the thinking for us. That's another area where the universities could help themselves—by acknowledging that they're thinking along with the bishops, not instead of them.

You referred to a divided Catholic voice in America. One example came in the debate over health care reform, where the bishops were opposed on the grounds that the legislation could open the door to new federal funding of abortion. The Catholic Health Association, the main resource and advocacy group for the country's more than six hundred Catholic hospitals and sixty-one Catholic health care systems, and Network, a Catho-

lic social justice lobby in which women's religious orders are heavily involved, came out in favor. Is that the sort of thing you have in mind?

Yes, it makes the point very well. When we bishops tried to press legislators to vote against the reform bill unless it included a clear bar on new federal funding for abortion, you couldn't call a senator or member of Congress who wouldn't say back to you—not in a "gotcha" way, but sincerely—"Archbishop, you're telling me that Catholics oppose this, but I'm looking here at what the sisters just said." The two things they would quote most often were the Network statement, which was signed by a number of sisters, and the Catholic Health Association. Obama is a skilled politician, and he knows the classic way to succeed is by dividing your enemy.

In your opinion, did the CHA cross a line?

Yes, I think it did. Had the CHA said, "If you are seeking a more definitive public voice on the official Catholic position, you must consult the bishops. However, in our prudential judgment, the fears we have expressed that this health care bill could be used to further the abortion license have been quelled by the president's assurances." I think I could have lived with that. But to allow themselves to be elevated to a kind of parallel voice to the bishops was a big mistake.

In principle, you're willing to concede that predicting the consequences of a piece of legislation isn't covered by your teaching authority?

Yeah, I would say that. I would say that in this area, we're dealing with prudential judgment.

Is there a way the CHA could have expressed its prudential judgment that would have avoided the impression of undercutting the bishops?

Yes, I think that if anything they stated had been prefaced with a disclaimer that we do not claim to speak definitively, that we are not the definitive Catholic voice. Only the bishops are. Bart Stupak was right, although he didn't say it very well, when Chris Matthews brought up the statement from the sisters [the Network statement]. Stupak said, "If I want to know where the Church stands, I don't ask some bunch of nuns. I ask the bishops." He was absolutely correct, although he certainly might have phrased it more gently.

Cardinal Francis George is big on the notion of *communio*. There needs to be an ecclesial *communio*, and that's at the heart of what Catholicism is about. As bishops, of course, we're the ones who have the supreme duty and responsibility of protecting that *communio*. Any Catholic group, I think, would have to be scrupulous about never wanting to fracture that *communio*. Network and CHA may have put that at risk. Of course, that doesn't mean there can't be very legitimate debate on prudential matters, for example, on health care or the minimum wage. Obviously that takes on a much more heightened tenor when you're talking about something intrinsically evil, like abortion. I'm not one of those who say that abortion is on the same level as immigration policy, because it's not. Yet I do believe the whole question of how to translate our faith into public policy is one of those areas where we bishops need to listen more to the insights of our laity, because that too is part of fostering a *communio*.

You're not interested in pursuing disciplinary consequences against the CHA?

I'm very interested in pursuing how catechetically, and relationally, we can restore that fractured unity. There are other ways rather than bringing down a hammer. I have enough respect for people such as Sister Carol Keehan [president of the CHA] to believe that if we are dogged enough in sitting down with them and saying, "Look what's happened. How can we make sure this doesn't happen again?" I think we'll make some progress.

Now, are there going to be exceptions? Sure. Hypothetically, a group that claims to be Catholic and says, "We feel we have as much right to teach in the name of the Church as the bishops do, and we look forward to a whole future of disagreeing with you," then I think a lot of bishops would reply, "Pardon us, but we have to be concerned with truth in advertising, and so it's our responsibility to say that you can't call yourself Catholic anymore." Occasionally, will it come to that? Yes, but my posture would be, I hope those cases are rare.

You believe you'll get further by presuming people's goodwill?

Yes, and there will be people who call me terribly naïve for that reason. They'll wonder, "When are you guys ever going to learn?"

Fundamentally, are you glad health care reform passed?

I'm certainly for the idea of reform, but not this particular bill. We bishops found ourselves in a very tough position, because this is something we've advocated for since 1919. Now it's on the brink of becoming reality, and we find ourselves unable to be exuberant about it, because there's a very fundamental and critical part of it that scares the life out of us.

Listen, I went through the nightmare of worrying about access to health care with my own niece Shannon. As a little girl she came down with cancer and required extensive treatment, which left her parents, whom I love dearly and know to be decent and hardworking people, drowning in debt. Because of that experience, I'm a guy who not only is for health care reform theologically but personally. I don't want any family to have to go through what my sister's family went through. I wish I could be jumping up and down right now, but I can't, because I fear that the legislation will also open the door to further assaults on defenseless unborn life.

In general, you seem committed to keeping lines of communication open even with people with whom you have political disagreements.

I just had a dustup with a bishop I really admire, and a guy I think is a darn good bishop. He told me that when he goes to a parish, the pastor usually tells him, "By the way, Senator So-and-So is going to be there, and Assemblywoman So-and-So is going to be there." This is a lovable, popular bishop I'm talking about. He tells the pastor that if these politicians are aggressively against us on pro-life, and if they're arguing on the floor of the assembly for a rollback on the statute of limitations [on litigation against the Catholic Church over sexual-abuse claims], then "I don't want 'em here." He said, "I'm not going to eat fried chicken with them, and I'm not going to have my picture with them outside at the dunking booth. They want it both ways, and it's time they saw that their actions have consequences." This bishop told me, "The Jewish community does that. They're not going to honor some guy who consistently votes to cut off funds to Israel, and it's time for us to act that way. Right now we're patsies . . . they take us for granted, and they don't take us seriously."

There's something to be said for taking a tough stance like that, but at the end of the day, is it the best way to go? Or might it be that because I ate a hot dog at the parish picnic with a guy who's not with us on pro-life, that I can call him later and ask, "Hey, there's a bill coming up. I know we don't exactly see eye to eye, but is there maybe some wiggle room here? Can I ask you not to vote for that?" Do I have more of an entrée because we had a hot dog and beer together? I hope so.

I don't want to reduce this entirely to a political strategy, because I also believe that as a pastor of souls, I can never reduce another person entirely to his or her political positions. Part of the reason I don't like to shut the door to conversation is precisely because I'm trying to relate to the whole person, so my concern isn't just with how a particular vote turns out. It's with this person, and my hunch is that I'll have more luck trying to nudge them closer to what the Church considers to be the truth if I'm in contact, in dialogue, than if I'm standing off to the side tossing rhetorical bricks. A bishop in this day and age does have to be a shrewd political tactician, but we must never forget that fundamentally we're pastors, not lobbyists.

SIX

Authority and Dissent

Most organizations have fights about both substance and process, and the Catholic Church is no exception. Controversy swirls around not only what the Church teaches but who gets to shape that teaching and how much leeway Catholics have to dissent from it. There's endless argument not only over what bishops should or shouldn't do but about whom they ought to consult before they do it and even how bishops get selected in the first place. The same debates surround how much power the Vatican has versus local bishops and bishops' conferences, relationships between the clergy and the laity, and so on. Fundamentally, these are arguments about authority in the Church—where it comes from, how it's exercised, how it might be curtailed, expanded, or regulated by some system of checks and balances, and what the limits of legitimate protest and disagreement are.

Though the contemporary Catholic scene is far more complicated than a simple division into left and right, let's start there. For many liberal Catholics, the whole idea of authority is a problem, since an allergy to authority is often part of the DNA of the political Left. Add the fact that Church authority is often experienced by liberals as cutting in an increasingly conservative direction, and the problems are compounded. In fact, for those liberal Catholics who wish to remain within the bounds of the institutional Church, authority and dissent have become the core concerns. They're resigned to not seeing the Church adopt their preferred canon of reforms, at least anytime soon, so the key question becomes, can I hold these views—on women, on homosexuality, on the politics of abortion, on liturgical practice, or on whatever the issue may be—and still hold a place at the table in the Church? Or is the circle of acceptable belief going to be tightened to such an extent that I'll find myself on the outside looking in?

Conservatives typically don't have the same ideological hang-up with authority, but they can often be even more disgruntled with how authority is actually exercised. For example, convinced pro-lifers often lament that bishops are not more aggressive in cracking down on what they see as Catholic politicians who don't walk the talk on the abortion issue. In early 2010, for example, a delegation of pro-life Catholics led by the renowned activist Randall Terry traveled to Rome to stage a protest at the Vatican demanding sanctions against Cardinal Donald Wuerl of Washington, D.C., on the grounds that Wuerl had not publicly refused House Speaker Nancy Pelosi, a pro-choice Catholic, the right to receive Communion in the archdiocese. (As fate would have it, Terry's delegation was in Rome at the same time that members of the Survivors Network of Those Abused by Priests, joined by a few liberal European Church reform groups, were converging on the Vatican to protest its handling of the sexual-abuse crisis.) Privately, some bishops and other Church officials grumble that conservative Catholic activists sometimes come off as "more Catholic than the pope," yet when the bishops actually call them to obedience—for example, asking them to accept Church teaching on the death penalty or immigration reform—they often balk. Sometimes Catholic conservatives seem to resemble President Woodrow Wilson, of whom it was said that he loved humanity but couldn't stand actual people. In the Church, some conservatives seem to like the idea of authority but often don't care for the actual authority figures.

In many ways, the issue of authority and dissent in the Church is linked to one of the defining trends in Catholic life over the last quarter century, which I've defined as "evangelical Catholicism." In essence, it holds that in order for the Church not to be seduced by the hyper-secular ethos of the contemporary West, job number one has to be to recover a strong sense of distinctive Catholic identity—the traditional markers of Catholic thought, speech, and practice that over the centuries have set Catholics apart from the rest of the world and told them who they are. Such markers range from simple visual signs of identity such as priests wearing Roman collars and nuns wearing habits, to complex matters of liturgical practice (such as a new English translation of the Mass, much closer to the Latin original) and doctrine (for example, insistence that Christ is the unique and lone savior of the world). The practical impact of this evangelical wave coursing through the Church, from both the top down and the bottom up, is that there's no zone of Catholic life today immune from pressure around Catholic identity. As those pressures grow, space for alternative visions of Catholic identity, or for dissent from the official version of Catholic identity, can become increasingly hard to find.

In turn, this frisson over identity points to a core debate in Catholicism vis-à-vis its future in the secular West. One version of the evangelical Catholic movement holds that it's possible to have an impact on secular culture, and therefore the Church ought to leave the door open as wide as possible without compromising its distinctive sense of self. Another believes that in the present cultural climate, the better strategy is to think in terms of a "remnant church," meaning one smaller in numbers but more pure in faith, which can better resist the corrosive effects of secularism. The former instinct tends to suggest a kinder, gentler exercise of authority, one in which clarity about identity goes hand in glove with generosity toward those who aren't quite able to embrace that identity fully. The latter cuts in the direction of a firm hand with respect to dissent, in the service of ensuring that the Church does not become like salt that has lost its flavor. In some ways, this tension could be framed in terms of how to understand Benedict XVI's model for Catholicism in the contemporary West as a "creative minority," a term he borrows from the historian Arnold Toynbee. One wing of the evangelical Catholic movement tends to emphasize the "creative" part, another wing the "minority."

Dolan is a bridge builder by inclination and a historian by training, both of which give him a passion for "both/and" solutions. Unsurprisingly, therefore, he sees something to like in each of the two options sketched above. Having imbibed a rock-solid sense of Catholic identity, Dolan feels in his bones the urgency of fostering a Church clear about what it stands for and unafraid to proclaim it. In practical terms, that means he knows there will be times he has to pull the trigger in terms of enforcing authority and squelching dissent, in order to protect the clarity of the Catholic message. Yet he's also inclined toward a "hermeneutic of charity," meaning he'll work hard to avoid arriving at that point. At bottom, his ecclesiology leans more in the direction of the open door than the remnant church. Dolan also realizes that being the archbishop of New York makes him a role model for other bishops, so how he balances identity and generosity, clarity and compassion, will inevitably set a tone for the leadership style of a growing cross section of American bishops.

Let's start with the role of theologians, who traditionally have been the "R & D department" of the Church. Some people say that the litmus tests for orthodoxy are becoming so strict these days that only a narrow circle of the elect can pass, which shuts down creativity. Is there any merit to that argument?

Could one see where that perception comes from, given the stances of some Catholic leaders? I suppose. But in general, I think the bishops would say to theologians, "Go ahead and ask. It's your job to ask. Just please also know that you're asking, and not teaching." When I was at Kenrick-Glennon Seminary in Saint Louis, I was a good friend of a moral theologian who was feeling pushed out because, he said, "they don't want me to teach dissenting opinions." I replied, "I don't think anybody's worried about your alerting the students to them as opinions. But your role as a theologian is to say, 'Here's the clear teaching of the Church. Here are dissenting opinions, with which you better be familiar. You better have digested them and considered them, and know how to respond. And here are some questions about the teaching of the Church. Go ahead.'" I have no problem with theologians who take that approach, which I actually find very helpful and appropriate. What I do have a problem with are theologians who would present their opinions as magisterial teaching.

Take somebody like Father Charles Curran, who was forced out of Catholic University in the 1980s. What he would do in the classroom was to present the official teaching of the Church and then offer his own opinion—which, as you know, was often critical. What do you make of that style?

I would say one could defend that give-and-take style, as long as one taught the teaching of the Church as normative and true. One could then say, "Here are some areas where the Church needs to do a better job of presenting it. Here are some things that still have to be developed, to give the Church enhanced credibility in teaching what it holds." As long as the theologian protects, fosters, develops, and promotes the uncontested teaching of the Church, bravo. Can one then say, "Class, you need to know that there are people who disagree with this, and here they are. You need to know that even in some of my work, I've asked some particular questions about this, and here they are. But you also need to know that this is the teaching of the Church that faithful Catholics would accept, and I think it enhances our ability to make an act of faith if you know some of the questions associated with it."

There is a difference, don't you think, between catechesis and theology? Both are needed. The big problem today is no longer with theology, if you ask me, but with catechesis. We can no longer presume that somebody's been catechized. That's the big difference with the sixties, when the catechesis was rather presumed and the big problem was with theology. Now you don't have that substratum of accepted faith anymore. Whenever I meet with theologians at our Catholic universities, they will be clear to say, "We're not catechists, we're theologians. We presume the faith." Now, they're actually the first to know that most of the time that's an invalid presumption, but they say that's a little bit beyond our control. We're supposed to present the mature reflection on that faith as it seeks understanding. That's where the tension comes in, doesn't it? I think where we got into trouble in the sixties, seventies, and eighties was that the bias was almost on the authority of the dissent rather than on the authority of Church teaching.

I remember in the seminary during the 1960s, when theological writers such as Hans Küng and Karl Rahner were all the rage. I found it terribly exciting, and I learned a great deal from those figures that has stayed with me to this day. One of my regrets, though, is that because of the time, we read those writers as our main theology, instead of being grounded in what you might call the Church's tradition and then reading the new thinkers of our era to enhance that. Rahner, and Küng, and Schillebeeckx, and guys like Anthony Padovano, Gene Kennedy, and Andrew Greeley became for us what Augustine, Aquinas, and Bonaventure were for my pastor at Holy Infant, Jerry Callahan. My sense is that those who were grounded in the tradition of the Church were able to assimilate what happened in postconciliar Catholicism in a healthy, nuanced way. Those for whom the postconciliar Church is all they had, it became tough.

Consider the case of the late Belgian Jesuit Father Jacques Dupuis, whose writings tried to offer a positive Christian theological analysis of other religions. Some objected that Dupuis watered down traditional Catholic theology about Christ and the Church for the sake of détente with Hindus and Buddhists and so on. His work was never condemned, though the Vatican issued a statement in 2000 citing "ambiguities." If Dupuis were still alive today, could he get a job teaching in a Catholic institution in the Archdiocese of New York?

I don't want to comment specifically on Dupuis, but let me give you my general rule of thumb. If the Holy See has formally said that a given theologian can't be relied upon to present the authentic teaching of the Church, then no, I don't think that person would be welcome or should be welcome in any of our universities. But if the Holy See has simply said that there are certain areas of this theologian's corpus we have some questions about, but the theologian was not censured or silenced, then I'd be open to it. If that person wanted to come here under the terms of something like what the authorities once said to John Courtney Murray, which was keep teaching, just don't talk about the church/state stuff, that I'd be at peace with.

[Note: Jesuit Father John Courtney Murray was a twentieth-century American Catholic theologian whose work focused on reconciling Catholicism with religious pluralism and modern democratic states. He was widely credited with influencing the decree of the Second Vatican Council on religious freedom, *Dignitatis Humanae*. In 1954 Murray was ordered by the Vatican to stop writing on religious freedom, although his views would be largely vindicated by Vatican II ten years later.]

You know there's a view that we need to get smaller in order to be strong, and that if a lot of these people were to take their religious business elsewhere, in the long run we'd be better off.

There is that view, yes. I would buy it to the extent that I do believe that one of the great problems we have today is a dilution of the essentials of the faith. I would be inclined to think, however, that the real challenge is for us to be much more creative, much more thoughtful, much more positive in the way to explain that, rather than telling people to get lost if they don't agree. In general, my inclination is to see telling people to take a hike as our last option, not the first thing we do.

At the level of popular ecclesiology, there seem to be two competing models. One is that you want as many people as possible to walk through the front door of the church, because then we can work with them. The other model is that you don't want everybody to walk through the door, because that's going to end with confusion. What we want is people who are in full agreement with what the Church teaches, because then we can move forward effectively. Between those two models, what do you think?

I'm probably in between! It's all both/and, rather than either/or. I've heard it expressed another way: Your ecclesiology depends on whether or not you like the song "All Are Welcome." Or how do you react to the James Joyce description of the Catholic Church as "Here comes everybody"? For myself, I would reply, "Yes, bravo, what a beautiful poetic description of the Catholic Church." On the other hand, you can also ask, what does *here* mean? To what are they coming? Or, all are welcome, sure, but to what? We've got to stand for something. We've got to be clear about what all are welcome to; we've got to be clear about what the "here" is to which everybody is coming. They work together.

One of the reasons everybody comes, of course, is that they know there's something definite to go to. The attraction of the Church is precisely that in a confused world, we stand for something. So we've got to be firm, clear, indefatigable, in defending that "here," defending what the house stands for to which all are welcome. But there's a different emphasis. At times you're going to say, now we need to emphasize the welcome part, because we've been so clear for so long. You could apply a reading like that to Church history. From Trent to Vatican II, we were working on what the "here" was to which everyone is welcome. After Vatican II for a while, it was, no, we're more concerned about "all are welcome" and "here comes everybody." Then I think John Paul concluded, great, we can never forget this evangelical mission of the Church, but now we have got to also be attentive to the "here" to which everyone is welcome. The trick is constantly to strike the right balance, and veering too far in one direction or the other is always going to end in something that isn't fully Catholic.

You're not wholeheartedly on board with the view that we need a Catholicism that's smaller and more compact?

I would think any good pastor would be hurt, or would be worried, when people stop coming. That touches our pastoral heart. It bothers me when I see Mass attendance go down; it bothers me when I see people leaving the Catholic Church. I don't think that's a good thing, so it's never something we should embrace or celebrate. On the other hand, I also find myself swayed by John 6, from where I take my episcopal motto. In that scene from the Gospels, Jesus allowed some people to leave because he was not going to compromise on the integrity of his teaching and his eucharistic doctrine. That's the Catholic genius, isn't it? The right answer is somewhere in between the two extremes. You can see it in American religious sociology, where you've got the fundamentalists on one side and you've got the main-line Protestants on the other. Catholics, I think, have to find their place in between those two.

In his farewell address as president of the United States Conference of Catholic Bishops, Cardinal Francis George of Chicago identified the authority of the bishops as a core concern. Do you agree?

I do. There was a fine editorial recently in *Our Sunday Visitor* on the Catholic Health Association controversy. Without getting in to what caused it, the editorial more or less said that this is another example of the chiseling away of episcopal authority. Are we turning into Congregationalists, or Anglicans? Are we losing the uniquely normative value of the magisterium of the bishops?

Some people would say you're picking exactly the wrong moment to push the authority button, since the moral authority of the bishops has been badly compromised by the sexual-abuse crisis. How do you press that issue in the current cultural climate?

You're on target, and it's something Francis [George] has always said. What I admire about Francis is his complete lack of hesitancy in speaking bluntly and calling the question. He's said to us, "Brother bishops, this is the issue of the day. They simply want to neuter us. They want to take away episcopal authority." He's right. The only thing uniting both poles in the Church today is their hatred of bishops. For both sides, the only red badge of courage that's given out in the church today is for taking on the bishops. That's true both in *The Wanderer* and *National*

Catholic Reporter, whatever you want. Even apart from the theological issue of the primacy of the episcopal magisterium, we have come across as such clumsy administrators and teachers over the recent decades, highly exacerbated by the sex-abuse thing, that many people will say, "Not only do we wonder theologically about the unique normative value of your magisterium, but even if we were to believe that intellectually, the way you have run the Church is so awful that you don't deserve to be listened to." Both sides say that: "You've blown it. Don't be like kids in the corner stamping your feet and wondering why nobody will listen to you anymore. You should know why they don't."

Thoughtful, perceptive guys like Francis George will say that: "Brothers, it's not all their fault. We have given them sufficient cause." But the fact of the matter is that if we're going to be loyal to our Catholic birthright, we must defend the primacy and the normative value of the episcopal magisterium.

How can you do that effectively?

It seems to me that we've got to do two things. First of all, we have to be fearless. We have to say, look, it's not a question of whether or not we've done it right. It's a question of this is our sacred responsibility. It's necessary for the identity and integrity of the Church that the bishop has the defining voice. We're more than happy to admit that maybe we haven't done it the best way, but that doesn't change the fact that we have to do it, and in Catholic polity, we are in fact the only ones who do it.

Number two, we need to regain our credibility, not just theologically by defending the unique value of the episcopal magisterium, but also in our style. We have to try our best to do it with graciousness, and with a sense of contrition. What we have to do, and the bishops have to lead us in it, is one big fat mea culpa. We can't get tired of that, and we have to mean it. We know we don't do it right, we know that sometimes we are as awkward as the original twelve bishops. But that doesn't diminish the fact that very close to the heart of Catholic identity is the unique role of the bishop. If we lose that, we've lost something integral to the mission of the Church.

By the way, this isn't just about asserting our authority with others, but also recovering it within ourselves. One of the unintended consequences of the abuse crisis, I think, is that we have become gun-shy about being clear teachers. Deep down, we wonder, "How can I stand up and speak about this?"—whether it's defense of marriage, our pro-life teachings, the decline in the sacrament of marriage, widespread immorality, whatever—the question we're tempted to ask, deep down, is "How can I dare say it after what we've done?" We know that in the court of public opinion, it's like Nixon giving a talk on clean government! Like it or not, I'm afraid we bishops unconsciously say that to ourselves. We have to get over this sense of being gun-shy. We have to recognize anew that teaching with authority is part of our sacred responsibility.

Speaking of how authority works in the Church, I want to ask about the relationship between Rome and America. There's a perception that you bishops are more concerned with how you stand in Rome than with the pastoral good of your people in the United States. True?

I don't think so. Are there some bishops who would be? Yeah. In general, however, I don't think so. I think most bishops are at their heart pastors, and they're more worried about their dioceses and their people. Do they see Rome as a partner, as an ally, in this? Yes. Do they think that an irreplaceable part of their mission and mandate as bishops is to be attentive to Rome and in union with the successor of Peter? Yup. But if you're talking more about ambition, where do we stand in Rome, what's Rome going to think of us, no, I don't sense that. We may be interested in the goings-on in Rome in the same way we're interested in how the Yankees might look in spring training, but that's about it.

One thing that influences my thinking on this is my years in Rome. I saw the position of the Church in Italy, which, to be honest, was fairly weak. Growing up the way I did, when I went to Rome I was thinking, "Geez, this is going to be Holy Infant on steroids." It's just not, and I found myself wondering what that's all about. You get into the history of Church/state relations in Italy, which I gobbled up, and you're thinking about centuries of theocracy and the *non expedit* [the decree by which the Vatican forbade Catholics from voting in elections in the new Italian state after 1870] and all that. I sort of became this raving John Courtney Murray–ite, thinking, "Hey, ours is really the better way." If the question is whether I'm trying to impose a Roman model on the American Church, I would say if anything it's the other way around — that I believe Rome and the universal Church can learn something from the American experience of reconciling a very strong commitment to the faith with making our way in a very pluralistic culture, in which we really can't rely on being propped up by the power of the state.

How many American bishops do you think read the daily *bolletino* from the Vatican?

Very, very few.

How many American bishops do you believe would recognize Cardinal Tarcisio Bertone, the Vatican's secretary of state, and therefore theoretically the second-most important figure in the Church after the pope, if he were walking down the street in plain clothes?

Almost nobody.

So the notion that you bishops are hanging on Rome's every move is a myth?

Look, if the question is whether we're basically comfortable with the idea of a chain of command in the Church, the answer is yes. If you're asking whether we deeply value the role of the successor of Peter as the guarantee of unity in the Church, again, the answer is yes. But if you're asking whether bishops are obsessively following which way the winds are blowing in Rome to be sure they're on the right side, I really don't sense that. My impression would be that for the most part, bishops don't really think much about Rome until something specific forces them to do so. I know people tend to think that whenever we bishops do or say something, it's because somebody in Rome pressed a button, but honestly that's just not the way the Church works. The myth is that we're rigidly centralized and tightly authoritarian, but the reality is that the Church is much more loosely organized and decentralized. Many of the big issues we've wrestled with in the bishops' conference in recent years, in fact, stem precisely from the fact that it can be difficult to get all the bishops marching in the same direction!

There's a similar perception about the North American College, that it's a factory for turning future American priests into closet Romans with careerist ambitions. What's your experience?

One of the constant themes in my rectors' conferences at the North American College, which I assume came both from my philosophical approach to priesthood and my blissful experiences in the parishes, was that "You're here to be trained to be a parish priest. The only difference between this seminary and any one at home is the address." Now, I was also pretty candid. I told them, "As a matter of fact, some of you are going to be sent for graduate work. Some of you are going to be asked to work for the Roman Curia. Some of you are going to be asked to work in chanceries. Some of you are going to be monsignors, and some of you might wind up as bishops. But that should all be because you were good parish priests." I would often say, to the point that it became the laugh line in all the student skits, "If you are not enthusiastic about spending the rest of your life as a parish priest, go home." I don't think the college causes guys to "go native." If anything, we probably don't take as much advantage of the eye-opening experiences Rome has to offer about the global Church as we should.

How much reality do you think there is to the perception that younger priests these days, especially the kind who go to the North American College, are more clerical and authoritarian?

I would say my experience with the men at the college was analogous to my experience with the men I met in the Vatican diplomatic corps when I worked at the nunciature. I just found them healthy, wholesome guys. I think most of them just wanted to go home and be parish priests. The bigger problem with the college, I think, is a chemistry such that a guy knows that when he's chosen to go to Rome, it's a big deal. His bishop has put great trust in him, and the guy has heard oohs and aahs from everybody else. When he gets over there, the temptation is to think that ordination is a fait accompli, and that now he can't really afford to wrestle with the question of whether or not he should be a priest because as a matter of fact that choice has already been made. How could I disappoint everybody at home? I think that's a greater danger in Rome, and that's why I would constantly say to them, "Fellas, you can't really choose to be a priest until you've talked about not being one."

To ask the question from the other end of the equation, what about the charge that you bishops are becoming more authoritarian because you're threatened by the rise of a theologically literate and professionally competent laity?

I'll answer that in a way that's probably going to be a little delicate, but it needs to be said. For the last forty-five years or so, we priests and bishops have spoken about lay leadership in the Church, and we meant it. Pretty basically, however, most of our people still want a clerically led Church, and they are at peace with it. For example, when I sit at the Finance Council of the Archdiocese of New York, you're talking about high-powered folks. They can give you wonderful advice, and they will give me incisive observations about the budget. If I ask their opinion, they'll give it. But the underlying presumption is, "Archbishop, we trust you. You're doing a good job. Keep at it." Now in a way, alleluia! But it seems to me that leadership by bishops, priests, and nuns—by the institutional Church—is so ingrained in our Catholic laypeople that they're happy to let it continue. They'll say to me, "You bishops need to start fighting back. You bishops need to start getting the good news out there." If I say, "Actually, you need to do it," they don't quite understand that. It's sort of like, that's not our job, it's yours.

But if laypeople take you up on that, don't you run the risk that they may say some things you don't like? For example, they may have a different view on health care reform, or gay marriage?

The presumption when you hear that usually comes from the insular nature of the Left, presuming that a "lay voice" is automatically left-wing, and that whenever we bishops listen to a lay voice and "hear things we don't want to hear," it's always the predictable leftist agenda. You know the reality: If I sit down at a parish and ask people to open up, they're going to hammer me about closing parishes, about a lack of passion about Catholic schools, maybe a dilution or lack of passion about the pro-life message. If they get into the sex-abuse crisis, they're going to talk about why Father So-and-So was removed, we hear it wasn't done right, he was such a popular and wonderful priest. As I've told journalists here, you want to go with me to Saint Charles Borromeo, to Wally Harris's parish, and talk about the Church being lax when it comes to removing priests? They'll skin you alive. They're furious because their priest was removed, and they think we bishops are without justice and mercy. That's what you hear more often than not from the laity. [Note: Monsignor Wallace Harris is a prominent African American priest who was suspended in the summer of 2008 on the basis of allegations of sexual abuse. He had served as pastor of the Church of Saint Charles Borromeo in Harlem for almost twenty years.]

Now, will you also sometimes hear "Why are you bishops hung up on the same-sex marriage thing? Let it go. We know what the Church believes, but who cares what people do in the privacy of their own bedrooms?" Yeah, you will hear that. Will you hear from some, "Why does everything always boil down to abortion with you bishops? We can't understand why you would have thrown overboard the best piece of health care legislation we could have ever dreamed about, something you guys have been in the forefront of pushing, because of some abortion clause that even thoughtful people disagree on." You will hear that. I'm not afraid of hearing that myself, and I don't think most bishops are.

I don't think it's true that we bishops are scared, nervous, and driven to recapture some authority that we know we have lost over the last two decades. Are there some bishops who shake in their boots, unwilling to confront people who might challenge them? In general, I don't think that's the case. Take a bishop like Charles Chaput [the recently appointed Archbishop of Philadelphia, who's known as an outspoken conservative]. You know he'd be as comfortable talking to the Voice of the Faithful meeting as he would be on EWTN.

Sure, but that's not what I mean. We're trying to figure out why laypeople aren't more willing to step up, and I'm asking if it's partly because bishops haven't encouraged it for fear of not being able to control where it might go.

As if we control it now? How much worse could it get? If you've got some common sense about you, you know that where it really counts, laity are controlling things anyway—in the way they raise their kids, the way they share their married love, the way they want to pass on a whole culture of prayer and a system of values. That's where it's taking place, if it all. Those are the most fundamental things of the faith, aren't they?

〜

CATHOLIC FAITH
AND LIFE

SEVEN

Affirmative Orthodoxy

If one were to pick a modern pope to whom comparisons with Timothy Dolan seem most natural, the obvious choice would be John Paul II. First of all, Dolan is a "John Paul bishop" in the literal sense that his first appointment as a bishop, as an auxiliary in Saint Louis, was made by John Paul II in June 2001. Moreover, in most analyses of contemporary Catholicism, it's commonplace to distinguish between "Vatican II" Catholics and "John Paul" Catholics, categories that roughly (and inexactly) correspond to liberals and conservatives. In that taxonomy there's no question that Dolan belongs in the John Paul camp, and he'll often describe himself as a "John Paul II guy."

At a personal level, one could go on at length indexing the qualities that John Paul II and Dolan share:

- A kind of swashbuckling, daring, "man's man" personality

- A lively sense of humor

- An instinctive genius for communication, making both men "rock stars" in terms of their charisma and media savvy

- Personal fearlessness, rooted in a rock-solid sense of who they are. Nobody would ever compare John Paul or Dolan to Hamlet, constantly agonizing over which path to take

• Both men almost perfectly incarnate their respective national characters; Dolan is American the way John Paul was Polish.

There are, of course, a handful of fairly obvious differences, including the fact that whereas the young John Paul II was branded "God's athlete" because of his physical vigor—a mountain-climbing, skiing, swimming, dynamo of a man—the roly-poly Dolan isn't exactly the one who would pop to mind if one were imagining which bishops could produce their own fitness DVD. Yet the overall similarities between John Paul and Dolan are so striking that at one stage I actually thought about titling this book *American Wojtyla,* a reference to John Paul's given name.

At first blush, Dolan and Benedict XVI don't seem such a match made in heaven; they're not the sort of personalities that an online dating site such as eHarmony would likely flag as naturally compatible. Dolan has a deep affection for Benedict, not to mention a fierce sense of loyalty—witness the uncharacteristically testy fashion in which Dolan came to the pope's defense in March 2010, when Benedict XVI was under fire for his handling of the sexual-abuse crisis. In terms of personal dynamics, however, the two men remain an odd couple—Benedict shy and cerebral, Dolan ever the backslapping extrovert.

Yet in one key sense, the two men are simpatico, and that's in their commitment to what I defined in the introduction as affirmative orthodoxy. The term refers to a complete embrace of Catholic orthodoxy—the traditional elements of Catholic belief and practice—expressed in the most relentlessly positive fashion possible, so that the Catholic message comes across fundamentally as a yes rather than a no. The accent is on what the Church is for rather than what it's against.

In Benedict's case, the emergence of affirmative orthodoxy as the scarlet thread running through his teaching has been something of a surprise. Upon his election in April 2005, the stereotypes surrounding him seemed to point in a different direction—this was supposed to be "God's Rottweiler," "the German Shepherd," the Church's primary "enforcer." The expectation was that in Benedict, the Catholic Church had elevated a man who would preside over a tough, bruising pontificate, what one frenzied blogger described as a "global smack-down on heresy." In the main, that's not what Benedict's papacy has produced. By any reasonable standard Benedict is a conservative, but his main concern seems to be to systematically reintroduce the building blocks of orthodoxy, trying to dust off centuries of controversy and legalistic gloss in order to lift up the positive ideas at their core. For Benedict, this commitment to affirmative orthodoxy flows from his diagnosis of the cultural situation in the West, which is that in Europe particularly, too many people think they know what Christianity is all about—a rigidly legalistic system of rules and restrictions, intended to shore up the crumbling authority of the Church's clerical caste. In that context, Benedict believes the only way to get a new hearing is to stress the deep Catholic *yes* beneath the familiar litany of things of which the Church disapproves.

That, at least, is how insiders and those who pay careful attention to papal teaching would describe what Benedict is doing. Relatively little of that has registered in the outside world, however, because of the various crises, scandals, and PR meltdowns that have plagued his papacy. Perhaps a century or so down the line, affirmative orthodoxy will be what historians associate with Benedict XVI, but in the here and now it's hard to think of much beyond the sexual-abuse crisis, tensions with both Muslims and Jews, debates over condoms in Africa, a Holocaust-denying bishop, and the other assorted upheavals that seem to occur with disheartening regularity. (To be fair, that's not always been the case. Benedict's three encyclical letters to date, the most developed form of papal teaching—*Deus Caritas Est*, *Spe Salvi*, and *Caritas in Veritate*—have played to broadly positive reviews, and the pope won high marks for candor and kindness during his April 2008 trip to the

United States. Those moments, however, represent exceptions rather than the rule in terms of public perceptions and media coverage.)

For Benedict, affirmative orthodoxy thus seems to be the product of conscious reflection, perhaps coupled with the biographical fact that for twenty-five years he played the role of Dr. No, chief doctrinal cop, for the Catholic Church, and now he's free to offer a positive presentation of the faith rather than forever correcting error. For Dolan, affirmative orthodoxy seems more a matter of personal instincts and temperament. In other words, he doesn't have to think about it, because his own life experience has disposed him to see Catholicism primarily in terms of adventure, romance, and fellowship, and it almost requires an act of will for him to think of it any other way.

With apologies for the obvious dissonance of the comparison, one could almost say that what Mark and Lenin were to communism — Marx the theoretician, Lenin the practical implementer — Benedict and Dolan may be to affirmative orthodoxy. Benedict is laying out the intellectual and theological vision but sometimes has trouble translating that teaching into the postmodern marketplace of ideas. The agora, however, is where Dolan shines, which raises the prospect that this quintessentially John Paul bishop could also turn out to be a highly "Benedictine" figure — in the sense of being the American prelate best able to offer a living, breathing model of what affirmative orthodoxy looks, sounds, and tastes like. Whether that will be enough to win over the secular world remains to be seen, but if affirmative orthodoxy is to have a fighting chance, Dolan may well be its best hope.

You know the sound bite: The world knows too much about what we say no to, not enough about what we say yes to. Do you agree with that?

Oh, boy, do I ever. I think Benedict XVI has put his finger on it. I hope it's clear that for me, from the biographical point of view, my

Catholic upbringing, the Catholic ethos, the Catholic chemistry, what-ever you want to call it, has given meaning, purpose, and direction to my life. It's the pearl of great price. It has given me a worldview, a sense of joy and direction, and an excitement about life. In my mind, it's the healthiest, happiest way to live, so I don't find anything constraining or oppressive or choking about it.

This is what Benedict is saying, this is what John Paul II said, and this is what I think: Look at our literature, and drama, and sculpture, and art, and liturgy, and poetry, everything that's great in the Catholic worldview. The Catholic Church affirms, strengthens, expands what's most noble, most beautiful, most sacred, in the human project. That's what affirmative orthodoxy means to me. I like to quote a line from Father Robert Barron, that the Church only says no to another no, and two no's make a yes. It's only when the yes of humanity is threatened that the Church will say no, to protect the yes.

Talk about what the Church says yes to.

Sometimes I fear that you sink into platitudes, sounding like a Hall-mark greeting card, but I think we say yes to everything that's decent and honorable and noble in the human person—all the dreams, all the yearnings. I spoke about this yesterday at Mass, where Saint Paul talks about the longing for eternal life that's in the human heart. I said I'd just returned from Ars, and I used the story about John Vianney saying, "You show me the way to Ars, and I'll show you the way to heaven." I said that's what the Church is all about.

There's a great story about Archbishop Fulton Sheen along these lines. Sheen was supposed to give a talk at Independence Hall in Phila-delphia, and he said, "I'll walk there. I know the way." He got lost and ended up in a bad neighborhood where these toughs are out there drinking beer and smoking. He said, "Pardon me, can you tell me how to get to Independence Hall?" They said, "Yeah, it's three blocks that way." One of them said, "Hey, Padre, what are you going to talk about?" He said, "How to get to heaven." They said, "Hell, you can't even find Independence Hall!"

That's what we say yes to, that deep desire in people for something infinite, something beyond themselves. Sometimes I wonder if deep down, what we're really about is the restoration of what human beings were meant to be. You hesitate to use the word *restoration,* because that's a loaded word these days, but I'm using it as an artist would. Father George Rutler spoke about this on our retreat in Ars. He reminded us that for the Church, in the beginning was the Garden of Eden. This is the way it was intended to be, when man and woman were walking in intimacy and comfort with God. There was happiness, there was peace, creation was well ordered, and the affinity between divine and human, between creature and creator, was well ordered. The Church's project is to restore that. The mission of Jesus was to restore that, of course, but the Church continues that mission — the restoration of the greatest work of art ever, which is the human person. That has been tarnished by original sin, and continues to be threatened and tarnished, but the Church is always in the process of restoration. It's so beautiful theologically when you think of the Blessed Mother as the new Eve. It's almost like we're rewinding the video now. Once again, at the Annunciation, we have an angel appear to a woman, and we're going to set things right; God's going to give it another chance.

When I spoke at midnight Mass in New York, I was a little intimidated, because you've got senators, governors, mayors, you're on TV, and it can be overwhelming. I simply spoke on this: Today we celebrate the fact that we have a God who will not take no for an answer. He just keeps trying, he wants to break through to us, he wants to get through to us. Finally, he said, maybe they'll listen to a baby, because nothing changes lives like a baby. That's what the Church is all about, this tremendous, beautiful act of restoration.

Here maybe is where the Americanist in me comes out. Anything we see in culture or in society that contributes to restoring the beauty of human life—whether that be education, civic reform, public service, community building—you can figure that the Church is going to roll up its sleeves and be there. Anytime we see a degradation going on, and sort of a rollback in the restoration project, we're going to say, "Uh-oh, wait a minute."

Why do you think the Church's "wait a minute's" carry so much more weight in the court of public opinion than its affirmations?

I'm afraid it's sometimes because what they do is validate the stereotype, which is that the Church is primarily in the business of saying, "wait a minute." The impression is that we're the yellow light, if not the red light, of the human race. At our best, people might say we're a yellow light, but usually we're the red. It only validates the impression, which grew up in the Enlightenment, that when it comes to science, to any sort of progress in thought and reason, the Church is going to be scared. The Church is going to see itself threatened, because it has a bastion of control over the minds of people that it will not give up. My point is that nothing could be further from the truth. In reality, it was the Church that created universities, that formed scholars, it was our great thinkers who did all this stuff. We're one of the good guys. The head of our Church wears a white hat, so we're one of the heroes! Please look at us like an ally, and see us that way. I'm very fond of that quote from Paul VI: We are "expert[s] in humanity." We've been around for a long time, and we know something about the mysteries of the human heart.

I'm criticized for it sometimes, because people might think this is slightly uncritical or overly romantic, but I love the phrase "Holy Mother Church." She is a wise, loving, tender mother, who periodically has to say, "Kids, be careful. Don't go outside without a hat on, okay, because it's going to be cold and windy today." We've been around a long time, and we want nothing more than for our children to be nourished and cared for, so they can grow into thinking, responsible adults. There will be times, of course, when some people find that "mothering" to be excessive, perhaps overly protective and even stifling. What I hope people would understand, however, is that it's born out of love.

Have there been occasions in the past when the Church has not been good at letting go? Yeah, I'm afraid that's true. I think we serve society well when we admit that, where we don't show ourselves defensive when people bring up our failures. I remember once in Milwaukee being in a dialogue with Muslims, when we were speaking about religious freedom. I simply remarked, "You're talking to the representative of a church that had to learn this the hard way. When we look back, there were centuries in our history when we shared your view, that it's impossible to have a coherent, productive society without some type of theocratic government, where there would be a union of throne and altar. We learned from bitter experience that it doesn't work." Part of the genius of Catholicism in the United States is to serve as a counterexample to the notion that the faith can't thrive unless it's wedded to the power of the state. Now we're held up as an example of a faith that embraces religious freedom. Remember when John Paul II went to Paris for the first time . . . I think it was Richard Neuhaus who said that Voltaire must be rolling over in his grave, because now you have probably the most articulate expression of the good side of the French Revolution coming from the successor of Saint Peter! The pope was once thought of as the antithesis of everything the French Revolution stood for, and here he was extolling the positive vision of liberty, equality, and fraternity. Those are values the Church not only shares but that in a certain sense it pioneered.

I realize, of course, that there are plenty of people I love and trust for whom the experience of the Church is not as positive as mine. For them, Catholic identity is a drag. It hurts them, because it's been more of a straitjacket than a liberation. I have to admit that, and I have to say that for them, their ambivalence about the Church is probably justified, in the sense that I'm sure they did experience it that way. I wish Cardinal Avery Dulles were still around to redo his classic book *Models of the Church*, because I think the one we need today is "family."

You know who developed that model? It was the African bishops at the '94 synod: "Church as Family of God." It's more or less their native ecclesiology.

I wasn't aware of that. We've really got to work on that, because when we look at our families, do they ever tick us off! They're the source of our deepest wounds. How many times in a family do people slam down a telephone and basically stop talking to each other? But when it comes down to it, we're going to be there at Christmas, we're going to show up at Thanksgiving, even if there are people about whom we're thinking, "We've got to go through *that* again?" But our family gives us meaning and purpose, and in general these are the memories that give warmth and tenderness to life. That's how it is with our supernatural family, the Church.

I think we shouldn't be afraid of being branded romantics, especially when it comes to marriage. In my usual marriage homily from when I was a parish priest, I preached that we in the Church are hopeless romantics. We are foolish enough to believe that this young man and young woman mean it when they say they're going to love each other for the rest of their lives, and that they're not going to love anybody else in the same way that they love one another, and if possible, they're going to bring new life into the world. Come what may, they believe their love is more enduring than anything external. That's hopelessly romantic, but darn it, that's the business we're in. In some ways we should be proud that we're not "realistic," that we have not caved in to the exigencies of modernity.

You're savvy enough to realize, of course, that "romance" is not the first thing that occurs to many people when they think about the Catholic Church.

That's right. Unfortunately, many people are looking for that sense of uplift and meaning elsewhere, in other churches and in other models of life. They never absorbed the ingrained sense I was given that while there may be some things I don't understand about the Church, and there may be some things I do understand that I don't find particularly palatable, at least I'm conscious of a coherent and meaningful worldview.

I know a lot of it depends on how you were raised. Yesterday was Valentine's Day, and I was thinking about my mom and dad. I think I told you, they were always like two teenagers in love. Somebody recently told me that she never saw her mom and dad hug. That certainly wasn't my experience! Every time my dad came home from work, he would go in to embrace my mom and give her a kiss. It wasn't a peck on the cheek, either. It was a pretty good . . . well, antipasto, I guess you could say! It was beautiful, and I think all of that was part of what you'd call a Catholic values system.

A turning point in my life, which is the kind of thing one discovers only in retrospect, came on July 10, 1962. It's easy for me to remember because that's the day my sister Lisa was born, the fourth child of Bob and Shirley Dolan, and because it was the All-Star Game. My mom was in the hospital giving birth. My grandma, Martha Troy Dolan, my dad's mom, was babysitting, as she would when Mom was in the hospital. Dad came home from the hospital fairly late, about ten P.M. He and Nonnie Marty, as we called her, sat at the table. He had a couple of beers, she had something too, and I was eavesdropping. Dad was pretty down. He was out of work, he had just lost his job, and they had just had their fourth baby. I guess it was getting to him. I can remember my grandma saying, "Bobby, we've been through it all before. You'll get through this. Things will work out."

Thinking about it later, I realized this went a little deeper than just "Ah, come on, kid, you'll make it." This was a worldview. This was a hope, a trust in providence. Underneath what Nonnie Marty was saying to my dad was a values system that tells us, "We are children of a benevolent God and things will work out." In my own mind, I suspect that was pretty well cooked in the crucible of famine Ireland. Something tells me Nonnie Marty heard her grandmother say that, about the famine.

Anyway, take everything I just said—would that not give rise to a sense of affirmative orthodoxy? I find meaning, joy, hope, promise, purpose, dare, adventure, in a Catholic worldview.

Given all that, how do you explain the fact that more people leave the Catholic Church in the United States every year than enter? Why don't people seem to respond to this sense of promise and adventure?

God only knows. I have a hunch that it's because we have abandoned this whole Catholic worldview, and that we are too absorbed in the externals of the Church. For instance, let's say I'm going to a Priests' Council meeting on Thursday—which are very good, by the way, I enjoy them—but we're not going to talk about these larger questions. Instead, it'll be "These two parishes should join together, and we can't keep all these schools open, and what are we going to do about vocations?" We're into the quantitative stuff, and we don't talk often enough about a revival of our sense of daring.

Now, some places are doing it, big-time, and I applaud them. When I went down for the first Sunday of Advent to Saint Joseph's Parish in Greenwich Village, which is serving as the student center for NYU until we can get our Center for Catholic Life up and running, I got seven P.M. Mass. It's the Sunday after Thanksgiving. I said to my priest secretary, "What did you schedule it now for? None of these kids are going to be here." When I got there, however, it was standing room only. The music was beautiful, and the kids participated thoroughly. They were incredibly attentive at the homily. I was stunned by the list of projects they've got, whether it be a lecture on the Shroud of Turin or a book discussion on *Diary of a Country Priest*. These kids got it. They also have a number of service projects, so a young woman got up to talk about their Christmas project coming up to feed the hungry. I was thinking, "This is sort of what I had in mind." They're not belly-aching about the fact that they don't have a student center; they're not complaining about the fact that we had to sit in the back of the church to have hot tea and pound cake because we didn't have anywhere to go. That would be what the Priests' Council would talk about, what the Parish Council would talk about. I'd like to think that those kids at Saint Joseph's have enough of a sense, maybe, of what the real myster-ies of the Church are all about; they know this is a heck of a lot more important than the structures.

I think part of the problem is our temptation to give all our at-tention to the mechanics, to the *how-to,* rather than the *what,* of the faith. That's a particularly poignant temptation for Americans, because we thrive on a kind of pragmatism and functionalism. We American Catholics have been darn good on delivery, but I sometimes think we get the means and the ends confused. The purpose for all of our proj-ects, our initiatives and buildings and programs—those are means to an end, right? The end is what I just described, this Catholic worldview. Of course, at the core of all this is a person, Jesus Christ, the second person of the Blessed Trinity, who is the Way, the Truth, and the Life. We're not talking about a *what* but a *who.* Yet we are now so hung up on the how that we've forgotten the *what* and the *who.* What was sup-posed to have been the means to an end—to prop up our preaching the Gospel, to revive it, and God knows, to pay for it—has become more important than the end.

The choking problem we bishops face, without articulating it— and pardon me, this is an A-1 cliché, but it's as true as it can be: We are exhausted by maintenance, and we've forgotten the mission, not to mention the mystery and the message. As important as structures are, few people are going to surrender their lives to a structure.

Right now in New York, the odds are we're going to lose our only Catholic hospital, Saint Vincent's. Technically, legally, it's not ours, it belongs to the Sisters of Charity in the Diocese of Brooklyn, but obviously it's still a Catholic institution. It took an article in the *New York Times* a couple of weeks ago to remind me that Saint Vincent's was an icon of what we're talking about—this personal, gritty commitment to the person. The headline almost seemed a little caustic, but I thought it was powerful: A HOSPITAL THAT DIDN'T KEEP UP WITH THE TIMES. They meant it as a compliment. This is a place where you still knew people's names, where people have worked for forty years. Maybe you might have to go down three floors for the MRI, but people liked going there. The hospital was almost like a neighborhood unto itself, and sadly it's going down the tubes. I thought, "Wow, this is what Catholic health care is supposed to be." I'm afraid we've lost that. I'm not sure now what the difference between some of our mega-hospitals and NYU would be, but this is a hospital that didn't lose it. There's an example, maybe, that we got so lost trying to prop up the externals that we became distracted from the mission those externals are meant to serve. At its best, the institutional Church is supposed to be the engine that drives this adventure, but I'm afraid our structures become not the engine anymore but the final destination.

Looking around, where do you see a spirit of adventure in the Church?

One example would be World Youth Day in 1993 in Denver. You know the story. The American bishops were skeptical about this whole thing: "This ain't going to work, Holy Father. You are going to be mightily embarrassed. You're whistling 'Dixie' here, because we're not going to get that many kids, and they're going to be less than enthusiastic. You're going to be in a heavily secular, almost pagan place, full of the nouveau riche. This just ain't going to work." John Paul just sort of grunted and said, "Well, we're doing it." I have to admit that I shared some of the skepticism, until I walked into this center where they had a big tent simply for eucharistic adoration. When I saw thousands of kids in graveyard silence, with a tangible sense of adoration, the transcendence, the beyond, I thought, "This is going to work." John Paul knew what he was doing. There was a pope who knew that we're talking about the mystery, the message, and the messenger, Jesus Christ. Basically, what he was saying to us was, "You American bishops, God bless you because you've been a gift to the universal Church, but you're hung up on the mechanics."

Let's draw a political analogy. No matter how much you may have disliked him, nobody criticized Ronald Reagan for being unable to articulate this dream and dare of America. He knew what America meant, and we had lost it. It's ephemeral for us, but he was able to articulate it. I remember that I was in Florida when the shuttle exploded [in 1986]. That night I watched Reagan's speech with two brother priests who hated his guts, and they were both crying. They said, "Damn him!" As much as they hated to admit it, they were moved by him. He spoke to the angels within. He was just able to articulate what the higher aspirations of America were all about. John Paul was that way, and the Church has got to be that way.

I worry that we've become a glorified Rotary Club. We're so stumbling over the *how* of Catholic life that I think we've lost the *who,* meaning Jesus. I know how that sounds, and I know it's tough to define, but we had it once upon a time, didn't we? Didn't we sort of have it in grade schools? Without going back to a simplistic or childish piety, somehow we have to recapture the notion that the Church isn't primarily about running institutions or winning political debates, as important as those things are. It's about reaching deep inside the human heart and stirring what's best in it, and then boldly going out into the world and insisting that the better angels of our nature can prevail, that cynicism and ego don't have to be the last word about the kind of culture we pass on to our children, and that the Church is an ally in every positive stirring and hopeful current in that culture. That's a vision worth devoting one's life to, and if that's not affirmative orthodoxy, what is?

EIGHT

Beyond Purple Ecclesiology

Though some Catholic voices complain of media bias when it comes to coverage of the Church, the more common problem is ignorance. Many reporters and pundits don't know the Church from the inside, and so they form impressions based only on what they can see, which is usually the latest thing the pope has said or done, or the latest statement from the United States Conference of Catholic Bishops on some hot-button political topic, or the latest cause célèbre—a pastor refusing to admit the children of a same-sex couple to a Catholic school, for example, or a charismatic TV priest caught making out with his girlfriend on a public beach. Those things are all real, but they are hardly the only realities of the Catholic Church. Talking about religion in the secular press sometimes seems analogous to trying to represent a three-dimensional object in a two-dimensional space, in that only bits and pieces will be visible, and the impression one gets is therefore terribly distorted and incomplete. Another way of putting the point is that the problem with most secular conversation about religion usually is not text but context. Media accounts and academic analyses, or even simple conversation around the water cooler, often have the facts basically right but lack the context in which those facts can be properly understood.

Perhaps the chief index of that missing context is what one might call the widespread "purple ecclesiology" that plagues most public discussions of Catholicism. *Ecclesiology* refers to how one understands the Church, and *purple* is a bit of Catholic slang referring to bishops. (In Italian papers, journalists will often use the term *il porporato*, "the purpled one," on second reference when writing about some member of the hierarchy.) By "purple ecclesiology," therefore, I mean a view of the Catholic Church that puts undue or exaggerated emphasis on the bishops, leaving virtually everyone and everything else in the Church out of view. A moment's thought suggests how distorted a picture that will inevitably produce. There are slightly more than 5,000 bishops in the Catholic Church worldwide and some 1.1 billion Catholics, which means that the bishops account for .0005 percent of the total Catholic population of the planet. Granted, bishops exercise considerably more influence in setting the tone in the Church than that arithmetic might suggest, but nevertheless, a purple ecclesiology cannot help but place the vast majority of Catholic life, even Catholic leadership and vision, in shadows. In a sound bite, the problem is that when people say "the Church," what they really mean is "the bishops."

This purple ecclesiology is part of the Church's image problem, because as long as all the outside world sees is the bishops, much of the positive spiritual and humanitarian work of the Church will escape notice. Here's a classic example: In 2002, the white-hot period of the sexual-abuse crisis in the United States, media outlets rightly invested enormous resources in bringing to light hidden stories of how the Catholic Church over the decades had failed to protect a galling number of children from predator priests. Yet in that same year, Catholic schools in America educated 2.7 million children, a disproportionate share in poor urban areas; Catholic Charities assisted 10 million people, the majority being low-income women and children; and Catholic hospitals provided $2.8 billion in uncompensated charitable care, with the bulk of it going to women and children. If one wanted to tell the whole story of the Church's approach to child welfare, all of that should have been in the mix. One of the reasons it wasn't is that most of that activity is carried out by laypeople, not by bishops, and therefore it rarely registers in the popular mind as something "the Church" is doing. That's the toxic consequence of purple ecclesiology in a nutshell.

Dolan says that he's as frustrated with this state of affairs as anyone, agreeing that it will be tough to bottle and sell affirmative orthodoxy—that is, to recapture what he calls a sense of Catholic adventure and romance—as long as this purple ecclesiology obscures what is truly essential about Catholic life. The question is what such a high-profile prelate might be able to do to lift up the rest of the Catholic story. Is a great irony possible—that it may take a bishop to demolish purple ecclesiology?

The outsider's perception of the Catholic Church is whatever the latest thing the bishops have said or done happens to be.

You got it. But that's not just a problem out there, it's in here. I went up a couple of months ago to Poughkeepsie, where we had a parish that in its heyday had a school, rectory, gym, the whole deal. Now it's decimated. Over the last year, Catholic Charities took over the old gym and now we've got a day care center on the ground floor and a food bank on the second floor. On the third floor we've got an immigration center that does English-language instruction, immigration services, all that stuff, because there's a large itinerant Hispanic population out there. That's been humming for a good year. I went up to bless it, and I was just blown away by what I saw. I was talking to the staff, who are dedicated Catholic people, and who are proud of what they've done, but who were also a little critical. Of course they thanked me for being there, but the edge of their remarks was, "Where has the Church been? You're here now after a year, but where has the Church been? Why hasn't the Church been more supportive of this?" I'm getting more and more frustrated, and finally I blurted out, "What are you talking about? The Church has been here already. You are the Church. This is the Church at its best. This is what we're all about." Of course what they meant was, why hasn't the purple been here for a year? Even our own people are thinking like that. I don't mean to dismiss their concern, because I think anytime our Catholic people experience a lack of concern or support from their bishop, that's something we need to take seriously. My point instead is that we need to flip the perception around—to see the kind of thing that's happening in Poughkeepsie as the real expression of "the Church," not so much wherever the bishop happens to be.

I also think that sometimes people outside the bishops' ranks have a better grasp of what's truly fundamental than we bishops do. When I was down in Haiti in the aftermath of the earthquake, for example, we spent late Saturday afternoon with three hundred or so Catholic Relief Services workers. CRS didn't just parachute in. Even before the earthquake hit, we had three hundred people on the ground. Ken Hackett [former CRS president] told me that one of the reasons we were going down there was to shore them up. So we sat on this hillside. The CRS building was not damaged, because it had been built according to code, but there was destruction all around us. I had seen all the work these people had been doing for the last twenty-four hours. Many of them are Haitians, and had lost family members and homes, so they were personally devastated. They're all exhausted, they're all frustrated, they're all saying, "How are we ever going to get out of this?" We talked for a couple of hours. Ken was tremendous on the mechanics, saying, "This is what we're going to do to help you all get through this." I tried my best to be a cheerleader.

As I was leaving, I looked out at these three hundred people and asked, "Is there anything more I can do for you?" I'm thinking about medicine, money, blankets, maybe getting messages home. One girl says, "Yeah. Could you say Mass for us tomorrow morning?" I'm thinking,

"She gets it." This is the Church at its best. I'm the one who had capitulated here to the "how," to the function, because I'm thinking that's all they were worried about. Of course, I didn't want to come off as pie-in-the-sky, saying, "Just kneel down and I'll give you my blessing and everything will be okay." But they were the ones telling me, the best thing you can do for us is to give us some meaning here. The best thing you can do for us is to tap into our faith, in this act where we believe we are united to the dying of Jesus on the cross and to his resurrection. That girl may not have used that vocabulary, but she knew it deep down. Her theology in that question would rival Thomas Aquinas's "Office for Corpus Christi." If that's not "the Church" in action, what is?

The question is, how do we get people to think about that CRS worker in Haiti and not just about guys like you when they think "Catholic Church"?

Here we go again on strategy. Well, to begin with, I suppose those of us who already have an entrée with the media should talk about this more. I should talk more about what the Church is doing in Haiti, or about the Cardinal McCloskey home here in New York. We're talking about a constitutive, constant, consistent feature of the life of the Church, and one for which we probably don't get nearly enough credit.

One of the things I've said for a long time is that we need a resurrected sense of apologetics. We Catholics sometimes are far too timid. We don't know how to respond when people throw out these silly, caustic remarks about the Church. We might just smile instead of rising up to say, "Enough of that. That's simply not accurate." Somebody sooner or later has got to blow the whistle on this. For example, there's this idea that the Church is phenomenally wealthy while people are starving, and we're completely indifferent to their fate. When I see from Hollywood critics of the Church, for example, one-millionth of a percent of the charity I see coming from the Catholic Church, maybe they'll have a little bit of credibility with me when they badmouth the Church. The jewelry you're wearing right now—why don't you sell that, if you're so big on this? Maybe we need a little bit more of a brass-knuckles approach. You don't want to come across as defensive or stern, but sometimes you just have to say, no more of this.

There's also another dimension of the problem with this purple ecclesiology worth thinking about for a moment. So far, you've been asking me about how to lift up the organized, institutional good works of the Church, and that certainly is important. Yet the truth of the matter is that we're living in an era in which the institutional reach of the Church is in decline, so an increasing share of the faith formation, evangelization, charitable work, and so on is being done by Catholics out in the world and in the marketplace, without any identifiable institutional structure behind them—and that, of course, makes it all the more invisible.

For example, the Church really isn't in the orphanage business anymore, but that certainly doesn't mean that Catholics aren't involved in caring for orphans. Just anecdotally, I actually think that the greatest percentage of foster parents today is probably Catholic. I remember visiting what used to be an orphanage run by an order of sisters in Milwaukee, and I'm thinking, "Boy, isn't it a shame that we don't have this anymore?" But as I'm walking through, person after person is telling me, "I go to this parish or that parish." "I went to this or that Catholic school." What we now have is ordinary Catholic people acting as the genius, the muscle, the brawn behind all this stuff. It's Vatican II working, if you want to look at it that way. We have now formed the people who are doing this. The problem is that because they don't trumpet their Catholicity, and because they're not part of some organized Catholic movement or group, most people would not look upon this as something "the Church" is doing.

Just look statistically at what's propping up most of our Catholic charities. We have a budget in the Archdiocese of New York that's approaching $700 million, and most of that is federal and state and community money. At one level, bravo to our government for recognizing that the best people to carry out much of this humanitarian work are people of faith. That's a great compliment, and we do it well. Yet it also means that in some ways these aren't church resources, and if they're ever withdrawn, you wonder what might happen. We've seen that in various places around the country, where a city or a state adopts a law that the Church opposes—on domestic partnership, for example—and the Church says, "If you force this down our throats, our charities will have to close." More and more, some legislators are saying, "Fine, we'll take our business elsewhere." They're calling our bluff. My point is that with the dilution of the institutional Church, we're losing some of the immense credibility that we used to have because we put our money where our mouth is as Catholics. To some extent that's being compensated for by individual Catholics simply living their faith in the world, but people are much less inclined to see that as "the Church." We've got to become more creative about how to spotlight the contributions that so many Catholics are making under their own steam, simply as an outgrowth of the faith and the sense of daring they've imbibed from the Church.

I published a booklet for Liguori a few years ago about untold stories of the Catholic Church, made up of short profiles of Catholics in various parts of the world: a nun in Honduras who runs the country's largest orphanage, with thousands of stories about kids' lives she's saved; an American Jesuit who founded a home for AIDS orphans in Kenya, again with amazing stories; a Catholic layman in Nigeria who founded a conflict resolution center in Nigeria with an imam, both of whom used to be heads of rival armed gangs and now they work to stop violence. **Why don't people think about this stuff when they think "Catholic Church"?**

I wonder if we've swallowed, even our Catholic people, the caricature of the Church? Have our own Catholic people swallowed the idea that at our core, we're probably corrupt, scandal-ridden, lethargic, authoritarian, hypocritical? In other words, has the "whore of Babylon" been such a powerful myth, especially in American culture, that we ourselves have absorbed it? There's almost a failure to believe the good news about the great work the Church does.

There is so much positive energy out there beyond whatever we bishops may be doing at a given moment. I'm thinking of a variety of things, even if none of them are pure, because you're going to have give and take. For example, what I see sometimes in homeschooling. I know there's a lot of criticism of it, and without a doubt there are some zealots out there. But right now I'm going through the process of calling about twelve prospects for the seminary, to encourage them and to see if there's anything they want to talk to me about. Six of them are homeschooled. I have to admit that right away, that causes some flares to go up for me. But in general, I find these people have absorbed affirmative orthodoxy. Are a couple of them hyper-defensive, into that whole good-guy/bad-guy thing? Yes. But more often than not, I'm seeing people who are literate when it comes to the poetry, the art, the worship, the prayer, the *why*, the *who*, of this Catholic worldview.

We've got a fellow who's now a second-year man at the seminary, whose [dad] was a New York cop. It's a big family. This is one of the happiest, most wholesome guys in the world. He's in his late twenties. You're talking about a family that read the Bible together, prayed the rosary together, made a holy hour together once a week. They talk about this, not in a bragging way but just in a refreshingly open and honest fashion. You just know this guy has got it. Now, skeptics would say, he drank the Kool-Aid. My response is, no, this is what the Church is most about. This guy is going to be an exceptionally effective priest, because he's absorbed a Catholic ethos that gives meaning and purpose, without any angst or hysteria about it but just a basic serenity in the face of life's challenges. Now, I frankly think that this guy, as well as the many more like him out there, represents an important story about Catholicism today, but it's tough to get people to see it. That too, I suppose, is part of the fallout from this purple ecclesiology. Nobody will pay any attention to this guy unless he becomes a bishop!

Another problem with purple ecclesiology is that it can often make it hard to explain why Catholics stick around. After all, the Church loses people, but it also holds on to an enormous number of people. Often, outsiders don't understand why. Sometimes many Catholics don't see it, or maybe they choose not to see it.

They can sense it sometimes. Yesterday at ten-fifteen Mass, when we go in, it's down one side aisle, and then we come back up the other. As I'm going in, I see this huge group of ragamuffins in their late teens, and I see them all sitting there, and we've got time before the procession starts, so I ask, "Nice to see you, where are you from?" They reply, "England." We're talking about maybe a hundred kids or so. All through Mass they were on my mind, as we're singing the creed in Latin, clouds of incense are billowing, and so on. It's a pretty high liturgy at ten-fifteen on Sunday. It's beautiful, and we have other elements too, such as hymns in Spanish, so it's got a rich diversity. In general, though, it's pretty high. I found myself thinking, "Uh-oh, we must have lost these kids. They must have their earphones on by now." Afterward, I made it my business to go back over to them, and I teased them about it being Washington's birthday— "You know, he's the one who won the Revolution against the British," that sort of thing. I was amazed at the way those kids reacted to the Mass, their interest and attentiveness.

They began to ask me questions. "Why do you wear that?" "What's with the white smoke?" "Was that Latin?" I hope I wasn't just imagining this, but I thought I could see a bit of a connection with the transcendent there. I thought, "Ah, they've just been in the household of the faith." In other words, that fleeting contact with something utterly beyond but also something that's deep within each one of us is what the Church is all about, and it happens far more often than many people understand. The question is how we make that part of the cultural conversation about the Church, as opposed to just our scandals and political fights.

I suspect the typical person walking around these days doesn't really get why anyone would want to be Catholic, because that person's image is that it means sitting around and arguing over gay marriage and abortion. To that person, it's like a debating society.

You're on to something. I think about the icon we've got right next door in Saint Patrick's Cathedral, okay? To this day, I can't walk in there—and pardon the schmaltzy sound of this—without a sense of the beyond, of what's real in life. That is what Saint Patrick's provides for the greatest metropolis in the world, and in a way it's a microcosm of the Church. When people walk in there, there's a sense of the divine, of providence, of somebody listening to me, of trying to recapture some childlike innocence and adventure in life. I'm told that we get close to fifty thousand people for ashes on Ash Wednesday, that it's round-the-clock. What's that all about? From a worldly point of view, that could be ridiculed, that here are these crazy robots who once a year have some strange tie to their church where they get smudged. We know that's not true. We know that somewhere deep down people are saying, "I'm back holding my mother's hand crossing the street, because she's going to take care of me and get me safely to the other side."

It's a reminder of our mortality, and our immortality. People know that, there's this sense there.

I think about my experience in Haiti. I'm sure you've heard about the crucifix that was left unscathed in front of the cathedral, which has now become a symbol. I was walking to the funeral Mass of Archbishop Miot, which was in that destroyed square in Port-au-Prince, and I'm seeing dozens, hundreds, by the end thousands of people around the cross. They were praying there, crying, touching it, and I'm thinking, "This is Calvary. This is the Church, this is what we're about." Yes, we're also about the Pétionville Club refugee camp, where Catholic Relief Services is taking care of eighty-five thousand people. But we've been animated and propelled to do that by that mystery we've experienced at the foot of the cross. That's the core Catholic experience, but you're absolutely right that too often it's obscured by a focus on the latest political debate—the latest standoff between Bishop [Thomas] Tobin and Chris Matthews, or me and the *New York Times*, or something like that.

In a way, though, isn't that the same challenge that Jesus had? What did they ask him? Every time he tried to preach His message, all they cared about was, "Oh, by the way, are you now going to restore the Kingdom of Israel?" They were into that reductionism as well, weren't they? It's the question they asked Jesus in the Gospels: Are you going to give us a sign? I suppose that was the version of purple ecclesiology he faced in his own time, so perhaps we can at least take consolation in the notion that the problem is hardly new!

You know when I most experience "the Church"? Every other Saturday morning I walk down, in street clothes, to a Franciscan parish near Penn Station. There I stand in line, usually eight or so people in front of me, for confession. Nobody knows I'm a bishop. I watch the street people waiting for the soup kitchen to open; I see a mom and her little girl light a candle and say a prayer; I look into the church and see dozens of faithful there in silence before the exposed Eucharist; there's a young couple leaving the parlor after their marriage prep; there's an elderly lady crying in front of Our Lady's Chapel; over in the corner is the drop-off table for baby clothes for the young moms with a troubling pregnancy. And here I am, a sinner in line with other sinners, just wanting to take Jesus at his word that he welcomes and forgives me. Bingo! This is the Church! Nothing purple about it.

NINE

Tribalism and Its Discontents

It's become commonplace in discussions about Catholicism in America to refer to the Church as "polarized," meaning that Catholics are divided into Left and Right, between liberals and conservatives. Certainly there are a number of issues that can be analyzed in those terms, especially as it applies to the intersection between the Church and secular politics. In trying to understand how Catholics react to President Barack Obama, for example, or to health care reform, or the war in Iraq, or any number of other issues, one sees that the division of opinion in the Church does often neatly parallel the fault line between Left and Right in the wider culture.

Yet if a hypothetical sociologist from Mars were to land in the United States to study the Catholic Church, he or she (or it) would likely conclude that American Catholics aren't so much polarized as tribalized. Looking around, what one sees are a variety of different tribes dotting the Catholic landscape: pro-life Catholics, liturgical traditionalist Catholics, Church-reform Catholics, peace-and-justice Catholics, Hispanic Catholics, Vietnamese Catholics, neocon Catholics, Obama Catholics, and so on, to say nothing of the simple meat-and-potatoes Catholics out there. Each of these tribes has its own heroes. Each sponsors its own conferences, reads its own journals and blogs, and worships in its own community. They've moved so far down separate paths that quite often they seem to be having completely separate conversations, operating on the basis of separate and often contrasting impressions of what's actually happening in the Church. The consequence is that when members of these various tribes accidentally rub shoulders, it can be difficult for them to sustain a conversation because they often lack any common set of reference points beyond a few lines from the Nicene Creed and some shared spiritual practices.

In principle, of course, all this diversity is both healthy and inevitable. There are 67 million Catholics in the United States and 1.1 billion worldwide, so complexity is unavoidably part of the picture. This is a church, after all, not a sect. The diversity becomes a headache, however, when these tribes stop communicating with one another and instead begin looking upon one another as suspect, if not as outright enemies. Often enough to be noticeable, that seems to be the American Catholic situation. A quick story makes the point. In 2005, the BBC broadcast a three-part documentary called *The Monastery*, about five young men with little or no experience of either Catholicism or monasteries who were chosen to spend forty days living the monks' life at Worth Abbey in England, run by the Benedictines. It was a ratings hit, and Abbot Christopher Jamison later published a book about the experience called *Finding Sanctuary*. In 2006, Abbot Christopher came to the United States for a series of lectures based on the book. I happened to be in London shortly afterward and spoke to him over lunch. The abbot said that as he moved around, he was struck by a peculiar feature of American Catholicism. Rather than simply accepting his identity as a Benedictine monk, he said, many Catholics in the United States seemed to want to know more. Specifically, their question seemed to be "What kind of Catholic are you?" Was he liberal or conservative, charismatic or traditional, with the pope or skeptical of him? In some cases, Abbot Christopher said, it almost seemed as if people wanted him to declare the tribe to which he belonged.

The trick is not to eliminate these Catholic tribes, which would require a bulldozer and which would end up impoverishing the Church through the imposition of a bland sameness. The trick is instead to get them talking to one another, helping them to see that the Catholic whole is inevitably bigger than any given tribe, even if it encompasses and embraces the best that each tribe has to offer. That's a job for a bridge builder, something that in theory ought to be right in Archbishop Timothy Dolan's wheelhouse. How well he's able to accomplish that bridge building may constitute an important measure of his legacy in the American Church.

When people look in at the Catholic Church from the outside, what they often see is Catholics at one another's throats. Is that part of why you've said that an important "smell test" for you is whether a given parish, or seminary, or wherever, has a happy feel?

Sure, it needs to feel like a good place to be. We're talking now about atmospheric issues rather than projects, causes, or initiatives. Let me tell a story to make the point. I recently had a couple come in for an appointment who had been asking to see me for a long time. When I would ask about them, some cautioned, "Ah, they're kind of on the fringes. This might not be a good idea." Finally I sat down with these two people, and they really moved me. They're happily married, they've got their own kids, and they've adopted some kids too. About twenty years ago they gave up their middle-class lives, got this run-down house in the Bronx, and founded a small community, almost a sort of *Catholic Worker*–style place. They're very much into Catholic piety, such as eucharistic adoration. People off the street come in, and they've got a couple of these wagons where they go around at night with coffee and sandwiches, so they're also into the active part of it. More or less, their style is, "Come be part of this. You don't know where life's taking you? Come on in, you're welcome here. Be one of us." They reported that the heart of their week is to be Monday night, where they get together for Mass, a common meal, prayer, and a holy hour together. This is the real thing.

Now, would we in the archdiocese tend to ask, "Well, you know, they've never been audited. Does their pastor know about this? We don't really know what they're doing. We hear there's some flaky stuff going on." I guess so, but that's like when the disciples came back to Jesus and said, "We saw some guy who was casting out demons and he's not one of us," and Jesus said, "Hey, if he ain't against us, he must be for us." I'm saying, let it go—let the flowers bloom. My God, we need these kinds of things. This couple weren't mad that I've never shown up before. They're not mad that they've never been listed in a Catholic directory or recognized officially. What they're doing is the kind of thing we ought to affirm. Those are the kinds of things I ought to encourage, those are the kind of places I ought to be on a Monday night. The key point with respect to your question is, these are Catholics who aren't mad at anybody, and they're not waging these *ad intra* battles. They're happy, committed Catholics, and that's enough.

Building a happy place is rarely an accident. Have you ever had to fight to preserve it?

I can tell you a story from when I was a parish priest in Saint Louis. After Immacolata, I went to Little Flower Parish, where the pastor was George Gottwald, who at the time was also an auxiliary bishop of Saint Louis. We became very close, but he could be very testy and rather glum. We butted heads a few times. I remember once we kind of came to a parting of the ways. We had a great Legion of Mary in the parish. I loved the Legion of Mary; you heard me say the other day that I always think that if a parish has the Legion of Mary and the Saint Vincent de Paul Society, it's in great shape, because they'll take care of the spiritual and corporal works of mercy. Anyway, I was visiting with a family that had drifted away from the Church, and I kind of talked them into coming back, through the grace of God. They wanted their two kids in the school but couldn't pay. I said, "You need not worry about that. I'll see that your two kids are in the school." The dad said that he was a painter, and he'd be happy to come up to paint the classrooms and do anything we needed in lieu of tuition. He said, "I can give you four or five hours a week," and I replied that that was great. After I arranged it, [Gottwald] called me in and said, "You must tell them no. We have a strict rule. If he can't pay tuition, the children may not come in." I said, "Well, Bishop, you've asked me to do this administration of the parish so you can be an auxiliary bishop. If you don't trust me to make these decisions, then I think you'd better ask for another assistant, because it's not going to work out." To his credit, he backed down. As I mentioned, we ended up being close, and as a matter of fact, he gave me his bishop's crozier, which I still use today.

I'm not the kind of guy who goes looking for conflict, but if you're asking me if I'm willing to take a stand sometimes in order to try to keep the Church's door open as wide as possible, then the answer is yes.

Often when outsiders look at the Church, what they see is anger and infighting, and almost nobody wants to be part of that scene.

You're absolutely right, and I think that gets to the heart of the vocation problem. Who wants to join a group of crabs? If you're thinking about the priesthood and you're in the sacristy and hearing guys gripe about these new translations, or the bishops, or who knows what, that's going to get to you, isn't it? We have to project the image—and of course, it has to be more than just an image, more than just a PR technique—that fundamentally the Church is a family, where we certainly have our differences, but there's also a great deal of love, respect, and mutual support, so that at its core it's a warm, affirming place to be.

By the way, I imbibed that spirit in Immacolata Parish in Saint Louis, under the pastor at the time, Connie Flavin. Connie was right down the middle. It was not a conservative parish. He wanted to do things right, but it would have defied categorization. Connie was into everything. He told me once that he wanted me to be in charge of the charismatic prayer group. At that time, in 1976, charismatics were still thought of as suspect. I replied that I might be a bit uncomfortable because I don't consider myself charismatic. He said, "Well, neither do I, but we should have it. It's part of the Church, so let's do it." We also had a very active human rights emphasis. There was an African American neighborhood in the parish, and Connie was very aggressive about reaching out to it. He told me that for my first summer, he wanted me to knock on every door in the black neighborhood of the parish. He was really concerned that we not let them be dwarfed by the fact that ours was an affluent parish. He was a real middle-of-the-road kind of guy. He liked everything. He was not an ideologue at all. His spirit was that if the Church says we do it, we do it. The parish under him was a very happy place, and what I found was a tremendous warmth of the people. Some of my happiest times were getting to know those families, who to this day are still some of my best friends.

One of my best priest friends is a guy named Jay Johnson, who was at Immacolata. He was only assigned there; he was a full-time teacher in a high school. He became a good friend, and one morning we were sitting at the breakfast table roaring with laughter about something. Monsignor Flavin came in, and we got a little quiet because we thought we were laughing too hard too early in the morning, and maybe we woke him up. Jay said, "Sorry, Monsignor, were we too loud?" He said, "There's nothing I like better than hearing the priests laugh." That was a happy house, and I just loved it.

Does your style in any way also reflect your midwestern roots? I ask this as somebody raised in western Kansas.

I never really comprehended what that meant until I went to Rome. We would often say at the North American College that you're sent to Rome to get a sense of the wider Church, but in your first year you're stuck on the diversity of the American Church. You're comparing one another, and all the differences. Midwestern guys seem to have a reputation for practicality, kind of a no-nonsense "Let's just get this done" attitude, hospitality, informality, and simplicity. I know when I went to Rome the guys always said that Dolan's the one who will have us in for a beer after *pranzo,* or if we want to get a card game or a party going, Dolan will do it. In my mind, it was just what my dad did in the backyard with the barbeque pit. The neighbors would come around, the priest would show up, and everybody would have a good time. There did seem to be a real sense of hospitality, simplicity, informality, almost a sort of "aw, shucks" approach to life. Did I know that growing up? No, but as I look back now, that's probably a big part of who I am.

We are in some ways a badly fractured church in America. What kind of dialogue do we need to address that?

I'm a cheerleader for dialogue. I believe we can never have enough of it. I worry that dialogue has become such a bromide that it's now sort of toothless—it has become the aspirin we prescribe for everything. The other fear I have about dialogue is whether we have a hangover from the days when dialogue meant that we start with the lowest common denominator.

That's why *dialogue* has become a loaded word, because some people think it means going soft about Catholic identity.

They think it can mean, sadly, what can we give up and what can you give up, in order to arrive at some sort of bland tea-and-cookies stuff on Sunday afternoon? One guy who I think has reinvigorated dialogue is Benedict XVI, constantly saying that true, respectful dialogue starts with a clear understanding of the truth that you bring to the conversation. We insult our partner, our respected, cherished partner in dialogue, if we feel that they are expecting us to soft-pedal the truth. That to me is very, very important. Another thing we need in dialogue, especially for us believers, is a certain amount of fearlessness. That we are not afraid, that the truth shall set us free. We have the promise of Jesus that he'll tell us what to say when we're in trouble, and we have the promise of Jesus that he's going to be with us all days, so what do we have to be afraid of?

Your reputation as a bridge builder was in some ways forged in Milwaukee, where you came in with a reputation as a conservative yet somehow managed to appeal to the liberals too. How did you pull it off?

Keep in mind that I truthfully thought I'd be there the rest of my life. I went there at fifty-two. I was thinking, "I'm an archbishop now and Milwaukee is a darn important archdiocese. There are seven hundred thousand people here; it's the nineteenth-largest diocese in the United States. You've got your work cut out for you, but you're going to be here for a long time, so you've got the luxury of time. Even if I'm not going to be here for the rest of my life, I'm certainly going to be here for fourteen or fifteen years, probably until my mid-sixties, and then who knows?" Anyway, my thinking was, "Dolan, take it easy." That led to criticism from those who could have been my allies, who were

/ 159

disappointed that I didn't move more quickly. But strategically—and not that I concocted this—the [criticism] actually helped build a bridge to the other side. They said, "Wow, Dolan's getting attacked by our enemies. Maybe he's not that bad."

So when you saw Benedict XVI attacked from the right after his first year, you could relate.

I said, "Been there, done that." But here's the ultimate thing: My years in Milwaukee, too, were very happy. I miss it. In the final farewell with the priests, I was in tears. I love those guys. With a very few exceptions, these are wholesome, hardworking, zealous guys. When some of them were asking questions about optional celibacy, when they're asking questions about lay parish directors, when they're asking questions about reconfiguring parishes or about general absolution, they weren't in it to push some radical, Dutch Catechism agenda. Were there some like that? Yes. But in general, it's because they're good priests worried about the sacramental and pastoral life of the people.

As I'm looking back now, one of the things that perhaps most troubled me coming into Milwaukee is something that Rembert Weakland talks openly about. Rembert has a perceptive talk on what he calls "Catholic culture." His thesis would be that Catholic culture is gone. You can say great things about Catholic culture, you can say negative things, but whether we like it or not, it's gone. In that light, he asks, why waste our time? Now, by "Catholic culture" I think he meant the way things were up to December 8, 1965, the closing day of the Second Vatican Council. He was glad it's gone.

Rembert thought that the best thing we can do for the Church is to expedite the demise of all these external props that bolstered a Catholic culture and to substitute them with something better, because that culture is gone. So, anything that had to do with a traditional Catholic culture—a classical seminary, clerical garb, rectories, or even the promotion of what you might consider explicitly Catholic issues such as individual confession or natural family planning, marriage and family—you're probably at best treading water, at worst spitting into a tornado. You weren't going to bring that culture back, and so we might as well replace those externals with something that we know is going to see us into the future. There's no use trying to resurrect these artifacts of the past.

John Paul II, on the other hand, I think would have said that approach tosses out the baby with the bathwater. Do these things need to be cleaned up, purified? Yes. But they're still good. So when I came in and started talking about liturgical norms, sound catechesis, pro-life issues, marriage and family, vocations, confessions, eucharistic adoration, and so on, that was obviously a new agenda. Some guys said, "What's going on here? I thought that was all gone!" I had to convince them that none of what I was suggesting had to come at the expense of all the good things that had been accomplished in Milwaukee before I arrived, that it wasn't a matter of an either/or but a both/and.

What I found in Milwaukee too is that these guys like a scrappy fight. They don't like me to just say, "Oh, thank you for sharing." I can remember meeting with a group of great priests critical of my agenda and saying to them, "You know, you guys think you're way ahead of the Church. The truth is, you're way behind. There's been a catechism since the Dutch Catechism. The Church has passed you by, and you're freeze-dried at the day after *Humanae Vitae*. We've got to get with the Church. All the things that are taking off and giving life everywhere else, we look upon with suspicion here. We should obviously preserve what's been done well here, but we can do that while also opening up to other possibilities." They appreciated the candor, the challenge. In the end, I think most of them were at least willing to talk about it, and we got past the business of thinking in terms of good guys and bad guys.

Was there anything you thought you would change coming in but you were converted to it once you got there? In other words, did you change your mind about anything?

I don't know if I was converted, but there were some things that I came to see were not as deleterious as I had thought. For instance, priests not living in rectories. When I got there, I thought, "This is going to have to go, and I'm just going to bide my time." I was not prepared to find that it's not as bad as I thought it was. We did some studies. In my years there, I never got a complaint that a priest wasn't available, nor did I ever see it, with one or two exceptions, as an abuse. I never saw a guy saying, "Oh, I'm sorry, Archbishop, but I can't take that assignment because I've got my condo here and I'd have to drive forty-five minutes." Never. The priests would say, "Okay, sure, I'll go. You realize that when I wrote in to the personnel board, because I knew I'd be up for a new assignment, I'd asked [for something closer] if possible. But no, I'll go, that's our understanding." The priests were loyal, and they understood that. They told me that in a way, living somewhere else enhanced their priestly ministry by allowing them to live outside the parish setting while still being fully immersed in the life of the parish. They also thought it was kind of a practical way to prepare for the future. If they're going to retire at sixty-eight, they'd better have a house or someplace to stay for the last fifteen years or more of their life.

You were persuaded?

I still do have some concerns. You know, I feel that the major crisis in the priesthood since the council is the reduction of the priesthood to a ministry, to a function, to a job. I was afraid that theologically, the fact that priests live apart from the parish damages something that I think is essential to the priesthood, namely, that spousal, paterfamilias role. I think that's close to the heart of the priesthood. I worried how that would come across. To tell you the truth, I never saw a problem in Milwaukee. Also, I still think that eventually this may evolve and living in rectories may return. We started some of that with what we called "apostolic houses," where some of the younger priests reside. The younger guys told me, "We want to live together. We like living in rectories." That's a natural, gradual kind of movement. That would prove the wisdom, I think, of some patience, trusting that what was good and artificially tossed aside will come back.

You seem to have a track record of being willing to talk with almost anyone.

Part of that is probably a strategic calculation on my part, that I don't want to give anybody ammo to say, "The archbishop won't talk to us." But I also don't go into these meetings reluctantly, because in the vast majority of cases I'm more than happy to sit down with anyone who wants to talk. One key to successful dialogue, in my opinion, is trying our best not to judge motives. Very often that's where the problem comes in. You think you know why So-and-So is coming in to see you, because she wants to accomplish x. Isn't it better to take her at face value and assume that she wants to come in for the very reason she's stated? In general, I try to give people the benefit of the doubt and assume that someone wants to see me because he would like to sit down in a climate of trust, among people who believe the same things, and get some stuff off his chest. I might find out in the meeting that this person does have an axe to grind, but actually I find that happens a lot less than people might suspect.

In principle, is there any group with which you would not meet?

As a theoretical matter, there's probably no one I would cross off the list a priori. I was raised in a climate in which you figure there's not too many things in life that can't be solved, or at least calmed down, over a couple of beers and a cheeseburger on the patio. There are times, however, when I can't meet with people for various reasons, and not just the basic fact of there being only so many hours in a day. For example, right now our high school union people would like to meet with me. I told my staff that it's fine with me, but there were red lights all over the place. To be fair, it's not just the lawyers. Also the superintendent of schools, my communications guy, the institutional-memory people in the archdiocese, are all saying, "We know you want to do this, and there will come a time for it, but not right now because there are complex and delicate issues that need to be hammered out before they come to you." More often than not, they're right. There are priests, for example, who want to speak to me, whom I can't meet with right now. For example, there's one guy who wants to see me who's been suspended under the terms of the Dallas norms. At their 2002 meeting in Dallas, the U. S. bishops adopted a tough "one strike" policy, vowing to remove a priest from ministry for even one credible charge of sexual abuse. I've had to say to him that I'm as eager to see you as you are to see me, but my advisers tell me that right now you're in the middle of a canonical process that is moving toward resolution. It would be in neither your interest nor mine to jeopardize the integrity of that case. In general, however, unless there's some specific legal or institutional reason that would get in the way of a meeting, I try to have as much of an open-door policy as humanly possible.

Is it your experience that people usually feel better about the Church after these meetings than before?

I'd say 95 percent of the time, with anybody, from the most bitter victim/survivor of sexual abuse to the most rabid/radical whatever, I find that sitting down in an atmosphere of trust and fearlessness usually accomplishes some good. Have there been times when it's not only not productive but actually counterproductive? Yes, there have been occasions like that, but not often enough that it's made me seriously question my instincts of trying to be as accessible as possible.

In deciding which meetings you'll take, or anything else for that matter, do you ever worry that you're setting an example that will put pressure on other bishops to do the same thing?

Yeah, you do worry about that, at least I do. I hate people saying, "Well, Dolan met with them. What's wrong with you?" But our pastors go through that, don't they? They go through it with something as simple as a funeral liturgy. People will insist, "Father O'Malley at Saint Mary's lets all the nephews give five-minute eulogies afterward, but here at Saint Joseph's you say we can't have any, or maybe just one. What's going on here?" If that's true of a regular pastor, it's obviously even more true for the archbishop of New York. I have to be aware that in a sense, everything I do sets a precedent. Has that ever stopped me from doing something? I don't think it has.

If you have to choose how to spend your time, between meeting with a group that's feeling marginalized and hurting about the Church and a group that's really gung ho—so you're choosing between healing old wounds and nurturing new life—what do you do?

That's obviously a hypothetical question, because you hope in practice that the answer is usually both/and. But hypothetically, if I had to make the decision, I'd probably go with those who are disaffected. I would see that as part of the missionary outreach of the Church, the evangelical dimension—that you're always going after the lost sheep. If you've got a choice to make between preaching to the choir and to those out on the front steps, you probably should go to the ones outside the door.

That reminds me of some tense conversations I've had since arriving in New York about Sirius radio. You know, we've got this Catholic channel on the Sirius satellite-radio network, and that's obviously a great blessing. When I first got here, I was fairly critical of how we're using it. I said, "I don't listen that often, but when I do, I find it frivolous. There's not much meat on the bone. I listen to them, and they're just joking and laughing. That's a nice style, but where's the beef?" Joseph Zwilling, my communications director, finally replied, "You may have a point, but you need to know the history." He explained that when this thing began, they asked, "Is this going to be EWTN, where we're preaching to the choir? That's obviously a legitimate choice, and bravo to EWTN for doing it. Or is this going to be more of an *ad extra* effort, where we hope to appeal to those who are driving down the road and channel-surfing, and who maybe get hooked into some light-hearted banter? If so, perhaps at the end of that half hour, they might have gotten a little warmer, cozier feeling about Jesus Christ and his Church." Zwilling said, "We went for the latter, and I basically think it's working. Does it need refinement? Are some of your observations true, and do we need to work at it? Maybe. But if you want to switch philosophies, I'm going to be tough to convince." He was probably right. Does that mean we can't do some serious refinement with Sirius radio? I think we can, but the philosophy is probably right.

Some might argue that you can waste a lot of time reaching out to people who are never going to come around, and your attention would be better directed to those who are already on board.

I'm open, maybe, to the critique that I should do more of that, and that perhaps you can go overboard trying to tend to the lost. It is a legitimate concern. Take personnel work with my priests, which I try to take very seriously. After almost a year [in New York], I'm thinking that I'm giving the same two dozen guys 90 percent of my time, because they're the ones hurting, alienated, and in trouble. I've got a guy on Staten Island, and hardly a week goes by that this good guy doesn't call. I knew him as a student in Rome. He tells me that every Sunday night eight or ten priests on Staten Island get together, make some pasta, and have a good time. He always asks me to come, but I haven't been able to go yet. Why? Because most of the time, I'm meeting a guy who just got out of Guest House, or I'm meeting somebody who's broken and hurt, or maybe just whining. Sometimes I think I'm ignoring the people who are fundamentally content, not giving them the time and attention they need. I would rather be with guys eating pasta! But it's that old prodigal son thing, right? Fundamentally, I'm of the conviction that time spent in dialogue and outreach, even if it doesn't yield immediate results, is almost never wasted. It may plant a seed of reconciliation that will take years to flower, but the fact that it's been planted is important. Sometimes we can get so caught up in a managerial way of looking at things, concerned with efficiency and returns on investment and so on, that we forget to also look at our choices through the eyes of faith. From the point of view of faith, time spent in reaching out to the lost and hurting is never lost time.

The broader point is that you're not willing to throw in the towel on building bridges, inside the Church or outside, in favor of focusing on those in your own tribe.

Correct, and that is a temptation today. In some ways it's reminiscent of what used to be known as the whole *Lumen Gentium* versus *Gaudium et Spes* argument, between Wojtyla and Ratzinger. Are we going to go back to the catacombs, or are we going to be in the marketplace? My answer would be both, but that we cannot give up on the *ad extra* evangelization of culture, constantly coaxing, inviting, wooing, even flirting. We can't do that, of course, if we don't also tend to those within, right? The people who are going to do all that have to be nurtured too.

That can sound awfully abstract, but it has very practical implications. For example, which invitation am I going to accept at a given time? Is it better for me to go to a Rotary Club luncheon or a Serra Club luncheon? Which am I more "bishop" at? My gut would be, it might be cozier and more enjoyable at the Serra Club, but I'm probably going to do more good at the Rotary. That's especially true in New York, where maybe some of these folks are going to go back to their highfalutin offices and say, "Dolan was there, and he actually made some sense." I would see more of the apostolic role in being there.

One could apply the same logic to choices I have to make inside the Church. Am I better off using my limited time to meet with a group of self-described "gay Catholics," for example, who are feeling marginalized, or to meet with some gung ho members of a new religious order that's in one of our parishes and happy as clams? Again, the right answer is to do both, but in some ways I almost think that between the two, the former is the higher priority. We need to constantly be reaching out, constantly be willing to talk, constantly striving to make our lofty language about the Church as a family a reality. If I can contribute to that dream, or if I can at least set an example, then that's where my time and effort needs to go. It's so obvious that moms and dads can immediately sense which of their children is hurting and needs their love most at any given moment. Holy Mother Church needs that skill. A bishop needs that talent.

TEN

Prayer and the Sacraments

"If you build it, he will come" was the aphorism made famous by the popular 1989 baseball movie *Field of Dreams,* in which an Iowa farmer named Ray Kinsella, played by Kevin Costner, is persuaded by unseen forces to plow under a significant portion of his cornfield in order to build a baseball diamond in the middle of nowhere. While that seemed the least productive use of Kinsella's time and resources imaginable, and it drove him to the edge of bankruptcy, he took a leap of faith. He believed that following his dream would lead to something big, even if the evidence for it seemed scant. The final scene of the movie shows a line of car headlights as far as the eye can see streaming to Iowa to watch a game—and to plunk down $25 for the privilege.

In some ways, "If you build it, he will come" can also apply to the idea that an overt concentration on prayer and worship can still appeal to a postmodern, ultrasecular, twenty-first-century culture—both in terms of the act of faith required and the actual outcome. To look around at the Catholic scene these days is to see that some of the most phenomenally successful undertakings have precious little to do with political organizing or debates over Church reform, but much more to do with feeding humanity's spiritual hunger. When Cardinal Carlo Maria Martini was still the archbishop of Milan, for example, he was famous worldwide as a leading progressive voice in Catholic affairs. Yet in Milan itself, he was probably best known for his weekly reflections on Scripture held in the duomo, which drew tens of thousands of sophisticated, worldly residents of Milan, the country's financial and commercial capital, to meditate on the meaning of God's word in their lives. Similarly, the Community of Sant'Egidio in Rome is famous around the world for its work in conflict resolution and ecumenical and interreligious dialogue, but in Rome itself its primary appeal lies in its weekly vespers service staged at the Church of Santa Maria in Trastevere. The hauntingly beautiful music, inspired preaching, and simple but elegant prayers offered by Sant'Egidio draw tens of thousands of young urban Romans, many of whom probably have not darkened the door of a church since their parents stopped compelling them to go.

It's not just Italy. In Brazil, Padre Marcelo Rossi, a forty-something former aerobics instructor whose CDs featuring pop-style songs of praise have sold in the millions and earned him a Latin Grammy, routinely draws tens of thousands of people to a former glass factory on the southern edge of São Paulo. Rossi's appeal has nothing to do with his political positions, which are actually difficult to discern, or with any network of social ministries. Instead, he blends high-octane "praise and worship" music with a deeply reverent celebration of the Catholic Mass, weaving in simple, homely observations on prayer and the spiritual life. Of course, anyone who has ever attended a World Youth Day, that massive gathering of young Catholics that seems one part *Canterbury Tales* and one part Lollapalooza, will also appreciate the point. At those events, Catholic youth turn out in huge numbers for the sacrament of confession and for eucharistic adoration. Their spiritual fervor never fails to alarm some Catholic insiders, for whom such traditional practices seem passé, if not a lamentable return to the past, and it flabbergasts onlookers in the secular world. Yet whenever and wherever the Church builds it, the young seem to come. The bottom line is that against all odds, prayer, the sacramental life, and the other spiritual resources of the Catholic Church—when packaged and presented effectively—still wield an enormous appeal.

Looked at in purely capitalistic terms, the "business" of spirituality seems to be doing just fine in the early twenty-first century, inside the Catholic Church and out. Consider, for example, that Tim LaHaye's Left Behind series of apocalyptic Christian novels, based on the book of Revelation, to date have sold in excess of 65 million copies. In 2007 the Association of American Publishers estimated the market for religious-themed books at almost $900 million just in the United States, with a spokesperson for the association saying numbers like that meant that religion is not just a "niche market" anymore. In a similar vein, Mel Gibson's controversial 2004 film *The Passion of the Christ,* despite taking a beating both from critics and from plenty of influential Christian and Jewish voices, took in $371 million at the domestic box office, putting it in twelfth place for all-time domestic earnings, and earned some $612 million internationally. The point is that there is an obvious spiritual hunger stirring, and those who know how to tap it successfully can capture the imagination of a broad swath of humanity.

Despite all that, bishops and other Church officials are sometimes curiously reticent to talk much about prayer and the spiritual life in public. To some extent, that may be because they're out of practice, given that the media are far more likely to want to ask bishops about the latest sexual-abuse scandal or gay-marriage bill than they are about the practice of eucharistic adoration. To some extent, especially in the United States, Catholics have long been a bit reluctant to speak too openly about their spirituality, for fear of it being compared to the sort of "Bible thumping" popularly associated with some fundamentalist currents within evangelical and Pentecostal Protestantism. Bishops in particular may sometimes shy away from overt talk about prayer and holiness for fear of being accused of being pietistic, either unable or unwilling to grapple with the real-world challenges facing the Catholic Church in the here and now.

Whatever the motive, the irony is that unless one goes to a priests' retreat or some other internal affair, it can actually be fairly rare to hear a bishop talking about his own experiences of daily prayer, or what the Mass means to him, or the kinds of experiences he's had with the sacrament of penance, either as a confessor or as the one making the confession. It's a bit akin to the CEO of the Dell Corporation rarely speaking in public about computers, or the manager of the Yankees only occasionally talking about baseball. In other words, the somewhat surreal situation facing the Catholic Church is that its most visible leaders often are reluctant to promote, or even talk much about, the Church's core products.

Even the normally voluble Dolan acknowledges some discomfort talking openly about prayer, particularly when it comes to his own prayer life. Yet he also recognizes that a core responsibility of any bishop is to offer a role model of holiness, including devotion to prayer and the sacramental life. As a result, Dolan agreed to talk not only in the abstract about the spiritual life but also to crack open a window onto his own prayer life and the meaning of the sacraments in a personal key.

Tell me about your prayer life. What's prayer mean to you?

Part of that Catholic culture I was brought up in, with the faith as the be-all and end-all of my life, is that one should be a little reluctant to speak about that kind of thing. We're talking about a dimension of our lives that's intensely private, and of course no one wants to come off as holier than thou by bragging about his prayer life. Since you asked me, however, I'll go into it. Prayer means everything to me. I move this chair [Dolan points to a rocking chair in his study at the residence at Saint Patrick's Cathedral], which was given to me by the Carmelites at Holy Hill in Wisconsin. Every morning I open these doors into my chapel and turn this rocking chair to the altar, the tabernacle, the crucifix, so that it's facing the chapel in the morning. I'm talking about a quarter to five each morning. I open up those doors, I'm in my robe and pajamas, and I sit there. To be perfectly honest, sometimes I fall back asleep. Sometimes I get a yellow pad and write out homework, things I better do today — don't forget to call that guy, and so on. But in general, I try to give prayer a good hour. I find that to be enormously liberating, freeing. Am I distracted sometimes, do I nod off, do I sometimes cut it short because I want to call somebody or get something done before I forget? Yes, I do all of those things. But in general, that time is very important to me.

How in concrete do I pray? I have some basic prayers I start off with that pretty much are what Sister Mary Bosco taught me in second grade. We're talking about "Jesus, I believe in you. I love you. You are everything to me. Thanks for a good night's sleep, and I'm trusting you to get me through this day." Since I became a bishop, I've also developed a great reliance on the prayers of Saint Peter. I will simply say, "Lord, it's good to be here with you. Lord, if it's really you, would you call me to come across the water to you? Lead me, Lord, for I am a sinful man. Lord, wash not only my feet but my head and my hands as well. You alone are the Christ, the Son of the living God. Lord, you know everything. You know that I love you. I don't know squat, but I know that you love me. Lord, to whom shall I go? You alone have the words of everlasting life." I'll repeat these, over and over, in very simple refrains. Then I'll go into my office, I'll do the office of readings. Ade Schilly, one of my pastors growing up, once told me, "Tim, you'll know you're getting old when you really enjoy the Psalms." And do I ever enjoy them, and the Old Testament, just the chronic story of sin and redemption, adultery and fidelity, that I see over and over again in my own life, and God's constant invitation to redemption.

I'll try to do a little meditation, and some spiritual reading. I'm captivated these days with Marmion, and I owe that to Justin Rigali. [Columba Marmion was an Irish monk and spiritual writer in the late nineteenth and early twentieth centuries.] Rigali reintroduced me to

Marmion. I think I read him in my twenties, and I'm rediscovering him now. Then I'll say my morning prayer from the divine office, and I try to take my time. At the end of the hour I've more or less got my office done, giving me a solid grounding to the day, and then I'll clean up and go over for Mass, the greatest prayer of all. By the time I get to the breakfast table at eight A.M. for some coffee and oatmeal, I've got a good anchor for the day ahead.

By the way, when I say, "Save me, Lord, I'm going to drown," I will then put in a subordinate clause, and I will begin to tag the waves. I'll say, "Lord, here are the wind and the waves facing me right now: Father So-and-So, Saint Vincent's Hospital, John Allen's coming today and God knows what he's gonna ask. . . ." That kind of stuff. I try to identify those waves, and say, "Lord, if it's really you, call me to come across the water." I like to imagine. I love Ignatius of Loyola, who dares us to imagine. He says, let your imagination run away, put yourself into the scene. Imagine yourself in that boat, or walking on the water. Insert yourself into the biblical event.

Have you done the Ignatian exercises?

Only the eight days, I've never done the thirty. At three different retreats in my life, I have done the classical eight days that I find superb. I've never done the thirty. I still find that a little intimidating. The eight days alone were hard to get through. I am not a contemplative person by nature, though I hope I have a contemplative dimension. I'm afraid that I would give in more to activism. By the way, I have a Lenten project every year of rereading *The Soul of the Apostolate*, which is one of my great ones. I think one day there could be a good doctoral dissertation done on the shift in Catholicism after Vatican II from Chautard's *Soul of the Apostolate* to Gene Kennedy's *Genius of the Apostolate* [co-authored by Paul D'Arcy]. Remember that, which came out in the mid-sixties? The spirit of the times was more or less, let's shelve *The Soul of the Apostolate,* because now thank God we're beyond that. I don't think

Gene Kennedy meant that, but that's sort of what happened as we got into the hyperkinetic approach. Now, I think, and I would attribute it to John Paul, we've recaptured that *Soul of the Apostolate,* from which *The Genius of the Apostolate* flows.

So, my prayer would be very gritty, as I would begin to get very, very graphic about the waves and the winds that are facing me. That's very important to me, to really get down and dirty. For example, I would talk about my weight, okay? I say things like, "Lord, I'm a little worried because I'm having trouble genuflecting. Something's happening now that I'm sixty and my knees are starting to go." I'll get really graphic, in my own mind, bringing these waves and winds to the Lord.

I can hear your doctor saying, "Prayer's great, but you might want to throw some diet and exercise into the mix."

Of course, you bet! Believe me, I'm trying.

What else happens during the day? I have to be honest with you, because often I'm not able to devote a great deal of time to prayer during the regular course of the day. Maybe it's a quick visit to the Blessed Sacrament, maybe in the car my secretary and I would try to pray the rosary together if we're going somewhere, but in general until I go to bed at night and do my evening prayer, and then night prayer and "Hail Holy Queen," that would probably be it. At least my day is bookended by some solid prayer. That means everything. I would try to expand that a tad on my day off, which I usually try to carve out from Friday noon to Saturday noon. I would try to spend a little more time in prayer, not so much in the morning, but at least throughout the day, and maybe a little more expanded spiritual reading.

What's also very important to me is the sacrament of penance. For God's sake, I'm not bragging. If anything, I'm embarrassed to say how much I need it. I go every other week, here in town. I do have a spiritual director, and maybe I should try to see him more often. I may see him about every two months, and when I see him, I'll usually use that as a chance for the sacrament of penance too. That's probably a little bit more pensive time, but in general I go down here to Saint Francis and stand in line. I usually go Saturday morning, because I go out and take a walk, so I'm in my street clothes.

You don't have a regular confessor?

No, it's whoever's there. I go behind the screen. They wouldn't know it's me, and I don't identify myself. Famous story: I was installed on Wednesday, and on Saturday I went out to take a walk and stopped in to go to confession. The confessor said, "Yeah, did you hear that sermon the new archbishop gave on Wednesday?" I'm thinking, "Is he going to assign it as penance or what?" He was actually kind enough to quote from it, which made me think that I needed to go to confession all over again to deal with a swollen ego!

As a kid, were there particular devotions or saints of which you were especially fond?

I was brought up on the centrality of the Mass, devotion to the Blessed Sacrament, and things like Forty Hours. When you hear Father Andrew Greeley speak about the Catholic imagination as it was expressed once upon a time in May Crownings, Forty Hours devotions, First Communions, serving Mass, it resonates with me. Those were big things for us. They were always thought of as liberating, uplifting, and you looked forward to them. As a kid, in the middle of the very harsh grayness of winter, we would look forward to January 31, the feast of Saint John Bosco, because of our teacher, Sister Mary Bosco. The liturgical calendar would mark time for us. I'm not talking about a Joseph Ratzinger–style Bavarian Catholicism, because this was the American post–World War II suburbs, but still it was almost what Charles Morris talks about as a state within a state, though not in a handcuffed or straitjacketed way.

Have you ever had anything you would describe as a mystical experience?

If you mean an experience of just utter, long ecstasy, as in the lives of the saints, probably not. If you want to talk about periodic epiphanies, yes. There are times in which I'm very aware that this is a moment of grace, that Dolan, you ought to shut up and just bask in this. There have been some of those. I'm afraid there would be many more if I would have the time and patience to let it happen, if I would give the Holy Spirit the entrée.

Talk about what those moments are like.

I'll tell you where I had one, though I hesitate to talk about it, because again people are going to think I'm spiritually proud. A couple of weeks ago, we had in the cycle of readings for the daily Mass the story of David and Uriah. Part of my morning prayer would be to look ahead to the readings, because I know that in just an hour or so I'm going to go over to Saint Patrick's and try to give a little two-minute *ferverino* on the readings. In preparing for that, I had an experience of a very acute appreciation of God's overwhelming mercy, to the point that there were some tears. If that's what you mean by a mystical experience, then yes, I suppose I've had them. They don't come a lot, which I think is more my fault than the Lord's. Am I a mystic? Forget it. Are you kidding?

So it's not like John Paul—if I came to your chapel in the middle of the night, I wouldn't find you prostrate on the floor in the shape of the cross?

Not unless I had fallen out of bed because I had too many beers! No, you would not find me like that. There would also be moments in my life of what you might call exhilaration, which I think is also part of the Catholic ethos. I find myself very conscious that this is something special. I had it last week, the first time I prayed in front of the confessional of the Curé of Ars. That was a very moving moment.

There are other Catholic touchstones in my life, some of which would also have occasioned epiphany experiences. Lourdes, for instance. Lourdes is one of my favorite places on the face of the earth. To be in that crowd and singing "Ave, Ave" is for me a theophany. Seeing the pope is another instance. As many times as it has happened for me, to see the pope remains a spiritually uplifting moment. I've always been a big fan of Don Bosco, who always said the Eucharist, the Blessed Mother, and the pope are the real hallmarks of Catholic identity. Fulton Sheen once said that the mark of a Catholic is to recognize the divine in a baby in the arms of its mother, in a piece of bread consecrated at Mass, and in the voice of an old man in Rome. That means a great deal to me, so those would be touchstone moments as a Catholic in which I would sense a theophany.

Grace also builds on nature, so sometimes my peak spiritual moments come from simple human experiences. For example, the other night, Saturday night, I came back from Ars and had a little free time, so I was finally able to finish reading my Christmas cards. People are very good about sending me cards, and I enjoy sending them myself. To read those cards, to see the pictures of families in whose lives I've played a small part over the years, can also be epiphany moments. Isn't that sacramental, in the best sense? There again is that Catholic worldview, to be able to identify God in all of this.

Getting back to we Catholics in the United States, I wonder if Cardinal Francis George is on to something when he says that in a way, we have become Calvinists. We do see this cleavage between the divine and the human, and indeed there is, but of course the Catholic genius is that they come together in the person of Jesus Christ, whose incarnation continues in and through the Church. The Catholic instinct is to be able to detect the incarnation in something like a Christmas card.

To see a world in a grain of sand, and heaven in a wildflower?

Yes, that's it. I don't know if we get that. Are we failing in some way to teach that? Though how exactly you teach that, I don't know.

By the way, my years at the North American College were a great boon to my spiritual life too, in this sense: Never ever wanting to be a hypocrite, and never wanting to tell anybody to do something that I wasn't doing myself, having responsibility for the spiritual progress of the seminarians made me a better guy. When I talked to them about prayer, when I talked to them about study, when I talked to them about apostolic zeal, when I talked to them about charity and courtesy and hospitality, all of that also became a personal agenda for me. I thought, "Dolan, you'd better walk the talk." *Nemo dat quod non habet.* [No one can give what he does not have.]

In some ways, being the rector of the North American College was like a seven-year retreat. It made me integrate what I was telling the seminarians into my own life. There were major decisions that only my confessor and spiritual director would know that I had to change in my life, things like habits of prayer. I had to make the decision that as much as I like going out at night, except for rare circumstances I wouldn't do it because it was not a good example. The guys needed to see me there, they needed me around, and they didn't need to see me groggy the next morning. They didn't need to see me walking out every night at ten after seven to have dinner with people. They needed to see me in chapel a half hour before Mass. Those were good things for me. Those habits have stayed with me, and thank God. Now more than ever, I need it. We've got our June meeting with the bishops, and this is one of those retreat meetings. They've asked me to give the first talk on priest and bishop, and that question of being a credible role model for our priests is a major challenge. We're to be to our priests what we expect our priests to be to our people.

Do you have moments of doubt?

Yes, I do. I have moments of self-doubt, though you wouldn't know it because people say I come across as very self-confident and knowing what I'm about, and I hope that's true. But I do have moments of self-doubt, where I wonder, am I up to this? Am I the right guy for this? Do I have the words to express this particular idea; am I going to be able to get this across? I think one of the things we should not be afraid to do is to let people know that we have struggles and we have doubts.

There was a powerful moment in my life when I was the associate pastor at Little Flower Parish in Richmond Heights, which illustrates the point. I mentioned before that the pastor was George Gottwald, who was one of the auxiliary bishops. He could come across as very aloof and very distant. He was away from the parish, theoretically helping run the diocese, though in this case spending time at his cabin. We had a tragedy where a little first-grade girl fell off her bike, banged her head against the curb, and died after twenty-four hours in a coma. Of course, the whole parish was in shock. Moses — Bishop Gottwald — came down off the mountain and took the funeral, which he usually never did. I had to talk him into it. I said, "Bishop, you gotta do it."

I will never forget what happened that day. The church was jammed, and here's the bishop, this sort of stern, aloof, distant figure, but who everybody recognized was a great preacher despite all the other criticisms. Gottwald starts off his homily by saying, "I presume a good number of you are here this morning expecting me to explain why this happened, to make sense of it. If that's the case, you're all going to be very disappointed, because I don't think I understand it myself and I'm having a tough time finding meaning in all of this."

He could have stopped there. That was one of the most powerful sermons I ever heard, and those people were very moved by that. Unfortunately, he continued for about a half hour! But everybody remembered that opening line. Here was the bishop, and there were still enough vestiges of this medieval aristocratic figure that they really only saw him periodically. He came off the mountain to be with the parish at a very difficult time, and he admitted his sense of utter helplessness and unworthiness to be there, and his frustration at being unable to give the people what they wanted, namely, a quick, ready answer to this terrible riddle of suffering. Yet in admitting his own insufficiency, he really moved us.

I don't think we should ever be afraid to let people know that. I think Benedict XVI has moments of that—I see that in some of his talks where he will speak about that. Look at the letter he sent around after the Williamson affair. [Note: Richard Williamson is a traditionalist Catholic bishop who has publicly questioned whether the Nazis used gas chambers. Benedict XVI lifted his excommunication, along with three other traditionalist bishops, in January 2009, triggering an international uproar. Afterward Benedict sent a letter to the world's bishops, admitting that the decision to lift the excommunications had not been "clearly and adequately explained."]

How frustrating that had to be for Benedict, that somebody who has staked his theological reputation on trying to bring us together did something that now has caused a serious rupture. You know, the letter was a real exposé of frustration and personal letdown.

That said, I don't think I've ever suffered from trepidation about any job I've ever had. I hope that doesn't come from cockiness or an inflated sense of self. What I really believe is that God never calls you to do something without giving you the grace to do it. My mom, God bless her—the older we get, the more we find wisdom in our parents. When I was asked to be archbishop of Milwaukee, I obviously told my mom a little earlier than the news became public. I was nervous about the whole thing, and I said to her, "I don't know if I've got it." I was a little worried, because obviously Milwaukee had some unique challenges. She remarked, "Well, you know, Tim, the people who made the decision apparently think you do have what it takes, so why worry about it?" That's advice I've always taken to heart.

One other thing I should confess is that as far as the priesthood goes, part of the reason I didn't have any doubts at the beginning is because it was somewhat strategically beneficial in my neighborhood to say that one wanted to be a priest. I often talk about a "culture of vocations," and that's what we had. Growing up, if I went to get my hair cut—and the barber, by the way, was not a Catholic—but if he were to say to me, "So, Tim, what do you want to be when you grow up?" and I said, "I want to be a priest," he'd say, "Hey, what a great idea. Good." Or the neighbors would say, "Hey, Tim, still want to be a priest? What a great idea." The people in my neighborhood who had the most clout were the priests. The first house I can ever remember entering that had central air was the rectory. The first time I ever saw a color TV was the rectory. What silly reasons to attract me to the priesthood! Now, these are obviously not the reasons I love the priesthood today, and they weren't even really the basis of my vocation back then. What they illustrate is the sort of informal support system for vocations we once had, and that's more or less disappeared. All of that also helps explain why I never really struggled with the decision to become a priest, because everything in my little world supported it.

Have you ever had a moment of doubt that it's all true?

No, thanks be to God's mercy, I've never had a moment of doubt where I questioned the whole coherence of the faith. I have, however, questioned the way God is running things. I think I told you why I chose my episcopal motto, *"Ad quem ibimus?"* (To whom else shall we go?) It comes from one of the most normative experiences in my life, when my niece Shannon was struggling with cancer. Shannon is now twenty-one, and she's a beautiful girl.

When Shannon was eight, she was diagnosed with bone cancer. [At this point, Dolan handed me a picture.] There you see her in the midst of chemo. I used to call her *gnochetta*, because she was a little dumpling—this chubby, beautiful, angelic little girl. She came down with this bone cancer while I'm over in Rome. Let me tell you, that was a tough one. Her leg and her very life were in peril. I went through the initial stages with her, so at least I was there for the first surgery, where it doesn't appear they're going to have to remove her leg. After that, I went back to Rome. You know the layout of the North American College. At that time we had a Blessed Sacrament chapel down on the bottom floor in the corner, so if you were walking in the gate, you'd see it on the right. I would sneak down there to pray, and this was weighing on me. You know how when you're away from home, you tend to exaggerate? I was thinking, they're not telling me the truth, she's going to die and they're afraid to tell me, they've probably cut off her leg already and they haven't told me. I found all that very intense. Part of the agony was watching my sister Lisa and her husband going through this at a distance. They're just such good, decent, simple people, Lisa and Chris, and Kelly, her sister. I was thinking, "My God, this is no way to run a railroad." That would be a moment of doubt. I never doubted that God was in charge, but I was really somewhat vexed at the way he was running this.

This was the anger of Job.

Yes, it was. I remember being in that corner chapel one day in Rome saying, "Lord, this is not good, this is no way to run things." Whereupon through the open windows I hear a mother wailing at Bambino Gesu [a pediatric hospital next door to the North American College]. She's wailing over her sick baby, and I get up to close the window, because that was bothering me. As I close the window I'm looking out the corner, and what do I see but a father carrying out a casket in his arms? You're talking about a casket maybe about as big as two shoe boxes. He's carrying it out and putting it in the back of this hearse. Well, that didn't help either. So I sit back down, and I'm really asking, what is going on here, Lord? At that moment, I finally surrendered, asking, "But Lord, to whom else shall I go? You and you alone have the words of everlasting life." That's what Peter said in a moment of frustration, remember, at the end of John 6? Jesus asks, "Are you going to leave me too?" Peter says, "Lord, we often feel like it, because sometimes we don't know what you're talking about. We've told you before you're not making much sense, and this is no way to run a campaign. These people are leaving, and you don't do anything except give us this tough teaching. Yeah, to be honest with you, we're tempted to take off too, to go for greener pastures, but . . . to whom else shall we go? *Ad quem ibimus?* You and you alone have the words of everlasting life."

I remember confessing that, making that act of faith. That prayer, "Lord, to whom shall I go? You and you alone have the words of everlasting life," that's to me the salve, or the answer to that doubt. There are times you, Jesus, don't make much sense at all, and I just love second-guessing you, but I've come to believe that even though sometimes it doesn't make a lot of sense with you, it makes utterly no sense without you, and I don't know where else I'd go. If you want to call that doubt, or weariness, or frustration, you certainly can, but I don't call it sinful. I think it's prayerful, and I think God likes us to talk like that with him.

He's certainly given us other examples in the Scriptures where people he's very fond of talk to him that way.

Let me push this topic one stage further. When you say that in the end you turned everything over to God, I suspect that's something a lot of people could share. What many have a harder time with is the idea that institutional Catholicism is the vehicle through which they ought to do that. Do you ever struggle with that?

Once again, I think you're on to something. When I was in Milwaukee, the first guy I sent to Rome, to the North American College, was a real bright guy. When it came time for him to choose his license topic, he asked me, "What would you like me to research?" I said, "You asked so I'll tell you. How about ecclesiology?" I really think the pivotal question today is ecclesiology. I don't hear a lot of people today having trouble with God, and I don't really hear a lot of people having trouble with Jesus. I hear everybody having trouble with the Church. In some way, we've got to reclaim the identity of Christ in his church. The burning question today is an ecclesiological one.

There's that famous essay by Ratzinger, in which he talks about the modern desire to say yes to Jesus but no to the Church.

As [Henri] de Lubac said, "What would I know of him without her?" For us, they are one. For us, we are on the road to Damascus, you know? "Saul, Saul, why are you persecuting me? I am identified with my church." Just as most people missed the divine in Jesus because of his humanity, so do most people miss Jesus in the Church because of our earthiness, because we are clumsy, we are sinful, we are awkward. But this is how Jesus continues to radiate his grace and mercy, through the Church. There's the leap of faith today. I think

Father Ron Rolheiser says it well: We want a king without the king-dom; we want a shepherd without the other sheep; we want a father, with us as the only child; we want a general without an army; we want to believe without belonging. There's that cleavage, isn't it, and that's the great challenge today.

What I'm asking you, who know the earthiness of the Church better than most, the pettiness and occasional corruption and all that, have you ever had a moment when you sat down and said, "God, I believe in you, but I'm not sure about this church?"

No. If anything, the grittiness, the awkwardness, the clumsiness, the dirt of the Church has only deepened my faith in the divine. I real-ize, of course, most people don't draw that conclusion today. Actu-ally, I think we ought to brag about the earthiness of the Church. I think we ought to say that when Jesus appeared to his apostles after Easter, the first thing he did, after saying "Peace be with you," was to show them his wounds. Yes, true, as the exegetes would say, to prove the reality of the resurrection, but also because just as we have a God who's wounded, we also have a Church that's wounded. We shouldn't be afraid to show off the wounds of the Church to the world, and we should boast that the wounds remind us of the healer. Thank God we are wounded, because that moves us to seek the salve, the oint-ment, the medicine, the antibiotics, that only God can provide. I do think we have a Docetism, a Gnosticism, today. John Tracy Ellis used to say, paraphrasing MacArthur, that old heresies never die, they just fade away and then come back under another name. I do think we have a touch of Gnosticism today, where the Church should really be the country club of the elite. Baloney! The Church is the hospital for sinners.

Not long after I was in Milwaukee, I got a letter from this couple saying, "We're happy to have you, welcome, but by the way we felt obliged to tell you that we've left the Church. We just find it way too scandalous and too corrupt and too icky. We're moving on to look for a church much more to our liking, a much more perfect church." I replied to them — and I've regretted it sometimes, because it was a little catty — but I said, "Thanks for your sentiments, and sorry you feel this way about the Church. When and if you find a more perfect church, don't join it, because then it won't be perfect anymore!"

Isn't that the temptation today? Somewhere there's this Gnostic, perfect church, that's cleansed of all the difficulties we see in the Catholic Church. We're going to find it, and if we don't find it, then we'll just settle for a cup of coffee at Starbucks on Sunday morning and reading the book review in the *New York Times,* and that'll be our moment of transcendence. Then what have we got? It's a church of our own making? You talk about something icky! That's the great temptation, I think. Instead of re-creating God and his church in his own image, we're supposed to let them re-create us in theirs. That's what we're not getting across. But I do think that strategically, we should not be shy about letting the "ickiness" of the Church show. Let's talk about it. That's the great cleansing of Church history, isn't it?

Who was it who said that after years of study I've come to reluctantly accept that the Roman Catholic Church must be divine, because no merely human institution governed by such imbecility could have survived a fortnight! [The line is from Hilaire Belloc.] I use that a lot. People are shocked, because they think we're supposed to defend the pristine beauty of the Church. My dad would tease my mom — for example, she'd say, "Honey, I went to the beauty parlor today. Do you like my hair?" He'd reply, "You ought to get your money back," teasing her. That's how we are with the Church. You grow old together, and as John Tracy Ellis used to say, you love the mystical body, warts and all. I tell priests when I'm preaching retreats, "We're married to her, you know. She's supposed to be our wife, and sometimes we see her with curlers and Noxzema. Sometimes she is a dazzlingly beautiful woman, who we picture walking up the aisle on her wedding day, and sometimes she's a nag. Sometimes she lets us down, and sometimes we think, 'How in the hell did I ever hitch up with this one?' But in the long run, she's the love of our life, and we're head over heels hopelessly in love with her."

You're not so bewitched by the adventure and the beauty of it all that you can't understand how someone could feel profoundly betrayed and abandoned by the Church?

I would consider it tragic, but I could understand that. I'd have to respond, "I'm sorry you feel that way, and from an earthly logic, I'm afraid you make sense." It would be tough for me to judge them. I've been invited to give an address to the priests of Ireland, and I'm thinking about what I want to say. What have we learned from the [sexual-abuse crisis]? Ultimately, isn't it that our faith is not in the Church? I don't make an act of faith in the Church. I make an act of faith in the Son of God, who said I will be with you always, until the end of the world, and that the gates of hell shall not prevail against the Church. I make an act of faith in that.

Archbishop Oscar Lipscomb told me a great story. You know Oscar, what a great raconteur. He once told me about a pivotal moment in his life, which was in a course on the Trinity at the Gregorian University in Rome taught by some world-renowned professor. At the close of the course, which was taught in Latin in the *aula* of the Gregorian, this theologian closes his notes, and as Oscar tells it, the dust and the butterflies and the moths fly out. The theologian takes off his glasses, and he goes into Italian instead of Latin, which means "Now I'm getting personal, boys." He says, "Gentlemen, you must hear me say that when all is said and done, I do not believe in the doctrine of the Trinity." There were gasps and ahs, people were nudging one another, and he said, "You heard me right. I do not believe in the doctrine of the Trinity; my faith is not in the doctrine of the Trinity. My faith is in the God who revealed it to us." Oscar said that was a pivotal moment for him. We have our faith in a person, not in a proposition. That's how it is with the Church, don't you think? My faith is in Jesus Christ, who has revealed himself as being alive and accessible in his Church.

What I used to say to the seminarians was, "If you ask me 'What is the Church?' the answer lies in rephrasing the question. 'Who is the Church?' is really more like it." The Church is the incarnation going on, it's the visible presence of Jesus Christ in the world today. I was just reading this idea in Marmion this morning; the incarnation continues. He was talking about the humanity of Jesus that is often scandalous. We have a savior who was born in a feed box, we have a savior who bled, who cried, who got irritated, who suffered and died. That's the folly, the scandal of the cross, yet that's our God. That incarnation continues in the Church. We have a church bleeding and beaten up and wounded, covered with sores and pus and everything else, but that's where we find God.

You would acknowledge, though, that we haven't always been very good at admitting to the "sores and pus" that cover the Church. Rosmini wrote *Of the Five Wounds of the Holy Church* a century ago, and they wanted to burn him at the stake, yet today they're getting ready to canonize him.

Sure, we can be a little slow. Connie Flavin, my first pastor at Immacolata, was a great convert maker. He was so gentle and good. I sat in once, and he would always try to find out where these people were coming from. They would say, "I believe in God," or "I'm an Episcopalian or a Methodist," and he would gently probe to understand their attraction to the Catholic faith. Often they didn't quite understand it themselves, so he would say, "You know, a theist is somebody who believes in God, a Christian believes that God became one of us in Jesus Christ, and a Catholic is one who believes that Jesus Christ continues in his church." Not bad. Not a bad syllogism for the essence of Catholicism.

Talk about what the Mass means to you.

It means everything to me personally, in that it's the moment of real identification of who I am as a priest. It's the time I am most vividly aware of my identification with Jesus Christ as a priest, even to say, "This is my body, this is my blood," not "This is his body, this is his blood." For me, it's a powerful daily personal reminder of who I am in the eyes of God. It's a reaffirmation of my vocation, my priesthood.

But if I stop there, that could get a little utilitarian and a little self-ish. The Mass isn't just my little tidy personal benefice, my personal shot in the arm. Like a married couple, you know, may have their cup of coffee together in the morning, and it's a reminder that this is the person I've chosen to spend the rest of my life with. But the Mass is also the sacred vehicle where his word is continually preached, and where his very Body and Blood is given to his people to nourish and to strengthen their souls, which is what this is all about. It's the Incarnate Word, where eternity and timeliness come together, the beyond and the here, the heavenly and the earthly; the above and the below are locked together in that one person of the Incarnate Word, and that continues in the sacred liturgy. Heaven and earth are joined. I know that may sound terribly poetic and romantic and theological, but to me there's nothing more practical or real than the Eucharist.

I would say that in the early days of my priesthood, fidelity to the daily Mass, the centrality of the Mass in my own identity and ministry and vocation, was probably something of a dream. I would think, "I know this is how it's supposed to be, and maybe one day it will be." Now it is. Now to me, it's very essential. I reinstituted the custom from

Cardinal O'Connor of daily Mass at Saint Patrick's. Cardinal Egan had not done that, for good reasons. I think he was very wise in saying, "It might be more important for me to get into a parish every Sunday morning." He was indefatigable about that, God bless him. I'm now trying to make my parish visits on Saturday nights and later on Sunday, so I don't miss that too. But for me, to be there daily, visible, at the cathedral, the very locus here in midtown Manhattan — it's like going to Nazareth. You've been to Nazareth, and you see that spot: "Here the word became flesh." That's what the Mass means to me.

Is it frustrating to you that this act, which is supposed to be — and which still is at the theological level — our supreme moment of unity, has become a political football?

Yes, very much so. A lot of that is our fault, a lot of it goes back to our temptation to functionalism and utilitarianism. We look at the Mass only as a project, an initiative, and if we do it right, if we have all the mechanics right, it's going to click. I once concelebrated a Mass for a dying friend on a hospital tray. We didn't have a liturgy committee that helped plan that liturgy, but it was very powerful. You talk about joining heaven and earth, about defining who we are — that meant everything.

I talked before about my frustration with myself and with us as shepherds, that sometimes we don't stare that in the eye. What has happened to our Sunday Mass? Why are only a third of us, on the best of Sundays, attracted to the Mass? If this is such a treasure, which I believe it is, why isn't it just radiating? Now, granted, when you look at a diocese this size, that's not bad. You've got close to a million people who worship every Sunday. Still, we have to be honest enough to admit that the majority of our people are not participating on a regular basis in something we regard as the most sublime experience possible here on earth. We have to ask ourselves why that is.

Let's talk about the sacrament of penance. How often do you hear confessions?

Not enough. I try to hear them once a week, on Fridays. I talked to you about how often I go. There's another moment when I feel very priestly. They certainly don't need me—they've got a good bevy of confessors here. By the way, they do a great confessional trade here, as a good number of churches and parishes do here in Manhattan. I need it for myself, selfishly, because for me to be able to say through the ministry of the Church, "I absolve you from your sins" is a very defining moment. It's a moment of priestly identity, one that I need as I look for these booster shots, these affirmations of who I am. The sacrament of penance does that for me.

There's another critical issue. You've heard me say that from a historian's point of view, in terms of religious sociology, I wonder if we're going to look back and see the disappearance of the sacrament of penance as a huge loss. I think we need to be blunt about that, and I don't know that we are. I send out a little newsletter to the priests every couple of weeks, and recently I wrote to them about the sacrament of penance. I said, "Fellas, I don't have the answer here, but you know better than I do that to borrow the phrase from Mel Allen, the announcer for the Yankees, I'm afraid the sacrament of penance is going, going, gone. It may already be gone. We have to do something to reclaim it." This is one of those beauties and helps that we're blessed with as Catholics, which we don't trumpet enough.

You know who will help us recover it? The RCIA people. [The acronym stands for Rite of Christian Initiation of Adults, the process for preparing adult converts for admission to the Catholic Church.] If you ask the catechumens what they look forward to, or what attracts them about Catholicism, rather often they will mention the possibility of the sacrament of penance, which astounds us. Tragically, it surprises some of our professional catechists, who don't believe in the sacrament and who don't talk about it. But the catechumens feel an attraction to it, that there's something here at the very essence of our very relationship with God, namely, mercy, which is very tangibly expressed in this powerful moment of conversion and reception of divine mercy. I don't think we trumpet it enough. I wonder if we should speak about that more. Why are we reluctant about that? Why, as a preacher, don't I speak about what I just shared with you about the Mass more often? Why don't I speak about the mystery of the sacrament of penance more often?

You said you hear confessions on Fridays. How much time do you spend?

It's only a half hour, although I do more during Lent. I should be more available, for my own good. Now, I don't publicize it when I'm in there. Remember, poor John Paul did it on Fridays during Lent, and they had to choose ten lucky tickets to go to confession with the pope? It's not like that.

There's another aspect too. You talked before about the Church as an "expert in humanity." Over the centuries the basic place where priests picked up their expertise on the human heart was in the confessional. If they're not there, you wonder where they're getting it.

You're right. When we were in Ars, Father George Rutler spoke about John Vianney's familiarity with Satan. He said we all should have that. We should be on a first-name basis, because we're fighting on the same terrain for the same goal, to conquer souls. We shouldn't be comfortable with sin, but we should be very comfortable with sinners.

Did I ever tell you the story that in Milwaukee I once went to a home, state-run but under the auspices of Catholic Charities, to visit these extremely troubled young boys? These were boys who were so violent that when they went to school, the classroom had to have a policeman or a bodyguard on hand. When I visited we were looking in through the barred windows of the classroom, and I asked the principal if I could go in to chat with the students. She said you'd better not, but I kept asking and finally she said okay. I could see that my handlers were nervous, asking themselves, "What's this going to be like?"

When I walked in, there was this little kid, he had to be about nine or ten, and I went up and said, "Nice to meet you. Thanks for letting me come into your classroom and say hello to you. My name's Archbishop Dolan." He looked at me and said, "I am the Devil." Now, that's kind of scary. Of course, everybody gasped. I said back to him — I actually can't remember saying it, but every year when I would go to the fund-raiser someone recounted the story — "Nice to meet you, Devil. It's good to finally meet you in person, because I've known you for a long time. You've been bothering me since I was a kid, and I've been fighting you for a long time, so it's nice to put a face with the name." That startled the boy, because I didn't castigate him, or run out, or act repelled. There was a moment of softening there, so that we could chat a little while. I thought about that — there's a familiarity with sin, with evil, with suffering, that should characterize the life of a priest. We need to say that we are very much at home with those troubled people.

Since you bring it up, if someone comes to you and says, "I need an exorcism," how are you going to react?

I would be very receptive to them, although I might not agree with the vehicle of exorcism except in very severe and very grave cases. I hope I would be receptive to the plea for whatever is available in the vast spiritual arsenal of the Church to help them combat the evil in their lives. I'm close to a priest who does it, an exorcist in another archdiocese, and he's only done it three times in something like thirty years. He thinks two of those three probably hadn't risen to the occasion, but he's convinced one did. He'll always start with first things first: "Are you baptized?" If somebody's coming in off the street, and if we believe in the power of baptism, we ought to ask that first of all. Then he invites them for the sacrament of penance. He says, "You're asking me for help in applying the infinite mercy and power of Jesus Christ to the spiritual combat that you're experiencing, so let's tap into the well of the sacrament of penance." He believes that more often than not, that works, and that's where I would come down. There are other ways, without going to nuclear war, an exorcism, right off the bat.

As far as the whole scenario of spiritual warfare going on, I believe that, and I'm afraid we've lost that. I'm afraid that sometimes we kind of have this overly "I'm okay, you're okay." You know, it's a little embarrassing to get too graphic about the forces of evil versus the forces of good, but I believe that battle is going on. I love the quote that Satan's most powerful tool is having convinced us he doesn't exist.

ELEVEN

Why Be Catholic?

Once upon a time, most Catholics could go their entire lives without ever seriously pondering the question raised in a 1982 rock song by the Clash: "Should I Stay or Should I Go?" When Catholicism was coextensive with culture, and when one lived and moved in largely homogeneous Catholic families, schools, and neighborhoods, the question of religious affiliation generally never arose, except in rare individual cases. The typical attitude in Catholic culture was memorably captured by James Joyce, whose literary alter ego, Stephen Dedalus, at one point in *A Portrait of the Artist as a Young Man* realizes that he has lost his faith. When asked if he would now become a Protestant, Dedalus replies: "I said that I had lost the faith, not self-respect." In other words, even a lapsed Catholic of that era couldn't really imagine himself as anything other than a Catholic.

At least in the developed West, those days are long gone. One of the primary consequences of secularism is to erode homogeneous religious enclaves, so that religious affiliation shifts from being a matter of cultural inheritance to a matter of individual choice. Today, if one is to be a practicing, active Roman Catholic, it will generally not be the result of simple cultural momentum. In fact, in many ways the prevailing cultural winds pull people in the opposite direction, away from active religious commitment in general, and away from the Roman Catholic Church in particular. Certainly massive coverage of the sexual-abuse crisis over the last decade has not been a particularly strong selling point for Catholicism, and increasingly popular perceptions of the Church tag it not as an inclusive family of faith but as a right-wing political lobby. Whether that's congenial to one's politics or not, you don't need to belong to a church to advance that agenda. (The rise of the so-called "theo-cons" in Europe, many of whom are atheists but supportive of the conservative cultural positions of Catholicism, illustrates the point.)

All that comes on top of intra-Catholic developments over the last fifty years that have also eroded some of the traditional reasons people remained in the Church's fold. Theologians and Church historians rightly insist that Catholicism never actually taught *extra ecclesiam nulla salus* — that outside the Church there is no salvation. Among the Church fathers, Justin Martyr taught that ancient Greek sages such as Socrates and Heraclitus, who "lived according to reason," had been saved, and centuries later Dante described meeting Ripheus the Trojan in Paradise, describing him as a virtuous pagan saved by the mercy of God. Yet at the level of popular Catholic understanding, it was widely believed for centuries that baptism and membership in the Church were essential for salvation, which among other things fueled support for the Church's missionary activity. In the period after the Second Vatican Council (1962–65), that popular Catholic psychology crumbled in favor of the view that non-Catholics and non-Christians who try to live upright lives will be embraced by God in the afterlife. While that's arguably a much more generous view, it also inevitably softens the boundaries between religious options and induces some Catholics to ponder other possibilities.

And ponder they certainly do. A 2009 Pew Forum study on religion in America concluded that the Catholic Church in this country loses four existing members for every one new member it attracts. Even though the study also concluded that Catholicism has one of the highest retention rates among major denominations in America, its ratio of exits to entrances clearly constitutes a numbers problem. At the moment those defections are being masked by an enormous influx of Hispanic immigrants in America, two out of three of whom are Catholic. One may legitimately wonder, however, whether those Hispanic immigrants will remain Catholic into the second and third generation, as the effects of secular culture begin to take hold, and as the dynamic religious marketplace in America introduces them to other options (especially the rapidly growing panoply of Pentecostal Christianity).

Given all this, the odds are good that a growing number of American Catholics, at one point or another in their lives, will be forced to ask themselves, "Should I stay or should I go?" The ability of the Church's pastors, spiritual guides, and lay leaders to offer a compelling answer to that question will, therefore, have a great deal to say about Catholic fortunes in America.

The typical modern person may be open to God, to the idea of transcendence, to the idea of a spiritual journey, but they look at the Catholic Church and what they often see is a mess. Ultimately, why be Catholic? If you can have a relationship with God and spare yourself the heartburn, why bother?

I think we have to approach it in two different ways. First of all, we have to make the argument to those who are already Catholic: Why stay? Why take your Catholic religion seriously? Why be fervent in your faith, when we're so aware of the clumsiness, the sinfulness of people in the Church? As a matter of fact, we can look beyond us and see people whom we admire very much, who seem to be getting along with lives of virtue and piety rather well and pretty much on the road to salvation, yet not as practicing Catholics. So, why remain?

Let's take that one first. In some ways I think we have to reclaim a tradition that we're in danger of losing, one that is another great area of similarity with our Jewish brothers and sisters, which is that we're simply "born Catholic," and for better or worse it's a constituent element of who we are. I think the only traditions who would fall into this category are Muslims, Jews, Catholics, and the Orthodox, the so-called "inherited religions." There are dangers in that outlook, I know, and we've seen some of those dangers in the past, but the core idea is a good one—that being a Catholic is not something you choose, it's who you are. Jesus and his church have claimed us, not vice versa.

It's a birthright?

That's exactly right. We are a Catholic, or a Jew, simply because we were born one. You no more choose your way of approaching the Creator than you do your family. You were born into a supernatural family. For the vast majority of us, that happens to be the case. Of course, in contemporary religious sociology, that's regarded as a deficit. It means we can take our faith for granted, we can drift into a listlessness about it, and we never have to freely, deliberately, and responsibly choose that this is the way I want to spend the rest of my life. There is a challenge there, but I still believe we need to reclaim the understanding of Catholicism as a birthright. You didn't choose me, I chose you—or as the Jews say, we didn't choose to be Jews; we are the "chosen people." It's a settled part of our identity, so that it is part of our spiritual DNA to be Catholic. That's a catechetical challenge to which I don't think the Church today is rising. The way I try to make the point is that when I look out on Sunday, I say that as Catholics we are part of a supernatural family. Just as with our natural families, we may have our tensions and our frustrations, but ultimately this is who we are. Our fates are bound together, for better and for worse.

What about those who would say, "It's not that I don't want to be in the Church, it's that the Church doesn't want me in it"?

Sometimes we have that feeling about our natural families too, right? I may feel like I never wanted to walk away from the family, but they've made me feel unwelcome because I have a girlfriend, or I'm living with somebody, or whatever. Yes, there's something there. But when we say that the Church is a family, isn't that more about a kind of utter dependence because we have been chosen and adopted by God, not because of anything we've done or anything we've proved? We are simply clay in the potter's hand, and that can be very beautiful and liberating, can't it? The real analogy for being Catholic is not so much marriage as birth. You're born into this family. We have to recapture that in some way, with all its glory, though without denying some of the corollaries that are a little difficult to reconcile. To reclaim the beauty of that, the utter humility of that, is a good thing, without denying that all families have their problems, and God knows we've got ours in the supernatural family of the Church.

There's another point here worth making, in terms of what we say to those already in the fold but struggling with whether to stay. Recently I gave a day of recollection to the priests of the archdiocese for Advent, so we were up at Saint Joseph's [Seminary] at Dunwoodie. We had a great turnout of priests. I spoke on the three comings of Christ: history, mystery, and majesty. On the coming of Christ in majesty, in that twenty minutes of reflection, I said, "Brothers, there are certain things in this world, and in the Church, that are never going to be perfect until Christ comes again at the end of time. Even though our American sense of Puritanism, Pelagianism, and pragmatism thinks that we can make things perfect, we can't." I wonder if part of the problem today is that we expect a Gnostic perfect Church, and it frustrates the hell out of us when we don't have it. We have to be realistic without ever giving up our dreams. We have to keep our ideals without becoming ideologues, and we have to keep our zeal without becoming zealots. The Church is never going to be perfect, and somehow we have to make our peace with that.

That's what you say to those already in the family. What about those on the outside looking in?

In other words, why would anyone join this family, which often can seem dysfunctional? I just say, "Look, I don't know about you, but when it comes to my relationship with God, I need all the help I can get. It's awfully fragile, my relationship with God. I know it's at the core of my being, I know that life makes no sense without it, but as is often the case with life, those things that are most definitive and most normative about us are the things that we don't really cultivate or that we take for granted. That's certainly true with our relationship with God, so I need all the help that I can get to cultivate that, to understand that. I don't know of any institution on the face of the earth that helps to cultivate that and to bring it to fruition like the Catholic Church. If you really want to know, love, and serve Jesus Christ, as you've told me you do, I invite you into a great drama and adventure called Catholicism. If we do this right, it's going to help you know, love, and serve him in a way that you never thought possible. As a matter of fact, it's the way he's told us that he would like most people to come to know, love, and serve him. So, why don't you give it a whirl?"

Here's the pitch: Let me help introduce you to what I think is one of the more consoling, challenging ways to know, love, and serve Jesus Christ, who is the Way, the Truth, and the Life, the beginning and the end—who is, in the words of John Paul II, the answer to the question posed by every human life. Come on in, because this is the best way to do it. I don't know about you, brother or sister, but if you're like me, you need a lot of help, and I'll tell you where you can find it. Let's just say that we're in this together. If you're struggling down a path trying to get to a goal that you're not sure about, it's a heck of a lot better if you find two or three others on the same trail. They may have as many flaws as you, and they may not have the exact map either, but it's sure a lot better to be with some people trying their best to get to the same place. When we pool our talents and resources, we're probably going to be able to get there better. That's the mystery, the invitation, of the Church that I think we've got to pose.

Ratzinger once wrote that in the end, the only two compelling arguments on behalf of the Catholic Church are the artists and the saints it's produced. In a way, they are the proof, aren't they, that this support system you're talking about works?

You got it. The argument has to be that the Church will allow what's best in you, what's most noble and authentically human, to flourish. That's not to say, of course, that anybody who joins the Catholic Church is automatically going to become some great saint or artist, because the plain fact of the matter is that most of us aren't. The point is that whatever your spiritual and human potential is, there's a community here, a family, that will help you develop it, in a way that I frankly don't believe you can find anywhere else on the face of the planet.

At some level, is it a surprise to you that more people haven't walked away from the Church, given the blows to its public image in recent years?

In my mind, we cannot underestimate the common sense of our Catholic people. They're able to distinguish between the sins of priests and bishops, for example, and the bedrock of their faith. They know that the Church is filled with sinners, but the Church itself is something they would die for. It represents what is most pure, most noble, what gives meaning to their lives. In a way they're gritting their teeth and saying, "We're not going to let the sins of priests, nuns, bishops, even popes, take our faith away." Does every layperson say that? I've met enough people in my life who didn't have the favorable experience I had at Holy Infant Parish, who might blame a nun, for example, for the fact that they haven't been to a Catholic church since May Crowning in eighth grade. I know you can't always count on Catholics to be commonsense enough to say that the sins, the errors, the arrogance and corruption of certain people in the Church is not enough to damage their faith. Does it ever! But I think that in general, Catholic people are savvy enough to know that there's a big distinction here. I was inspired by a recent article by former New York governor Mario Cuomo, who wrote that priests and bishops have been sinners since Holy Thursday, and that such scandal, as real as it is, will never destroy his faith.

By the way, I'm convinced that such savvy is especially likely to kick in when people have been exposed to the basic Catholic ethos I've tried to describe. Let me tell a story from Holy Infant Parish that may help make the point. We often teased poor Father Callahan, our pastor, and this might be a parable for something. At the parish there was a huge field, a soccer and baseball field, and it was basically pure dust. Every year when the winds would come, the dust would blow, and yet every spring Father Callahan would have it planted by the men of the parish. Every year on the Major Rogation Day, which is in April, all the kids of the school would be out there with him in a cope and the holy water, blessing the barren, muddy field so it would grow grass. Nothing ever happened, but he would never give up. Every year he's out there, and we're praying and sprinkling holy water, and the men of the parish are plowing and planting seed. Sure enough, when the first quasi drought in Saint Louis would come in June, with the heat and the humidity, there would just be dust all over. The men would laugh and open a can of beer, and sit around and smile about it. The point was, you never gave up. There was a sense of hope, and it was your approach to life. In many ways, I discovered sort of an Old Testament approach to life, a confidence that things are going to work out. There are setbacks galore, there are imperfections galore, but God's in charge. There's a basic trust, and people who have imbibed that are much less willing to simply let it go.

At least for people who grew up in a Catholic family, I also think their attitude to the Church is often shaped by their experiences in the home, whether those experiences were fundamentally good or bad. If you were in a Catholic school like I was, and then went home to an old man who was drunk and who took his belt to his wife and the kids, it obviously would not have had a positive effect. When I went home, however, Mom was still there ironing. She was far from June Cleaver, but she'd have cocoa when we came home. Dad would come home and give my mom a kiss, then he'd open a beer and we'd sit and chat, or in the summer, play catch. Then it was all coherent, wasn't it? It all blended together. It was sort of the way it was supposed to be, the way that Christopher Dawson speaks about Christendom in the Middle Ages—a kind of seamless, complete way of life that, at its best, felt more like a warm blanket than a choke collar.

In trying to answer the question "Why be Catholic?" is it frustrating to you that it's often much easier to tell bad news about the Church than anything positive?

That's terribly frustrating. The exuberance, the warmth, the growth, the revival, that you see in the Church is not "the story." . . . That's news, but it's not out there. The boilerplate story about Catholicism in the United States, arguably since the false accusations against Cardinal Joseph Bernardin, so we're talking more than two decades, has been the sex-abuse thing. No matter where you're at, it comes up. I was up in Albany two weeks ago for the New York State Catholic Conference. We've got about two thousand people, probably half of whom are in their senior year in high school through college, ages seventeen through twenty-five. They're very interested in the pro-life message, very interested in health care, very interested in immigration, crowding our workshops. They're very interested in the schools stuff, very interested in good government, which is the crisis in Albany. They're reverent, attentive, and enthusiastic at Mass. But when I went to the press conference, question number one was about giving Holy Communion to pro-abortion Catholic politicians, and number two was the sex-abuse thing and the rollback of the statute of limitations. Does that make me want to pull the three hairs I've got left out of my head? Yes. Now, to say this might seem like sour grapes, and I suppose it feeds impressions that I am in an ivory tower and don't get it, or that I'm trying to guide us to a story that I want covered, and we're not about to do that because we're hard-hitting journalists. Yet if a reporter really wants to tell the story of the Catholic Church today, how can you come to an event like that and utterly ignore the passion and the goodness of those young people? Isn't that part of the mix too?

Obviously no reporter is going to take your word for it. Why do you think ordinary Catholics themselves don't tell that story?

A number of reasons. I've thought about that a lot. One, I think, is a theological reason. I don't think Catholics are comfortable talking about their faith. They were raised theologically in a way that meekness, humility, is considered a virtue, and we're not in-your-face Bible thumpers. Second, there's a cultural thing. I don't think we can exaggerate the fact that part of the Catholic ethos, the Catholic upbringing in America, is that we should avoid talking about religion in public. That's just how you're raised. John Tracy Ellis talked about "Maryland-style Catholicism, a distinctly American expression of Catholicism which bent over backwards to keep religion interior and to reassure a culture that's skeptical at best, and hostile at worst, that they have absolutely nothing to fear from us Catholics, because we're just like them. There's a cultural element there, meaning that we don't really want to talk about religion because it's not polite. Third, our people aren't equipped with a vocabulary to talk about this stuff. If I cornered a couple of people last night, at a vicariate gathering of hundreds of people for vespers and a reception, and said to them, "Isn't this great?" they would have replied, "Oh, yeah, we love coming here." But if I said, "Don't you think this is a great sign of the renewal that's going on in the faith that when you've got a clear, confident, joyful presentation of the Catholic message people will flock to it?" Their reaction would probably be to say, "We're not sure what that means. We're just happy coming here. The Mass is beautiful, the preaching is good, we really love the sisters, the priests are always concerned about us, the school is excellent, and we always feel welcome here." They wouldn't have a vocabulary to talk about a new springtime, or seeing something good going on in the Church.

Do you think we're destined to live with this disjunction between what outsiders see in the Catholic Church and what insiders actually experience?

I do. To get evangelical here, I presume, although I'm hoping it doesn't take that long, but I presume what we're going to have to do is what the early Christians did for the first four centuries of our existence—try our best to claim some credibility in culture and society, through love and joy. That's how Christianity eventually prevailed, though of course, Constantine helped! In general, that's the snowball effect that helped the Church grow in rather tumultuous times during the first four centuries.

When the prevailing culture was hardly friendly . . .

That's right. In some strange way, these Christians, this Church, represented something alluring, something cogent, something worth looking into, something that causes you to shake your head and say, "They've got something there worth investigating." Is that the only apologetic we're left with? Probably. But is that such a bad thing? Can we lure people in now through marriage — you know, you're marrying a Catholic, so we're getting a new Catholic, plus your kids are going to be Catholic? I doubt it. Can we lure people in anymore because we run the best hospital system, we got the best education system? I don't think so. That institutional bait really isn't there anymore, is it? So what do we have left but a real sense of love and joy?

Pardon me for being a name-dropper, but in my meeting with President Obama, he said, "The government can't give hope, and the government can't love. You in the church can, and please keep doing it." In the long run, isn't that the only thing we have to offer? Perhaps one of the things that Irish, Polish, even Bavarian culture maybe teaches us is that even when things seem to be clicking, even when you've got a hand-in-glove relationship with church and culture, is that the answer? Maybe not, because Lord knows what we're seeing now is the decimation of those cultures, to some extent through our own failures. Of course there are some who say no, that all the cultural problems of the moment began when the Church started losing its institutional grip, and it became "anything goes."

These are probably the same sort of people who 150 years ago were lamenting the collapse of the Papal States. Flash-forward a century, and Paul VI is saying this is the best thing that ever happened to us.

Sure, absolutely. My sense is that we are fated for the moment to live in a world in which the Church cannot rely on power or on a massive institutional apparatus to lure people in the door. The only selling point we have is building strong, healthy, loving, joyful communities that somehow "sell themselves" by being places people want to be, where they feel connected to the transcendent and to one another. That may seem like a steep hill to climb, but my sense is that it's when we're climbing that hill that we're at our best. I enjoy the novels of Dean Koontz, for instance. A few years ago I wrote him and suggested that he was writing of "Catholic things" in his novels. I wondered if he were a Catholic. The author kindly replied, informing me that, as a matter of fact, he had become a Catholic. He had been attracted by the worldview, the great art and literature, and the reverent worship. That's what I'm talking about: the allure of the Church.

TWELVE

Hope

In the movie *The Shawshank Redemption,* Tim Robbins plays a banker who is convicted of murdering his wife and spends a long stretch in a Maine prison. While there, he patiently sends letters year after year to the state legislature appealing for resources to expand the prison library. Worn down by his persistence, officials finally ship off cartons of books and records to the prison. The day they arrive, Robbins's character barricades himself in the warden's office and plays an aria from an opera by Mozart over the prison loudspeakers, an act of rebellion for which he is predictably tossed into solitary confinement. When he finally emerges, he tells his friends that he carried the memory of the music with him into the hole, and that it gave him hope. His best friend, played by Morgan Freeman, warns that hope is a dangerous thing in prison because it can get you killed. Robbins responds: "Hope is a good thing, maybe the best of things, and no good thing ever dies."

Here's another movie reference illustrating the same point. In the biopic *Milk,* about the life and death of the first openly gay elected official in the United States, San Francisco city councilman Harvey Milk, viewers see Milk in the early stages of his career angrily protesting the abuse of homosexuals by police, businesses, and even the political establishment. His message plays well among a certain core of activists, but

Milk routinely loses elections. Finally, one of his opponents pulls him aside to tell him that his pitch has to become more hopeful if he wants to stir hearts. "You've got to give them hope," he says.

Whatever one makes of those bits of Hollywood philosophy, they illustrate a lesson that every successful entrepreneur and leader, from politicians to used-car salesmen, from sports coaches to financial consultants, learned long ago: Hope sells.

One hardly needs to scour the Internet Movie Database or the annals of American politics, however, to absorb that lesson. Ultimately, what fueled the rise of Christianity during the early centuries of Church history was that amid the crumbling of the Roman Empire and the general dissolution of ancient Hellenistic culture, Christianity offered a message of hope—hope rooted in the steadfast conviction that whatever the vicissitudes of the moment, ultimately history is a story of salvation. Easter Sunday always follows Good Friday, so death is always swallowed up by resurrection. As Christian preachers over the centuries have often put the point, history is a story whose middle chapters may contain plenty of surprises, but we already know how it ends—and it ends well.

The appeal of Catholicism at any given moment in time, therefore, will to a great extent rise or fall upon the extent to which it successfully projects a message of hope. That was part of the logic that led Pope Benedict XVI to devote his second encyclical letter, *Spe Salvi*, to the theme of hope. The pope argued that Christianity offers a deep hope, a transformative hope, one that goes beyond what human effort alone can achieve, or what vague spiritualities without a personal God can promise. He contrasted the hope offered by Christ with the putative liberations of revolutionaries such as Spartacus, Barabbas, and Bar-Kokhba, arguing that Christ's emphasis on changing the human heart before the social order offers hope of transforming the world from the inside out.

In *Spe Salvi*, Benedict XVI may have outlined the intellectual and spiritual scaffolding, so to speak, of the Catholic understanding of hope, but it's an open question how much that message has penetrated to Main Street. Looking at institutional Catholicism today, many outside observers, and even many Catholics, may struggle to think of "hope" as the top note in the Church's public image. In other words, Catholicism needs someone who can take the content of *Spe Salvi,* and the long tradition of Christian hope upon which that encyclical built, "mass market"—effectively broadcasting not only a message of hope but also a compelling personal example of what a hopeful life looks and feels like. At the grass roots, plenty of Catholics already do that, but usually far from the public spotlight. Increasingly, some Catholics find themselves wondering if—indeed, hoping that—Archbishop Timothy Dolan's most important role in the Church will be precisely as such an "apostle of hope" on the American public stage.

As you look around at the Catholic Church today, where do you see signs of hope?

If you have eyes to see, I think you can find them all over the place. For example, my experience as rector of the North American College certainly gave me a revived sense of hope, even though as you know, my gas tank wasn't running low on that anyway. To see these young guys, 95 percent of whom are as wholesome and as hopeful and as genuine and sincere as you can get, I'm thinking, "God's taking care of the Church." Or, how about something as simple as Mass last night [Dolan celebrated Mass in Spanish at Our Lady of Guadalupe at Saint Bernard's], or Mass this morning at Saint Patrick's? These were packed houses, full of enthusiasm and life. Of course, I'm not naïve. I know there's a crisis. I know that unfortunately two-thirds of our people weren't at Mass this morning. I looked at our seventy-seven seminarians in the Archdiocese of New York earlier this morning, and I thank God for them, but I also know we could have three times that many and it would not be enough. I'm aware of the statistical challenges. But when I look around, I see enough positive energy to convince me that there's hope.

Of course, I also recognize that I'm inclined to see hope in the Church, because I look at her through the eyes of someone deeply in love. I told you about my friend who's buried in Rome at the Campo Verano. The only thing he wanted on his tombstone was DILEXIT ECCLESIAM, "He loved the Church." I would hope that it could be my epitaph too. I just have this romantic boyhood love of the priesthood and of the Church. By the way, that's made the whole sex-abuse thing personally excruciating for me, because I still have this altar-boy image of the priesthood. These days when somebody comes up to you and says, "I used to be an altar boy," you want to call the diocesan lawyer because you think, "What's the next line going to be?" Yet for me, that whole love of the Church is still there, and somebody in love is always going to be a hopeful person.

I suppose another element of my own hopefulness is that I've been blessed to know some really bright people in the Church over the years. For example, you know that I worked under Pio Laghi in the nunciature in Washington. Laghi was a "peasant," in the best sense of the word. When I use the word *peasant,* I truly mean it as a compliment. John XXIII and John Paul II were peasants, in that they were men of the earth. Pio Laghi was that way, as I think our last nuncio, Archbishop Pietro Sambi, is too—earthy, incarnational, sacramental, and realistic. I hope I have some of that. You can't come to know people like that and then succumb to the notion that everything about the Church is somehow bleak.

Laghi, by the way, also has a great sense of humor. I remember once I was doing some correspondence, and I wrote that the nuncio can't come in July because he'll be on vacation. It came back crossed out, and he said, "Nuncios never go on vacation, they go on 'extended consultations.'" So I wrote back that the nuncio will be in Europe on "extended consultations." I answered another letter once, turning down an invitation with too much emotion: "Even though in my heart I would have a passion for being with you, it is with the deepest of regrets that I must say no, even though it pains me to have to say I'm afraid I'll be unable to come." He crossed it out and said, "This is a little too much. We tell lies, but only if they are venial sins!"

Finally, I think some of my basic cheerfulness about my own life and circumstances comes from my own family. As is obvious from my book based on the conferences I gave at the North American College, I sometimes think there still is clericalism and guys are spoiled. To me, there's nothing more sobering than going to my sister's house, with their six kids. I mean, I'm going to complain? Her husband is working two jobs and then coming home and changing diapers. That's stress. They're in debt, they're borrowing money, and I'm going to complain? All I can think is, what a blessed life I have.

You've been in the spotlight for a long time now. What have you learned about how to present a message of hope to this twenty-first-century world?

I've learned a couple of things. On the theoretical level, the theological level, I have come to find out that merely to emphasize hope in itself, which obviously isn't a bad thing, doesn't do it. Hope must flow from faith. Faith has to be part of it. The reason I am a man of hope, the reason the Church is a people of hope, is precisely because of faith. My faith is that there is a God who happens to love us, who happens to hold us in the palm of his hand, who happens to have sent his only begotten Son to save us and to promise us eternity, and who assured us that he'll be with us always even to the end of days, and who inspired Paul to write that ultimately everything works to the good for those who believe. That's faith, okay? From that theological virtue of faith, hope will flow. Connie Flavin used to say that faith tells us there is a God, hope tells us that this God has made promises that he keeps. Faith and hope are essential. If you only emphasize hope, there's a risk of becoming some sunny, Pollyannaish cheerleader. It has to be intimately tied to faith.

Second, how we mirror and reflect hope usually comes more from who we are than from what we do. If you can exude a sense of confidence and serenity, and especially joy, right away that is going to be a teaser to people to ask, "Why is he that way? Why is she that way?" It's somewhat like Jesus in front of Pontius Pilate. Jesus amazed Pilate simply because of his serenity, his steadfastness, his utter clarity about his identity and his mission in front of a man who had all the power in the world and who literally could decide if he lived or died. That he found tantalizing. Our message of hope sometimes is simply how we come across, who we are. If people can see that in the midst of whatever you're going through, you still do seem to reflect a sense of faith, an assurance, a sense of serenity and joy, I think that accomplishes more than any sermon or any treatise.

Ultimately, it gets not to a *what* or a *how* but a *who*—namely, Jesus. I often feel like the Church today is reduced to Peter and John in the Temple square that first Pentecost with the beggar asking, "Can you give me some money?" The apostles reply, "Gold and silver I have not, but what I do have let me give you. In the name of Jesus, stand up and walk." That's the Church today. We somewhat have been reduced to having no more gold or silver, which isn't a bad place to be, if you think about it. What do we have anymore? Physically, what do we have institutionally, to give us any clout? Sure, we still have some. We still have Saint Pat's, we have the pizzazz of a Saint Patrick's Day Mass where people want to come. But in the long run, that's pretty much cotton candy, isn't it? What else do we really have but Jesus Christ? It's like the woman caught in adultery in our Gospel last Sunday. She looked up, and all she saw was Jesus. That's sort of where I'm at now, it's where the Church is at. Sometimes we regret that, but I'm happy about it. That gives us hope, doesn't it?

Hope can actually be a "new apologetic" for us. Some in the world do not see any reason for faith, but rare is the person who admits he or she does not need hope. As my friend Father Benedict Groeschel observes, "They tell me they have no faith, so I ask them if they have any hope. That's a starting point."

How successful do you feel you are in changing the point of departure for the public conversation about the Church, so it's no longer focused on the institutional dimension or management questions but on what's truly fundamental, which is the encounter with Christ?

How successful I am I don't know, but what I do know is that this is perhaps the critical challenge facing American Catholicism today. We can't take the bait of allowing culture to reduce us to a purely managerial posture.

How do you do that?

It's a strategy of trying always to return to the spiritual, to the person of Jesus Christ, and never allowing a situation to pass that you don't get back to that. You always try, sometimes desperately and often unsuccessfully, to get back to the root, to bring it back home. You almost try to see everybody you meet, as antagonistic or skeptical or just plain apathetic as they might be, as in some way really saying what the Greeks asked Philip: "Sir, we'd like to see Jesus." You always try to see that question in everybody and in every situation. That becomes almost a mind-set. That's the tools you bring, the hearing aid you wear. Everything somebody says to me, ultimately I'm going to reduce to the question "Sir, we would like to see Jesus." I've got to show them. Now, does that sound nebulous? I'm sure it does. But in my experience, it's actually terribly practical. For example, I try never to have a priests' council meeting without making sure that somewhere, somehow, in my remarks, we will get back to Jesus and his Gospel, to the salvation of souls and the extension of his love, message, and mercy. I will try my best to articulate that.

In terms of choices about how I spend my time, one thing I am conscious of is a preferential option for the spiritual. It's something that was probably always there, but it's something that I've now identified. For instance, when my secretary and I spend about an hour once a week going through invitations, I find myself perking up when a guy says, "Will you come and close Forty Hours devotion?" In the scheme of things, that's a relatively minor occasion. Even so, if I have a choice, and on that afternoon I could also be with some influential group that wants me to come by for supper, because they're also having the mayor and all, I'd probably still go with the closing of the Forty Hours. I do believe with all my heart and soul, "Seek ye first the kingdom." It's the same reason I celebrate Mass every morning at Saint Patrick's. Sometimes I get a little clash even in my office, let's say for breakfast meetings. They'll say we have to have this breakfast meeting at seven A.M., because that's the only time these people can come, and you've got to see them." In general I've said no to that sort of thing, because people need to know that the archbishop of New York has seven-thirty Mass every morning at Saint Patrick's. The rest of the schedule hinges on that, not vice versa, and that says something not only about my priorities but about what the Church is truly all about. That, to me, is a teachable moment. That's something I need to say. It's the same for Sunday Mass at the cathedral. As you can imagine, I get tons of invitations for Sunday morning. Will there be times I take one? Yes, but rarely. This is a priority for me. I think it says something to my priests and people that the greatest act I can perform is to pray with and for my people, with the greatest prayer that we have, and to do that in the mother Church is, to me, supreme. Rare would be the time when I would break that commitment.

We're talking about hope, but you can't be hopeful in every moment. When your heart is heavy, what do you worry about?

I like to draw a distinction between concern and worry. I'm concerned about a lot of things, but I think one can make a good case that pervasive worry is actually sinful. It's a sin against hope. I try not to worry myself silly about anything, because that would violate the hope that's a big part of my makeup. That said, my major concern would be that our focus is too much on what you would call the managerial and superficial things, instead of on Jesus Christ. At the end of the day, when I look back at what were the major things I had to deal with today, most of the time they're money, they're personnel, the latest headline and the latest crisis. It's the swine flu outbreak at such-and-such parish. So I ask myself, have I spent as much time trying to see that Jesus Christ is known and loved as I have on all that other stuff? We are lopsided in our concerns, so that we're tempted to forget the primary thing.

Is the fundamental way to offer hope to form communities alive with the encounter with Christ?

To form persons who see themselves in light of Christ, and then those persons will form a community. This is where we differ from the evangelicals, right? We don't stop with the formation of the person, because for us that individual person then becomes part of a people. I like the slogan from the United Way, even though the grammar's wrong: "Think of we instead of me." In the Church, we think of we instead of me. That's why I'm not looking forward to saying "I believe in God, the Father Almighty" on Sundays with the change in the creed, even though that is what Nicaea said, so I can see the logic for it.

In a very basic way, I believe with all my heart and soul that being a faithful, committed Catholic is one of the happiest, healthi-est ways to go through this life, and to spend eternity. I don't know what I'd do without my faith. When I go to wakes and the simplest truck driver in the world, who just lost his wife, says to me, "Father, I don't know what I'd do without my faith," he means it. I know what he's talking about. The corollary to that is that a particularly exciting way to spend that Catholic life is in the priesthood. I couldn't think of a better way to spend one's life than as a priest. Is it for everybody? No. I'm kind of glad it wasn't for my dad! To narrow it even further, a particularly exciting way to spend one's priesthood is as a parish priest. Only about eight years of my priesthood were spent in a parish, but they were probably the happiest, and it's the way I try to view my job description here. I'm a pastor of the parish that happens to be called the Archdiocese of New York. . . . I've always seen part of my work as a priest and a bishop as trying to extend the experience I had as a child, of a happy, loving family and parish, beyond, now that I'm able to do that.

I happen to have an upbeat, fearless, embracing view toward cul-ture, and I sometimes worry I'm not getting across that I'm not at all blind to the fact that there's a lot of diabolical, evil stuff there, and we have to be constantly vigilant. I'm not blind to the sin of the world. But we have to balance that with the steadfastness that allows us to keep trying and never give up. I know the message that the world tries to send much of the time, which is that lofty ambitions are a dead end, and the most we can realistically hope for is maybe a comfortable couch and a big-screen TV where we can be left alone. You know the saying: "You can't win, and you can't even tie!" God knows there's enough pain and failure and frustration out there to make that sentiment feel credible. Yet the amazing message of Christianity is "You can win!" In fact, Christ has already won, and so all the suffering and heartache we see around us is transitory. We can persevere, knowing that we're in the hands of a loving God. That's fairly simple to say and incredibly tough to live, but if we believe it and live it credibly, the world's going to look at us and see hope. Isn't that why the Church has grown so rapidly in the poorest, most war-torn, suffering nations in the world? Governments cannot give ultimate hope, nor can possessions or power. Yet a man who rose from the dead, and who wants to share that triumph with us in his church, sure can.

What This Book Is Not

This may seem an odd way to conclude, but I'd like to spell out here three things that this book is not—if for no other reason than to head off reviewers pointing them out for me!

First of all, this is obviously not a conventional journalistic profile of Archbishop Timothy Dolan, which would involve a careful reconstruction of his life and career, along with a variety of different points of view about what Dolan represents. There are some third-party observations scattered throughout the book, from the verdict of the Survivors Network of Those Abused by Priests about his record on the sexual-abuse crisis ("abysmal") to the comment from a former classmate that Dolan was marked as a rising star in the Catholic Church from the first moment he set foot on seminary grounds. Yet the overwhelming bulk of the book is obviously Dolan speaking in his own voice.

My aim here was not so much to profile Dolan as to share his thinking with a broad public, to deepen the familiarity with him for those who already know him, and to introduce him to those who don't. Whether or not one agrees with his worldview, either on the details or the big picture, this is a man destined to be a towering point of reference in the Catholic Church in the United States for at least the next couple of decades, and therefore it's worth knowing something about how he thinks. Rather than comprehensiveness, what I was aiming for is more akin to a painting by Monet—a sort of impressionistic portrayal of Dolan.

Nor was this a hardball-style interrogation, in which my primary aim was to press Dolan aggressively to account for controversial chapters in his own history or to defend the various failures of the Catholic Church writ large. There were some tough questions along the way, and we discussed most of the hot-button issues facing the Church in the early twenty-first century, from the sexual-abuse crisis to debates over the role of women in the Church, homosexuality, and the intersection of faith and politics. In the main, however, I wanted the book to be more of a conversation than a debate. I also wanted Dolan to be able to guide the conversation a bit, rather than imposing the structure myself. Allowing Dolan to follow his own lead, I thought, would be the best way not simply to get answers to the questions that might interest me but also to tease out what Dolan's real priorities are—and therefore where he's likely to invest his own time and treasure and that of the Church.

Second, this book is obviously not a kind of catechism, in which we exhaustively stepped through the core teachings and practices of the Catholic Church, with Dolan offering his gloss and commentary. Were that the aim, the book would have too many gaping holes to count. We touched on the creed only indirectly and in passing; we didn't spend much time on concepts such as sin, grace, and redemption, nor did we delve deeply into the theology of the bishop's office or the priesthood. We didn't discuss Mary, who plays a core role not only in traditional Catholic spirituality but in Dolan's own. Indeed, the subjects of half the chapters of this book are drawn not from Church teaching but from today's headlines. There is an abundant literature in Catholicism today composed of catechetical aids and resources, and anyone wanting to see Dolan at work as a preacher and teacher would be better served reading his own published works, such as *Priests for the Third Millennium* or *To Whom Shall We Go? Lessons from the Apostle Peter*, published in 2008.

Rather than the *what* of the faith, the idea of this book was to capture the *how*, at least in the sense of how Dolan approaches talking about the Catholic tradition and what it has to say to the contemporary world. In other words, my interest was more in presenting Dolan's method, his basic way of looking at things—or, if one must use a six-dollar academic term, his hermeneutics. As I've suggested throughout, that method can be captured with the phrase "affirmative orthodoxy," a term I coined with respect to the teaching of Pope Benedict XVI but that Dolan arguably incarnates as well as any other senior figure in the Catholic Church at the moment. What I was really interested in was this: What would an affirmative-orthodoxy approach look like with regard to, say, debates over gay rights? How would an affirmative-orthodoxy mind-set tackle the problem of tribalism in the Catholic Church? Can affirmative orthodoxy offer a credible message of hope, or is it simply a matter of trying to slap a positive spin on positions that at their core aren't particularly uplifting? The aim in each case was not really to offer comprehensive answers to any of those questions, because treating any one of them in the depth it requires would take a book all by itself. The goal instead was to suggest Dolan's way of taking up these questions and to at least hint at the psychology and vocabulary he applies to thinking about them.

The bottom line is that Tim Dolan is probably the test case par excellence for the fate of affirmative orthodoxy in the context of American Catholicism and American society in the next couple of decades. Whether that style of Catholicism succeeds or fails, whether it spreads widely or remains narrowly associated with Dolan himself—perhaps applauded but not really imitated—remains to be seen, but it's among the more intriguing currents in the Church, and I hope this book serves as a kind of primer for its basic style.

Third and finally, this book is not intended as the first draft of an eventual *positio*, the paperwork required to formally present someone as a candidate for sainthood. Though I think there's much to like and admire about Archbishop Timothy Dolan, I'm well aware that the guy isn't perfect. For one thing, he has an annoying penchant for hyperbole. To listen to him talk, it seems as if every person he's ever met had a "towering" influence and became a "close" friend. Every experience Dolan's ever had, from opening the mail to smoking another Macanudo, seems to have been "normative" for him. If that were really true, Dolan would have more norms than the Code of Canon Law! His habit of overstatement often makes it hard to know how seriously to take Dolan when he describes his reaction to some specific figure in the Church, whom he may characterize as "brilliant" and "a real churchman," or some new movement or proposal, which he'll often describe as "fantastic." Does he really mean it, or are those his functional equivalents of saying "just par for the course"? It's a question that I sometimes find difficult to answer.

I'm also not naïve, nor do I think Dolan is so lofty and spiritual as to be completely selfless. For example, he knows that his geniality and reputation as a nice guy work in his favor, greasing the wheels for whatever he wants to accomplish. While I believe that for the most part Dolan is simply being who he is, I also realize that his accessibility, his constant drive to make you feel special, can amount to a form of subtle—perhaps even unconscious—manipulation. To take just one small example, every time I traveled to New York to interview Dolan for this book, he invited me to stay at his residence at Saint Patrick's Cathedral. On the last such occasion, which was just a quick overnight trip, I finally took him up on it, largely to avoid the outrageous cost of hotels in midtown Manhattan. I ended up bunking in the same room Pope John Paul II had used when he visited New York. Granted, it's really just a normal guest room that's constantly used by all sorts of folks, but I still couldn't help drawing an analogy with Bill Clinton's famous habit of putting up donors and VIPs in the Lincoln Bedroom at the White House in an attempt to solidify their support. While I don't imagine that Dolan was consciously attempting to sway how I would approach this book, I also don't believe he's entirely innocent of the positive PR value of his demeanor and generosity.

In all honesty—and I say this with no pejorative intent whatsoever—*saintly* is not really the first adjective that comes to mind in describing Dolan. I've had the experience once or twice over the course of my career of meeting people widely regarded as living saints, such as Mother Teresa or Jean Vanier, founder of the L'Arche communities, which foster friendships with developmentally disabled people. Such personalities tend to radiate a kind of intensity, a near-obsessive focus on their mission, which can almost be frightening. That is not usually the impression Dolan creates. In fact, centuries of experience suggest that sanctity and being a nice guy are at best distant cousins, and sometimes they're just not on speaking terms. Father Ron Rolheiser, an Oblate priest and popular spiritual writer, says that he's spent many years studying the life and teachings of his order's founder, Saint Eugene de Mazenod, and on the strength of that research, he's drawn one inescapable conclusion: Mazenod may have been a great saint, but he was not the kind of guy with whom you'd want to sit down and have a beer.

The point about Timothy Dolan is that he is precisely the sort of guy you can feel comfortable with over a couple of beers. That comfort, however, doesn't come out of a bottle; rather it comes from the sense of being in the presence of a mensch—a human being who's flawed but who's also genuinely interested in other people and who's willing to step outside his own skin to consider how things look from somebody else's point of view. The comfort, in other words, comes from the sensation of being in the company of a bridge builder. Whether the bridges he builds will stand the test of time, and whether they'll be wide and sturdy enough for all the various tribes in American Catholicism to walk across them, remains to be seen. But in an era of "gated communities" of both the virtual and physical sort, someone able to blend strong personal convictions with real openness to alternative points of view is, at least, a refreshing change of pace.

That may not make Dolan a saint, but it does make him an eminently Catholic figure in the sense once described by poet Hilaire

Belloc, in a bit of doggerel that offers a fitting conclusion for this introduction to the mind and heart of American Catholicism's premier showman and apostle of hope:

> *Wherever the Catholic sun doth shine*
> *There's always laughter and good red wine.*
> *At least I've always found it so.*
> *Benedicamus Domino!*

ACKNOWLEDGMENTS

Obviously, the first note of gratitude goes to Archbishop Timothy Dolan for his graciousness in agreeing to this project and for making himself available for the extended interviews it required, with no limits at all on the nature of the questions or the topics to be covered. I also want to thank two of Dolan's collaborators, his priest secretary, Father James Cruz, and his communications director, Joseph Zwilling, for their logistical support and unfailingly positive spirit.

I want to acknowledge the wisdom and support I've received from my editor at Doubleday, Trace Murphy. This is my sixth book with a Random House imprint, none of which would have gotten off the ground without Trace's guidance and unflagging confidence in my ability to deliver a compelling read. *Tante grazie!*

As always, thanks are due to my colleagues at the *National Catholic Reporter*, including Tom Fox, Joe Feuerherd (whose death as this book was in production remains a great loss, both personally and professionally), Tom Roberts, Dennis Coday, Teresa Malcolm, Toni-Ann Ortiz, and the rest of the gang. You tolerated with great patience my occasional need to go AWOL and have supported my work through good times and bad. Each of you has my eternal gratitude. In a similar vein, I want to acknowledge my producers, bookers, and friends at CNN, especially Pam

Sellers and Maria Ebrahimji. I often joke that my formal title at the network, Senior Vatican Analyst, is meaningless, since I'm also CNN's only Vatican analyst. But the two of you actually make me feel special, even in a universe of one.

Finally, a note of thanks to my wife, Shannon, and our pug dog, Ellis. Only you two know the horrors of putting up with me when deadlines loom and the words don't want to come—and, of course, only Shannon can tell the tale. My thanks, therefore, not only for your support but for your silence! *Ti amo per sempre, ciambellina.*